D0992224

Out of the Northwoods

Out of the Northwoods

The Many Lives of Paul Bunyan

by Michael Edmonds

Wisconsin Historical Society Press

Published by the Wisconsin Historical Society Press
Publishers since 1855
© 2009 by State Historical Society of Wisconsin

For permission to reuse material from *Out of the Northwoods: The Many Lives of Paul Bunyan* (ISBN 978-0-87020-437-1), please access www.copyright.com or contact the Copyright Clearance Center, Inc. (CCC), 222 Rosewood Drive, Danvers, MA 01923, 978–750–8400. CCC is a not-for-profit organization that provides licenses and registration for a variety of users.

wisconsinhistory.org

Photographs identified with PH, WHi, or WHS are from the Society's collections; address inquiries about such photos to the Visual Materials Archivist at Wisconsin Historical Society, 816 State Street, Madison, WI 53706.

Printed in Canada
Designed by Moonlit Ink, Madison, WI

13 12 11 10 09   1 2 3 4 5

Library of Congress Cataloging-in-Publication Data
Edmonds, Michael.
Out of the northwoods: the many lives of Paul Bunyan / by Michael Edmonds.
p. cm.
Includes bibliographical references and index.
ISBN 978-0-87020-437-1 (pbk. : alk. paper) 1. Bunyan, Paul (Legendary character)—Legends. I. Title.
GR105.37.P38E35 2009
398.20973'02—dc22
[E]
2009005646

ENVIRONMENTAL BENEFITS STATEMENT

The Wisconsin Historical Society Press saved the following resources by printing the pages of this book on chlorine free paper made with 100% post-consumer waste.

TREES	WATER	SOLID WASTE	GREENHOUSE GASES
49	22,664	1,376	4,706
FULLY GROWN	GALLONS	POUNDS	POUNDS

Calculations based on research by Environmental Defense and the Paper Task Force.
Manufactured at Friesens Corporation

CONTENTS

List of Tables

Cast of Characters

Bartlett, William W. (1861–1933): historian of the Chippewa Valley who interviewed loggers, ca. 1913–1927, to gather Bunyan stories

Brown, Charles E. (1872–1946): director of Wisconsin Historical Museum who collected Bunyan stories, 1906–1946, and published fifteen booklets of them, 1922–1945

Charters, W. W. (1875–1952): Ohio State University professor who collected Bunyan materials as a hobby and corresponded with Bunyan editors during the 1940s

Dorson, Richard (1916–1981). Indiana University professor of folklore and the most vocal critic of the midcentury Bunyan mania

Laughead, William (1882–1958): advertising manager of the Red River Lumber Company, which issued more than 125,000 copies of his Bunyan stories, 1914–1944, and launched Bunyan's fame; invented the names of Bunyan's crew, including Babe the Blue Ox

Lovejoy, Parrish S. (1884–1942): forester with the Michigan Department of Conservation who wrote a series of Bunyan tales under the pseudonym Charles Albright for the *American Lumberman*, 1916–1918

MacGillivray, James (1873–1952): Michigan lumberman who heard the Round River tales in the Saginaw Valley in 1887 and drafted a text of them for his brother William's Oscoda, Michigan, newspaper in 1906

Rockwell, James E. (1883–1953): Duluth, Minnesota, reporter who published the first collection of Bunyan stories to reach a national audience, in the Milwaukee nature magazine *Outer's Book,* in February 1910

Shepard, Eugene (1854–1923): Rhinelander, Wisconsin, timber cruiser and northwoods promoter who claimed to have invented Paul Bunyan

Shephard, Esther (1891–1975): San Jose State College professor who collected Bunyan tales in the Pacific Northwest for a 1924 book, one of two that made Bunyan famous (no relation to Eugene Shepard)

Stevens, James (1892–1971): West Coast logger and public relations counsel for the lumber industry who in 1925 wrote the other book that made Bunyan famous

Stewart, Bernice (1894–1975): northern Wisconsin native who, as a University of Wisconsin undergraduate collected tales in the field between 1914 and 1916 with her English professor, Homer Watt

Watt, Homer A. (1884–1948): New York University professor who, while at the University of Wisconsin in 1914–1916, gathered and published with Bernice Stewart the earliest collection of Bunyan tales that was systematically gathered in the field

Preface

WHEN I RECENTLY ASKED MY ELEVEN-YEAR-OLD if she'd ever heard of Paul Bunyan, she answered, "Sure. He's that great big guy with the blue cow." She was less certain about why he was famous and couldn't remember exactly how she'd heard of him. Folklore's funny that way. Everybody knows it, but most of us aren't sure how we first heard it, and nobody seems to know where it comes from.

Although I'd encountered Paul Bunyan as a child in the 1950s, my professional curiosity about him was aroused only in 2005 when I stumbled across a 1916 newspaper photograph of a young woman under the headline, "Extracts from Paul Bunyan Yarns." She was Bernice Stewart, who, as a college student during World War I, traveled through logging camps to collect Bunyan stories from lumberjacks. As if that weren't strange enough, when I looked into her work further I learned that, although everyone recognized his name, no one actually knew where Paul Bunyan came from.

Here was a puzzle worth investigating, one that even had an analogue in a Bunyan tale from Wisconsin: "As a trailer of game [Bunyan] was unsurpassed. Once he came on a moose in the woods that had died of old age. Having some spare time, Paul in a short time traced this moose back to the place where it was born."

I, too, had some spare time, so I set out on his trail. I soon discovered that previous researchers had overlooked many early Bunyan publications and manuscripts from Wisconsin. These documents suggested that some widely repeated "facts" about the tales—such as that they started in Maine in the mid-nineteenth century, that a real-life Paul Bunyan had fought in an 1837 Canadian rebellion, and that the stories were first printed in Michigan in 1906—were mistaken.

From that point on, the game was afoot, as Sherlock Holmes would say. I spent much of 2007 and 2008 pursuing it, and at almost every turn a new mystery or paradox greeted me. If the stories were created by macho lumberjacks in all-male settings, why weren't there any dirty jokes about Bunyan? Where did Charles Brown, the most prolific Wisconsin publisher of the tales, acquire his stories? Why did the W.P.A. Wisconsin Folklore Project records on Bunyan disappear? How did the private jokes of working-class loggers—the Hell's Angels of their day—turn into the cutesy caricature that every eleven-year-old recognizes a century later?

As I ferreted out answers to questions such as these, I was astonished at the hold that Bunyan took on me. I've always been fascinated by the ways that knowledge travels across time and space, but I was surprised at how thoroughly I enjoyed digging up Bunyan's roots. The early stories themselves, with ironic touches reminiscent of Mark Twain and logical contradictions worthy of Lewis Carroll, had much to do with it. They are, quite simply, fun. And the people who produced, promoted, and perverted the tales were fascinating characters. More than one of them had lied, stolen, or cheated to make tales told by wilderness lumberjacks into a commodity that could be sold for profit. All told, Bunyan's strange career was a fascinating episode in American intellectual history.

I could uncover the true facts about it only because a network of meticulous collectors had preserved a great deal of primary evidence long ago. That evidence lies in their unpublished correspondence, interview notes, and other archival documents scattered across the northern tier of states. My hunt for records carried me from the sun-splashed hills of western Massachusetts during a glorious Indian summer to the icy, gray slush of Minneapolis on a hostile March weekend.

At crucial moments in my research, James Milostan (of the John Michael Kohler Art Center), Professor James P. Leary (University of Wisconsin), and Jim Hansen (Wisconsin Historical Society) each suggested strategies that cleared away obstacles and led to new evidence. Barbara Friend, granddaughter of Professor Homer Watt, generously searched through family papers and opened her home to me. Kurt Kortenhof (St. Paul College, St. Paul, Minnesota) answered many questions and shared his research files on Eugene Shepard. Timm Severud (in the aptly named town of Winter, Wisconsin) provided knowledge and documents about Chippewa Valley history and American Indian loggers. Marie Harvat, Meredith Gillies, and their staff at the Children's Literature Research Collection, Andersen Library, University of Minnesota, responded to many inquiries; promptly provided copies of letters, clippings, and other primary sources; and made me feel at home in their collections. Galen Poor and my daughter Rose Edmonds painstakingly examined hundreds of pages of distant manuscripts for me. My son Devin confirmed my instincts by laughing at all the right places in an early draft. Jim Leary generously read and critiqued the manuscript of the entire book.

My wife, Mary Fiorenza, questioned my methods, my arguments, and my prose but never my intentions. Instead, she smiled benignly as I wandered down yet another eccentric path in the bibliographical woods. As usual, she has been my best critic. Finally, I must thank our daughter, Julia, for patiently enduring hour after hour in the University of Minnesota archives while Dad tracked down the origins of that great big guy with the blue cow.

LOCATIONS IMPORTANT TO PAUL BUNYAN TALES

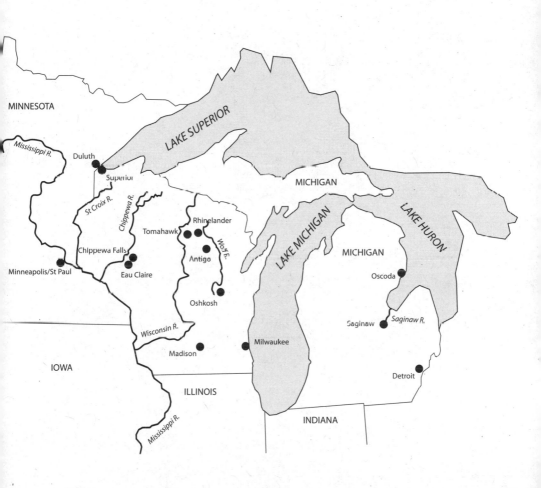

MINNESOTA

LAKE SUPERIOR

Mississippi R.

Duluth

Superior

MICHIGAN

St Croix R.

Chippewa R.

Rhinelander

Tomahawk

Wolf R.

Chippewa Falls

Antigo

LAKE MICHIGAN

LAKE HURON

MICHIGAN

Minneapolis/St Paul

Eau Claire

Oscoda

Oshkosh

Saginaw

Saginaw R,

Wisconsin R.

Milwaukee

IOWA

Madison

Detroit

ILLINOIS

INDIANA

Mississippi R.

CHAPTER ONE

Who Was Paul Bunyan?

"All lumberjacks, of course, believe,
*or pretend to believe, that he really lived..."**

MILLIONS OF AMERICANS immediately recognize Paul Bunyan's
name or face. Over the past century more than 300 books
have been written about him— never mind the 200 recordings,
videos, and musical scores or the half-million Web pages. His
name appears on countless restaurants, resorts, and tourist attractions from Maine to Oregon and has advertised everything from
construction materials to loaves of bread.

Bunyan is one of the most widespread icons in our culture, a
ubiquitous symbol of American power and ingenuity. His rise to
fame was meteoric, and his fate, like that of most celebrities, was
to be exploited by commercial forces. Where the Bunyan phenomenon started, however, has always been unclear. His progress from
private joke to public hero is a case study in how knowledge was
created, shared, and commodified in America during the twentieth
century.

Long before a single tree had been felled in the Great Lakes
forests, New Englanders told tall tales around colonial hearths
about cold so intense that words froze in the air or snow so deep

*This and subsequent chapter epigrams are quoted from the Paul Bunyan tales printed in
the appendix.

1

it reached the treetops. During the first half of the nineteenth century, many of these stories moved west with the farmers, storekeepers, mechanics, and laborers who wandered away from the narrow Atlantic seaboard into the heart of the continent. Paul Bunyan was not mentioned in any of them.

During the 1840s, Maine loggers brought equipment and skills into the virgin forests of Wisconsin, Michigan, and Minnesota in order to harvest their seemingly limitless stands of white pine. They brought with them songs and stories about logging back home in New England; these included "The Jam on Gerry's Rocks" and "The Logger's Boast." They had never heard of Paul Bunyan.

Over the next thirty years, Great Lakes lumberjacks combined these traditional folk tales and logging stories with accounts of new challenges they faced in the western wilderness. In the early 1880s, the lumber industry mushroomed and thousands of novice loggers entered the woods. Grizzled veterans in logging shanties from Saginaw, Michigan, to Duluth, Minnesota, began to tell tall tales about the old days, when things were *really* tough. Some of them claimed to have worked for a camp foreman named Paul Bunyan, whose unusual size, strength, and cleverness helped his men escape catastrophes or solve problems. Wisconsin timber cruiser Bill Mulhollen told the first reliably documented tales about Paul Bunyan during the winter of 1885–1886 in the upper Wisconsin River valley, at a logging camp a few miles north of Tomahawk, Wisconsin.

It's possible that Mulhollen heard them from fellow timber cruiser Gene Shepard, who claimed many times to have invented Bunyan. Shepard was famous throughout the lumber industry for captivating listeners with tall tales, and he spent the winter of 1882–1883 with a logging crew in the same area where Mulhollen told the first known Bunyan stories three winters later.

Unfortunately, Shepard was also a shameless liar who fabricated hoaxes, couldn't resist a practical joke, and plagiarized other people's work. Every statement he made in public has to be assumed false until proved otherwise, including his claim to have invented

Paul Bunyan. We will probably never know for certain whether he was the first person to spin tales about the mythical lumberjack hero, but he was certainly nearby when they were first told aloud in 1885–1886 and again when they were first printed, in 1904 in Duluth, Minnesota.

Between 1880 and 1910, Bunyan stories were told aloud in logging camps from Michigan to the Pacific. New tales about Bunyan sprung up among pipeline workers in the oil fields of Texas and among doughboys in the trenches of France during World War I. By then, at least seven collectors were gathering the stories directly from lumberjacks who had told them out loud for the preceding forty years.

Between 1904 and 1920, a handful of the oral Bunyan tales leaked into a few magazines and newspapers, but they didn't resonate with the public and slipped quietly into oblivion. For example, when Bunyan was first used in an advertising campaign targeted at lumber wholesalers in 1914, it flopped because most of them simply didn't recognize his name.

During the 1920s, however, two professional writers who'd worked in the woods as young men resurrected the Bunyan tales they'd heard and spun them into conventional short fiction. The country had just been catapulted onto the international stage by World War I, and Americans were eager to embrace an indigenous folk hero who could stand beside Hercules and Thor. Bunyan quickly became an icon of American power and ingenuity, and readers rushed to consume books, pamphlets, articles, and advertisements about the plucky lumberjack hero. Because "folklore" could presumably be created by anyone, entirely new stories were soon invented by writers who'd never set foot near a logging camp, in which a gigantic magical Bunyan performed fantastic feats such as creating the Grand Canyon or the Rocky Mountains.

After the American economy collapsed in 1929, corporate executives touted Bunyan as the ideal self-reliant worker who needed no unions or government handouts. At the same time, leftist organizers held him up as a symbol of the noble proletariat who provided the muscle and know-how to make America strong again. As the Bunyan mania continued to grow through the 1930s, elderly loggers were pulled out of retirement to perform songs, stage festivals, and host pageants. Depressed northwoods communities tried to lure tourists and sportsmen, and Bunyan's name appeared on billboards and landmarks all across the cutover region. When World War II erupted, American military propagandists quickly enlisted Bunyan to fight the Germans and Japanese. A Paul Bunyan craze had swept the nation.

But just after the war Bunyan came under attack. Academic folklorists, intent on proving that their new scholarly discipline was as rigorous as better-established ones, denounced the popularizations as "fakelore." When they discovered that the tales had first been widely circulated by ad executive William Laughead and lumber industry public relations officer James Stevens, some of them even concluded there had never been any authentic oral tradition at all. They threw the proverbial baby out with the bathwater.

Richard Dorson, dean of American folklorists, led this 1940s and 1950s campaign against the Bunyan mania. "He is the pseudo folk hero of twentieth century mass culture, a conveniently vague symbol pressed into service to exemplify the American spirit. He means different things to different vested interests: the soul of the workingman to the *Daily Worker*...; the efficiency of American capitalism to...the lumber companies; a gargantuan comic dummy for resort promoters; the invincible brute strength of America to some artists; a braggart and a blowhard, a fantasy, a performer of enormous tasks, a deified woodsman, to other segments of the American people. This is not popularization," he concluded, "but perversion."[1]

Of course, in a contest between historical accuracy and commercial interests the professors didn't stand a chance, and the protests of Dorson and his followers fell on deaf ears outside the academy. The forces of "perversion" finally triumphed in 1957, when Walt Disney Studios released a Bunyan cartoon complete with catchy songs, absurd caricatures, and childish plot. This Disney version was immensely popular and permanently infantilized the Bunyan stories in the public mind. In just fifty years, the hero of rugged working-class loggers had turned into pablum for toddlers in front of televisions.

Why should we care about the strange career of Paul Bunyan? First, because for most of the twentieth century he personified certain American ideals, especially the values and desires of common people who left few written records. Second, because his fate illustrates how grassroots culture was appropriated and co-opted by commercial interests. A similar process transformed Native American warriors into cigar store Indians, and black rhythm and blues music into Elvis Presley hits.

Bunyan began life as the private possession of unsophisticated working people. From the 1880s until World War I, he expressed the fears and aspirations of uneducated loggers as they risked their lives at a brutal occupation in the frozen wilderness. But after 1925, skillfully embellished tales about him by professional writers captivated the nation. This new Bunyan embodied not the values of working class woodsmen but those of middle-class editors, publishers, advertisers, and readers. Millions of Americans eagerly embraced him as their nation emerged onto the world stage, grappled with economic collapse, and faced up to a second world war.

By the 1950s, the generation that could personally recall frontier farms and virgin forests had dwindled away. In the age of the atomic bomb and Telstar satellite, few people could understand lumberjacks' jokes (or wanted to). Bunyan moved again, this time from the best-seller shelf of bookstores and libraries into the children's section. During the second half of the century, millions of kids fell in love with a sentimental Bunyan who entertained them in grammar school readers, television shows, and comic books.

As with the earlier versions, this final incarnation of the lumberjack hero expressed the beliefs, desires, and standards of value of his creators. He taught that the natural environment was merely raw ingredients to be chopped up, blended by machinery, and spit out as salable merchandise. He was a masculine role model for little boys until they grew big enough for John Wayne, the Marlboro man, or Bruce Willis. Besides the picture books, records, and cartoons featuring Bunyan's all-conquering strength, his name and image were used to advertise jackknives, fishing lures, baseball caps, hatchets, and other essential items of postwar boyhood gear.

Even today, Bunyan helps sell real estate, motel rooms, campsites, hamburgers, and pancake breakfasts to nostalgic tourists. There is a Paul Bunyan state park, bluegrass festival, snowmobile trail, bicycle club, sled dog race, driving tour, rifle club, scenic byway, marathon, and, of course, shopping mall (in Bemidji, Minnesota).

Other writers have thoroughly investigated how and why Paul Bunyan grew into a national icon.[2] But where did it all begin? How did the private jokes of lumberjacks become America's most popular folk hero? It was Richard Dorson who first suggested, back in 1951, that, "The most interesting folklore problem connected with Paul Bunyan lies in uncovering the early oral tradition."[3]

The remnants of that tradition can be found in the unpublished letters, interview notes, obscure pamphlets, and long-forgotten articles on which this book is based; the earliest and most detailed of these come from Wisconsin. Despite decades of academic interest in Bunyan tales from other states, the Wisconsin sources that document the oral tradition have been almost entirely overlooked by researchers. When they are examined alongside the better-known sources, it becomes clear that Wisconsin was at the center of the Bunyan legend.

Wisconsin anthropologist Charles E. Brown (1872–1946) first heard Bunyan tales in the early 1890s and began to systematically collect them from loggers in 1906. His unpublished letters, interview notes, and privately printed booklets contain dozens of the stories he gathered. Brown's role in helping to create Bunyan's reputation has been almost entirely ignored by academic folklorists (see chapter 9).

In February 1910, a Milwaukee nature magazine called *Outer's Book* printed the first collection of Bunyan stories to reach a national audience. They were gathered directly from lumberjacks by journalist James Rockwell (1883–1953). Wisconsin timber cruiser Eugene Shepard may have been one of Rockwell's sources, as his exploits are described in the article. Although the Milwaukee *Outer's Book* put Bunyan stories in front of thousands of hunters and anglers around the country and was quickly reprinted in newspapers, no historian or folklorist has previously noted it (see chapter 7).

From 1914 to 1916, University of Wisconsin undergraduate Bernice Stewart (1894–1975) and her English professor Homer Watt (1884–1948) traveled through Wisconsin lumber camps and northern towns collecting the tales. They were the first scholars who tried to systematically gather Bunyan stories, and academic folklorists still believe their 1916 collection contains the most authentic versions. Although their publication is often cited, Stewart's and Watt's research methods have never before been described in detail (see chapter 8).

Instead, historians concentrated on two more famous groups of tales. The first is the "Round River" sequence published in the small town of Oscoda, Michigan, in 1906 and reprinted in 1910 and 1914; these can be traced back to oral roots on Michigan's Au Sable River in 1887. The other group was created in Minnesota in 1914 by William Laughead for the Red River Lumber Company, from tales he first heard in Minnesota in 1901; when it was reprinted in 1922, Laughead's collection launched the national mania for Bunyan. During the 1950s and 1960s, the history of Laughead's Minnesota versions attracted much scholarly attention, and twenty-five years later so did the Michigan Round River recension, while the Wisconsin sources remained hidden.[4]

The neglected Wisconsin stories about Paul Bunyan were created earlier than the better-known ones from Michigan and Minnesota. They also reached a national audience sooner, differed substantially in their content, and provide richer evidence about the authentic oral tradition.

The chapters that follow first describe the logging camps where the Bunyan tales were born, explain how the stories were told aloud, chronicle their emergence into print, discuss how printing forever changed them, and locate them within the larger movement that made Paul Bunyan a household name. Chapter 11 examines the surviving evidence for claims about Bunyan's origin and uncovers the roots of the Michigan, Wisconsin, and Minnesota recensions of the tales.

More than one hundred of the earliest Bunyan stories are given in the appendix. Some are published here for the first time from manuscripts, letters, or collectors' field notes, while others are re-printed from privately printed, ephemeral booklets and obscure magazine articles. They describe a protagonist quite different from the familiar hero of later popular versions and children's books. They illuminate the values of the working-class men who, between 1880 and 1915, transformed ancient Great Lakes forests into lumber for the houses, churches, and storefronts that still surround us today. Those lumberjacks are all silent now, vanished like the virgin forests they entered more than a century ago, but their voices, their jokes, their fears, and their hopes can still be heard in the fantastic tales they made up around bunkhouse camp stoves on long winter evenings.

CHAPTER TWO

Bunyan's Origins in Fact and Fiction

"The crew on the pyramid forty was so large that Paul
kept one group going to work, one coming from work,
and one working all the time."

STORIES ABOUT PAUL BUNYAN were born in Great Lakes logging camps in the mid-1880s, as veteran woodsmen tried to impress gullible new recruits with remarkable feats they had supposedly witnessed long before. The stories about Bunyan grew from three interwoven roots:

- **Traditional folktales.** Many of the Bunyan stories' motifs—the central image or plot twist that makes a tale entertaining—had been used in much earlier folktales that didn't even mention logging or Bunyan. Many came from colonial New England, but some date back to Europe in the seventeenth and eighteenth centuries. A good example is the tale of the stretching harness (appendix, no. 44).
- **Early logging stories.** Other Bunyan tales incorporated early-nineteenth-century anecdotes from the logging industry in Maine or eastern Canada that memorialized remarkable events. These included stories and songs that

lumberjacks shared among themselves about death-defying logjams or legendary forest creatures; these were circulating before Paul Bunyan, as a character, had ever been imagined. Good examples are the descriptions of the hodag and the hangdown, predators that roamed around Bunyan's camp (appendix, nos. 85 and 89).

• **Original Bunyan tales.** The folk hero Paul Bunyan was created in the mid-1880s and inserted as the protagonist of traditional folktales and logging stories. Wisconsin timber cruiser Bill Mulhollen told the earliest reliably documented Bunyan stories north of Tomahawk, Wisconsin, in the winter of 1885–1886 (appendix, no. 5). As Bunyan became known among lumberjacks, new stories were invented specifically about his exploits. These later tales were set in logging camps, and their humor depended on familiarity with the industry's techniques and jargon. A good example is Otis Terpening's short sequence concerning Paul's problems making an ice road (appendix, no. 22).

The thousands of later books, articles, stories, advertisements, comic books, television shows, picture books, and tourist attractions about Paul Bunyan all grew from these roots.

Because the earliest Bunyan tales originally circulated in wilderness logging camps, readers can't fully understand them without knowing at least a little about the ways that white pine forests were harvested by hand and the unique jargon used by woodsmen in the nineteenth century. This chapter briefly describes how Great Lakes logging was performed, prints a lumberjack's own account of a typical day in the Wisconsin pineries about 1890, and examines early speculations about Bunyan's origin.

The North American logging industry began in the forests of Maine, Quebec, and New Brunswick in the early nineteenth century. Before the Civil War it spread south and west into upstate New York, western Pennsylvania, Michigan, Wisconsin, and Minnesota. As the great pines in those states were exhausted around the turn of the twentieth century, lumbering spread even further afield into southern states, California, and the Pacific Northwest.

In Wisconsin, lumbering started about 1830 and grew rapidly during the 1850s, after treaties were signed with the Ojibwe and Menominee Indians. At the time, the northern third of the state was almost entirely covered in ancient forests. A modern historian has calculated that the northern Wisconsin forests ceded in the 1837 and 1842 treaties with the Ojibwe amounted to 170 billion board feet of timber (a board foot measures twelve inches by twelve inches by one inch thick).[1]

But mere statistics cannot convey the power of the primeval forest. The first lumbermen around Rice Lake, Wisconsin, "were tremendously impressed by the giant virgin white pines that grew thickly, cut here and there by bands of hardwoods. While standing under the great pines near Cumberland, they took out their watches to learn the time of day, but the trees grew so thickly and cut off the light so completely that it was only with great difficulty that they were able to read their watches and see that it was three o'clock in the afternoon. For a distance of about a mile and a half the pines were equally thick. No underbrush or shrubbery was able to grow in such darkness. The great tree trunks, three or more feet in diameter, were as close together as they could grow, and between them the ground was covered with a thick and springy matting of dead needles and cones."[2]

The process of harvesting such trees was simple in theory but complex, difficult, and life-threatening in practice. After the federal government gained ownership of the forest from American Indians (usually through treaties signed under an implicit threat of violence), it offered the land for sale to lumber companies. Companies' headquarters were usually located in distant cities, so they hired local "timber cruisers" to survey the wilderness and assess its market value before purchasing. Timber cruisers mapped every square mile of the untouched woodlands, noting the species of trees, estimating the amount of lumber they represented, and then registering the company's purchase at the nearest government

Pines near Chippewa Falls, Wisconsin, 1905 WHI IMAGE ID 2196

land office. They also paid its taxes at the local county courthouse and monitored their clients' lands to make sure no competitor was illegally harvesting its trees. Hundreds of timber cruisers roamed through northern Wisconsin between the Civil War and the turn of the twentieth century.[3]

Once a lumber company had received the cruiser's map of its holdings, it sent logging crews into the woods to harvest the largest pines. White pine was in high demand by builders and factory owners, and it was the easiest species to transport because it floated well. Nineteenth-century loggers typically went into the woods in November or December, often poling against the current up streams and hiking miles through the forest. Operations began at a site where rough camp buildings had been erected earlier in the fall and nearby forty-acre sections had been marked off for cutting. Companies so often exceeded these section boundaries and took trees from neighboring tracts that lumbermen joked about "round forties" that produced astonishing yields of timber. Many Paul Bunyan anecdotes include his ability to harvest immense amounts from a single forty, particularly a legendary one that contained a towering, pyramid-shaped hill so high that "just to see to its top required twenty men."

Once established in the woods, pairs of sawyers chopped a notch in a tree about three feet from the ground on the side toward which they intended it to fall. They then sawed the trunk from the opposite side, inserting wedges to keep the saw blade from catching. Once the tree fell, a "swamper" stripped off its limbs so the sawyers could cut the trunk into ten- to sixteen-foot lengths (depending on the needs of the lumber mill to which it was contracted).

A "skidder" then wrapped a chain around the log and used oxen or horses to pull it out of the dense woods, sometimes on a small, pointed sled called a "go-devil." The men stamped the company's logmark, a unique symbol that served the same purpose as a cattle owner's brand on a free-ranging steer, into the ends of each log and stacked them on a large sled. These teams of four workers—two sawyers, a swamper, and a skidder—were the basic labor unit of white pine logging in the late-nineteenth century.

Sawyers felling a tree, location and date unknown   WHI IMAGE ID 2413

The team hauled the logs to the nearest river, which might be miles away from where they were cut, on rudely cut forest roads; to facilitate sledding a multi-ton load of tree trunks, logging roads were often iced. At the end of their journey the logs were carefully stacked at the "skidway" on a riverbank or on adjacent ice. "Teams hauling travois or logging sleds would pile the logs on the ice out in the lake until it would crack," Wisconsin logger Horace Drake recalled. "Sometimes the sagging ice gave way and men and oxen went through the ice into the lake. Orders were given that the dinner bell should be rung at such an emergency, and at that sound everyone left his job and ran to the landing to help in the rescue work."[4]

In the spring, when the snow began to melt and the rivers rose, all the logs were pushed into the current and floated downstream to a sawmill. Transporting logs to the mill on a river drive was a difficult and dangerous process that could last several weeks. It could not wait, because low water might strand a fortune in logs high and dry in the remote wilderness. Once begun, it could not be stopped, because the river carried logs downstream night and day. Many thousands of massive tree trunks had to be tumbled into the current and then herded downriver in a floating mass, around

Sawyers cutting a felled pine near Florence, Wisconsin, 1880 WHI IMAGE ID 3679

Teamsters skidding a log on a go-devil, Marathon County, Wisconsin, circa 1910

WHI IMAGE ID 58515

Teamsters decking logs on a frozen lake, circa 1880, location unknown
WHI IMAGE ID 6316

bends, across shallows, through gorges, and over waterfalls. Expert lumberjacks called "river pigs" rode the surging logs like surfers, while less-talented comrades tramped the banks and waded the icy shallows to push stragglers back into the current. Dams were often constructed by lumber companies to raise the water level and float logs over rapids and shallows in the spring.

But if the foremost logs snagged on a rock or caught in a narrows, the entire winter's harvest could pile up for miles in an enormous jam. Hundreds of thousands of huge tree trunks could mount several stories high and be dislodged only by workers risking their lives. Volunteers would remove the "key log" of a jam by chopping, prying, or dynamiting it, launching the entire mass down on themselves while they scrambled for their lives across an avalanche of tumbling tree trunks. Dismemberment and death were commonplace.

Virtually every step in this process spawned stories about Paul Bunyan and his crew. Chopping, sawing, swamping, sledding, river driving, and jam breaking all provided settings for Bunyan tales, and the earliest versions often depended for their humor on technical jargon or expert knowledge of tools and methods. Even

A five-mile logjam on the St. Croix River, 1886 (note loggers in center foreground)
WHI IMAGE ID 2364

the logging environment itself became a character, as rich forests, enormous trees, unusually harsh winters, memorable blizzards, and extraordinary cold snaps set up punch lines and paradoxes in the Bunyan stories.

Once the logs finally reached a sawmill, they were held in place by floating booms and sorted according to their logmarks. Then they were guided individually through huge, water-powered saw blades that sliced them into salable lumber of standard dimensions. The finished lumber was carefully assembled into rafts and floated or towed hundreds of miles downriver to wholesalers in cities. Trees felled near Eagle River or Hayward, Wisconsin, were sawed into lumber at Rhinelander or Eau Claire and taken by raft pilots all the way to

River pigs taking a break, location and date unknown WHI IMAGE ID 31453

Logs delivered to Scouler & Jacobson sawmill in Rosholt, Portage County, Wisconsin, circa 1905 WHI IMAGE ID 58512

A pilot guiding his lumber raft through rapids in the Wisconsin Dells, 1886

WHI IMAGE ID 4270

St. Louis for sale. Majestic pines that had towered for centuries over northern Wisconsin came to their ends flooring kitchens in Peoria, shingling roofs in Chicago, or lining boardwalks in Omaha.[5]

Perhaps the best way to grasp the material context of the Bunyan stories is to read logger Otis Terpening's unpublished recollection of a typical day in the St. Croix pineries of northwestern Wisconsin around 1890:

Morning, it was real hard to say when that time came, As few of us cared [carried] the old Bulls eye watches, And what few did where set with the camp time, so we could tell when the chuck hammer [dinner horn] would blow, But morning always came about three o'clock, In to breakfast. Buckwheat pan cakes on a griddle that covered the whole top of an eight lid range, Black Coffe sweeten with brown sugar, Did not have tin cows then—Hash warmed up potatoes fried salt pork, Cold Beans, black strap molasses, with a tin full of fried cakes, No talking at the tables only ask for what you wanted, And ever man in his own place, You could not change places ever meal. If you wanted to change places get permission from the cook, If you were a new man and got in a hurry and went in and set down, In some jacks place he would tap you on the shoulder, And say Pard I guess you are in the wrong stall, Move out. If you done it again look out for the but of your ear, For a man was look upon as a coward that would be driven from his place at the table. After breakfast back to the sleeping shanty, The rest of the crew would take a smoke and sit around about one hour, But us loaders would grab our mackinaws light our torches, The torches was a tin can holding about a quart of kerosene with a round wick in them And a place where we could stick a stick into them about seven feet long. The teamster would drive up in front of the camp and yell, Hey Hey Boys, day light in the swamp, And away we went to the decked skidway, stuck a torch in the snow on each side and steped to it. On a mile and a half haul we would load them up three times before daylight, The loads run from four to six thousand [board feet] to the load, when the last team was loaded we went in to dinner, And often the dinner horn would blow long before we started in. The rest of the crew went in when that blowed, [The dinner horn or chuck hammer] was made out of tin about four feet long no toungue in them you made the noise with the vibration of your lips, The same as a cornet player. On a still day it could be heard for miles.

Dinner, Teams put in and feed hay and grain, Ever body hungry and in a hurry to get in to dinner, But laughing and joking and talking over the doings of the for[e] noon, Wash and comb our hair, Take a few drags out of the old

Inside a logging camp cook shanty near Hayward, Wisconsin, date unknown
WHI IMAGE ID 1962

pipe, Every body engaged in jolly bantering one another, when the cookee [assistant cook] throws the cook camp door open and toots the horn, Ever body rushes for the door, If a light man gets in front of you picks him up bodly and hurls him back into the crowd, which brings forth yells of delight, When you step into the cook camp ever thing is still, If some one happens to laugh the cook whistles or raps with a knife handle and we all know that means silence. Potatoes brown gravy, salted beef (called Red Horse) Pea soup made from ripe Canada field peas, A pan of stewed Prunes or dried Apples, Take all you wanted, Rice pudding, Tins of fride cakes, with a little Ivory soap shaved and mixed into them to make them light, sweet cookies, A pint basin of tea and more if you wanted it, Back to the camp, Time for a good smoke (we always had pie for dinner, it was either dried apple prune or raisin baked in a ten inch tin and cut into four peaces, And each man took one peace)

After noon, Dinner seemed to put new life into the crew, The woods would ring with the blows of axes, And the singing of saws, And it seemed thet they would all cut loose a pine at about the same time and the woods would roar, Some gangs when the tree would start would yell W-A-T-C-H O-U-T while others would shout W-I-D-O-W M-A-K-E-R-S, others would yell T-I-M-B-E-R- The sleighs went growning and chucking down the sleigh road, And ever man was doing his best, And no shirking, Hear the logs sounding and thumping on the fly skidways, And as the sun got a little warm the air was filled with the smell of the pine, O why did God give this old Lumberjack a memory, Work until the moon or what we called the jobbers sun came up, And then back to camp with a feeling that we had done our best. The same rush and hurry to get ready for supper, If we had time would jirk off our rubbers and put on a pair of old Stags, (stags took in a lot of things it might be a pair of low rubbers or a pair of old river shoes with the tops cut off, And be sure to get your own, Had little poles hanging on wire above the stove and each man had a piece of his own to hang his wet socks and foot rags, Mits and such things, If you made a mistake once it was alright but the next time you found your stuff gently laid on top of the stove, And the Jack with flashing eye would look at you and say, Pard I can larn you something if this happens again, And if you say so can do it right now, Some time the challenge was accepted and it was clear the kitchen, That was at least what we said)

Supper, Bread old Mag. for butter boilt potatoes fried salt pork, (Sow Belly) Black molasses cake, And always the pan of dried apples sauce, And the tin of fried cakes, A pint basin of real coffee, And another one if you want it, salt was put on the table in a pint basin Pepper the same you took it out on your knife, Every thing still at the table the old iron handled knives and forks seem to play a tune, on the tin plates,

Back to the sleeping camp. Each man would sit on his own bunck, Their was what we called the Deacon seat a short bench for strangers, Often we had a hole through one end and a little peg with a pin into it and when the stranger sat over the hole some one was always watching to jirk the string from the other end and the stranger would go into the air, Lit up our pipes loaded with Peerless and smoked until the camp was blue. No games during the week, talked over the doing of the days and if some one had made a slob the whole crew would rost him, And often would add a little to the Myth of Paul Bunyan. At nine o'clock all lights out.[6]

Logging techniques evolved between 1850 and 1900 as an expanding market drove improvements. The earliest Wisconsin camps consisted of a single building and twelve to fifteen workers, mostly French Canadians and Yankees working under foremen from New

Moore & Galloway Company logging camp, Marathon County, Wisconsin, winter of 1891–1892 WHI IMAGE ID 58511

England. Soon after the Civil War, camps grew to house as many as thirty workers, and separate cooking and sleeping quarters were erected, connected by a covered passageway. By the 1880s camps with dozens of men from many different ethnic backgrounds included several buildings to serve different purposes—bunkhouse, cook shanty, blacksmith shop, stable, etc.[7]

During the 1870s, shallow trenches the width of a sled's runners were dug between the pine stands and the riverbanks. Filled with water, these "ice roads" considerably eased the hauling of logs, and stubborn oxen could be replaced by more easily managed horses. In the 1880s, logging railroads began to penetrate into forests far from riverbanks, and by the end of the century they enabled loggers to harvest trees year-round. In the 1890s, after nearly all the largest pine in Wisconsin had been cut down, lumber companies passed over the same acreage a second time to gather smaller trees (less than a foot in diameter); then, they went through a third time, after 1900, to take out the hardwood species. By then, camps might number up to 150 workers, most of whom performed very specialized tasks.[8]

Towns grew up wherever logs could be corralled out of the river's current and a sawmill could be powered by a waterfall or dam. The Wisconsin cities of Eau Claire, Chippewa Falls, La Crosse,

Stevens Point, Wisconsin Rapids, Wausau, Rhinelander, Oconto, Marinette, and Oshkosh all began at places where sawmills could transform logs into salable lumber.

In 1860, Wisconsin employed just 2,000 workers in the woods; in 1880, only 4,000. But between 1880 and 1890, demand for lumber skyrocketed, and the number of Wisconsin loggers grew more than fivefold. According to the 1890 U.S. census, more than 23,000 men were employed in Wisconsin's logging industry, 18,877 in logging and 4,597 in "transporting logs" (these latter managed nearly 10,000 oxen and horses). Another 32,000 workers staffed the Wisconsin sawmills that turned raw timber into finished boards.[9]

Each winter during the 1890s, these thousands of lumberjacks occupied about 450 Wisconsin logging camps and in the spring drove their timber downstream to more than 1,000 mills. A quarter of *all* Wisconsin workers were employed in logging or lumbering during the final decade of the nineteenth century. Lumber was the economic engine that drove the entire state's economy.[10]

The output of Oshkosh mills grew from an annual 40 million board feet in 1854 to 180 million in 1871. The richest harvests came from the northwest: during the 1860s, the Chippewa Valley's lumber output expanded from 60 million to 430 million board feet annually, and in the single year 1872, the Wisconsin side of the St. Croix Valley yielded 300 million. In 1883, nearly a third of the state's finished lumber and shingles came from the Wisconsin River valley, 18 percent from the Chippewa Valley, 15 percent from rivers flowing into Green Bay, and the remainder from the Wolf River valley and scattered regions. By the turn of the twentieth century, local officials keeping track of sawmill outputs estimated that more than 37 billion board feet had been harvested for lumber from central and western Wisconsin (not including shingles and lathes): just over 6 billion from the Black River, 7 billion from the Wisconsin River, 8 billion from the Wisconsin side of the St. Croix River, and 16 billion from the Chippewa River.[11]

At its peak around 1900, logging was no longer an informal, ad hoc activity but a complex, large-scale industry with highly specialized jobs and wage scales. At a typical logging camp in 1910, saw crews consisted of thirty-six men (eighteen pairs) who cut off every tree that measured four inches or more in diameter about a foot from the ground. Their logs were sawed to lengths between eight and twenty feet and skidded by teamsters to the nearest railroad spur, where crews loaded them onto cars. An average of eighteen cars was loaded each day and driven an average distance of fourteen miles to a sawmill. A typical Wisconsin logging camp in 1910 consisted of about 145 men, divided by function and wages as follows:

foreman	$100 per month with board
saw boss	$45 per month
special order boss	$45
two scalers	$40
one clerk	$35
two cooks	$60.00 & $45.00
five flunkies	$28.00
one bull cook	$26.00
two barn men	$28.00
one blacksmith	$50.00
one blacksmith helper	$30.00
one saw filer	$50.00
one filer's helper	$30.00
thirty-six sawyers	$30.00
fourteen skidding teamsters	$30.00
forty-five swampers	$26.00
ten skidway men	$26.00
four top loaders	$45.00
eight ground loaders	$40.00
four taylor's-in	$26.00
four teamsters	$30.00

A separate crew nearly as large constructed and operated the temporary logging railroad that transported logs to lumber mills.[12]

The presence of hundreds of such regiments of axmen swiftly cleared the ancient white pine forests of the Great Lakes. In 1890, the twelve-mile stretch of river between Saginaw and Bay City, Michigan, powered sixty sawmills; twenty years later, only five were left, and the industry's center had moved 600 miles west to Minneapolis. In Wisconsin in 1910, the lumber towns of Superior, Green Bay, Ashland, and Marinette were still thriving, but loggers and investors were already leaving. In 1900, Wisconsin was the number one lumber-producing state in the nation; just a decade later it was in eighth place and its annual harvest had fallen by 40 percent from its peak. "Conditions began to change in the nineties," one Wisconsin lumberman recalled, "as many of the class of men above named went to Minnesota, Idaho, Washington, California, Oregon, Canada, and the Southern States where they made good, as some of them are shipping lumber back to us."[13]

In a single generation, the majestic, ten-story pines that had stretched up into the Wisconsin sky for centuries were exterminated as ruthlessly and efficiently as the bison were swept from the Great Plains. By 1910, woodsmen had cut down two-thirds of all the trees in Wisconsin's ten most northern counties and stripped most of the state's other forests of their pine. In Douglas County, 95 percent of all trees were gone; in Marinette, Rusk, and Vilas counties, 75 percent or more had been cut down. By 1930, when the Depression hit, commercial logging in Wisconsin had almost entirely stopped and hardly any conservation or reforestation work had yet begun. Where an ancient forest had thrived for millennia, loggers left only stumps, slashings (trimmed branches and tops), and isolated, spindly trunks too small or crooked to harvest. Fires broke out across the barren cutover every summer, toppling the last trees and creating a landscape "of desolation and destruction that was most foreboding."[14]

During that same generation, Paul Bunyan emerged from the logging camps along with the two-by-fours and the shingles. Identifying the specific geographic location that gave birth to the stories about him puzzled folklorists for decades. The first collectors of the tales assumed that Bunyan moved with loggers from Maine and other northeastern states into the Great Lakes. But when researchers tried to test this assumption in the 1930s by interviewing elderly loggers, they were thwarted by several forces beyond their control.

First, many of the veteran loggers who had actually heard the Bunyan tales in logging camps had also internalized the popular versions created during the 1920s and 1930s. Their memories were unconsciously tainted with names, details, and motifs invented decades after they themselves had left the woods. Sincere though these elderly loggers may have been, their recollections of the oral tradition had been corrupted by the media.

Some aged lumberjacks also enjoyed treating young academics the same way they had treated greenhorns around the camp stove long before. With a straight face, but tongue firmly planted in cheek, they invented explanations to test the gullibility of naive collectors and innocent graduate students.

Finally, retired loggers often failed to distinguish between the tales' motifs and the hero of them. Many classic Bunyan stories, such as the harness that stretched in the rain or the corn that grew so fast it lifted men into the air, had been printed in eastern newspapers as early as the 1830s without Paul Bunyan as their protagonist. Informants remembered the motifs from their childhoods in the East and unconsciously conflated them with Bunyan tales.[15]

Nearly all of the early Bunyan researchers assumed that the lumberjack hero had probably originated in Maine. This assertion has been widely repeated in reference works ever since, despite the complete lack of evidence supporting it. Esther Shephard, who interviewed dozens of lumberjacks in the Pacific Northwest in the early 1920s, was among the first to question it. "[M]y first 'hunch,'" she told a correspondent in 1934,

> was that the original Paul Bunyan stories came from Maine.
> I changed my mind later. In talking with loggers here in
> the Northwest I found that those who came here from

the Middle States almost always knew about Paul Bunyan while, to my surprise, some men who had logged in Maine for many years did not know about him. This finding, or impression—no real proof, of course—was the basis for my belief in a Michigan or Wisconsin origin.[16]

Her notion was later confirmed by folklorists Richard Dorson and Horace Beck. For his 1946 book *Jonathan Draws the Long Bow*, Dorson meticulously searched eighteenth- and nineteenth-century New England newspapers, local histories, and manuscript collections for tall tales; he found literally none that mentioned Bunyan. Beck, who comprehensively researched the history of folklore in Maine during the 1950s, baldly concluded, "Paul Bunyan does not appear to have been known in the lumber camps." Maine certainly supplied crews, expertise, equipment, and capital to the Great Lakes lumber industry, but it did not contribute Paul Bunyan.[17]

Other researchers thought that the tales had started in French Canada. Author James Stevens believed an elderly Canadian logger who told him that Bunyan was a soldier in the Papineau Rebellion of 1837, when French-speaking residents fought their English rulers. But when folklorists Edith Fowke and Max Gartenberg tried to track down evidence about this claim, they could find no name resembling Bunyan in any of the voluminous archives relating to the rebellion. Stevens's 1925 error was widely accepted as true and appeared in a quarter of a million copies of his books. It was repeated in many standard reference sources, and this entirely fictitious Canadian fighter is still widely cited today as the model for Paul Bunyan.[18]

Not only was there no real Bunyan in the Papineau Rebellion, but there is also no mention of a fictitious Bunyan in French-Canadian folklore. Marius Barbeau, an anthropologist at the National Museum of Canada, plainly stated to researcher W. W. Charters that "...Paul Bunyan as such does not seem to be known in French Canada." Luc Lacourciere, director of the Folklore Archives at Laval University in Quebec, told Daniel Hoffman that "for my part, I have never found a trace [of Bunyan] in manuscript or printed records. His name is simply not found in them."[19]

The only evidence of Bunyan that Fowke or Gartenberg heard from Canadian loggers came from those who had worked in the United States. "On two or three occasions," Barbeau wrote, "I heard of a Paul Bunyan story from old people who had been in the lumber camps of Michigan or Wisconsin. One of them I met at Port Daniel, Gaspe Peninsula, in 1923. He was a native of that district and of Loyalist Scotch extraction. He knew some Bunyan stories and had heard them in lumber camps in Wisconsin and Michigan."

Lacourciere speculated that "Bon Jean," the name of a French-Canadian folk character, might have been brought into the United States by Canadian lumberjacks and transformed into "Bunyan." This explanation was advanced again in 1993 by Michigan author Laurence Rogers, but it is purely speculative.

Barbeau identified some French-Canadian motifs surviving in Bunyan tales, much as New England ones had: "I can recognize a number of elements which are familiar in French Canadian folk-lore. In the Bunyan stories the same style of exaggeration prevails as in the most familiar of all stories in the folk tales of French Canada, that is, in the P'tit Jean." But both Barbeau and Gartenberg pointed out the substantial differences between the larger-than-life Bunyan and the diminutive "Petit Jean" of Canadian tradition. Gartenberg and Lacourciere held open the possibility that the names might be phonetically connected, and Barbeau suggested some Petit Jean motifs may have inspired some of the Bunyan tales, but they were all confident that Paul Bunyan, the character, did not originate in French Canada.[20]

Some of the early Bunyan researchers assumed there must have been a "real" Paul Bunyan, an actual logger upon whom the folk hero was modeled. Discovering him proved as difficult as finding out where the stories had come from, because there were real Paul Bunyans everywhere. Esther Shephard discovered that "…some-one around a camp is often called 'Paul Bunyan.' From that source you get many statements as to the 'original' Paul Bunyan. One man told us that Paul Bunyan was the proprietor of five saloons at Flint, Michigan. Another statement is that 'Paul Bunyan' was a French camp cook in Michigan who was always bragging about the big logs they took out in the camp where he last worked. The American loggers began to tell stories to beat him and that is how the stories got started."[21]

Ontario researcher George Laidlaw uncovered several Paul Bunyans during a single month in 1924. "I ran across a lumberjack lately that has worked up around the north shore of Lake Superior, in the vicinity of Lake Nepigon," he wrote to Charles Brown. "He knew two Paul Bunyans, one a medium sized man who was an adept at singing French smutty songs and rendering them in English, also was a dancer. The other was a smaller man who was an adept at giving men names. These two men were lumberjacks. This man had not heard of the hero Paul Bunyan." Laidlaw concluded, "I think the name Paul Bunyan must be used quite a bit as an alias, probably, by lumberjacks, as these 2 with the foreman and the cook make four different men that have that name that I have come across."[22]

In 1993, Michigan writer D. Laurence Rogers claimed that Bunyan had been modeled on a French-Canadian logger named Fabian Joseph Fournier (ca. 1845–1875), who was famous throughout the Saginaw region for his brawling and acts of strength. Rogers quoted a 1951 letter in which James MacGillivray, author of some of the earliest Bunyan stories to be printed, described first hearing them from timber cruiser Jimmy Conn (1870–1940) and argued that because Conn worked in the same vicinity as Fournier, the latter must have inspired the stories. That logic is weak by itself, but Rogers's argument is further undermined by the fact that MacGillivray wrote elsewhere that he had first heard the tales in 1887, when Conn was only a teenager. Rogers also didn't know that by the time MacGillivray first heard them in Michigan, Bunyan stories were already circulating in Wisconsin.[23]

The earliest trustworthy mention of the name Paul Bunyan dates from the winter of 1885–1886, when two detailed, independent descriptions come from Tomahawk, Wisconsin (see chapter 5). There are dozens of recollections of Bunyan tales told after 1885 in logging camps in Wisconsin, Michigan, Minnesota, Ontario, Pennsylvania, New York, Idaho, Oregon, Washington, and California. When these references are all arranged chronologically, they strongly suggest that the tales began in the Great Lakes and spread simultaneously to the east and west. Wisconsin folklorist Charles Brown reached the same conclusion after decades of correspondence with retired loggers.[24]

As lumberjacks migrated each fall to new logging camps and left them each spring for mill towns, Bunyan stories spread not only from the Great Lakes to New England and the Pacific Northwest but also overseas. In 1918, when many loggers enlisted or were drafted into the First World War, Bunyan traveled to Europe with them. James Stevens went to the front with an Oregon National Guard unit whose members jokingly claimed that Paul Bunyan could have ended the war faster than the American Expeditionary Force (AEF). After it was over, the soldiers' newspaper *Stars and Stripes* ran letters to the editor comparing the army's camps and mess halls to those of Paul Bunyan, including one from a northern Wisconsin lumberjack. After the war, as logging became increasingly mechanized and lumberjacks were no longer an isolated population of workers with their own special skills and culture, Bunyan largely disappeared from their conversations. By then, he had already been appropriated by urban editors and publishers.[25]

CHAPTER THREE

Lumberjacks and Their Culture

*"...legends exist among the lumbermen of the Great
North, among a community shut off from the world for
months at a time..."*

T IIE BUNYAN STORIES did not arise spontaneously. They were invented by real people in actual places. This chapter investigates
the men who worked as Wisconsin loggers and spun the tall tales
about Bunyan long before they appeared in print. Who were they,
how did they live, and what did they value? In the pages that follow,
lumberjacks answer these questions largely in their own words.

In the 1840s and 1850s, as the forests of the Northeast yielded
up their last easily accessible pine, thousands of loggers moved
west into Michigan, Wisconsin, and Minnesota. Isaac Stephenson
came from Maine to the forests north of Green Bay in 1846, was
amazed at the amount of pine to be harvested, and went home
to retrieve experienced Down East loggers and equipment. Other
early Wisconsin woodsmen from Maine included C. C. Washburn,
Daniel Shaw, and Isaac Usher, who brought an entire crew west
with him in the winter of 1855–1856.[1]

Wisconsin's first lumberjacks, like their bosses, were mostly
Yankees from Maine or French Canadians who were displaced

when the fur trade moved west to the Rockies. Martin Page started logging on the upper Chippewa River in the winter of 1856–1857. "The woodmen were mostly French, Irish, and Yankees," he recalled of the early years, "many from the lumbering regions of Maine and Northern New York. There were very few Scandinavians in the Chippewa Valley at that time...There were a few Germans in the valley, but as a rule they did not take to lumbering." The same was true of the upper Wisconsin River valley: "When pine logging got under way in this section of the state," remembered William Alft, "many lumberjacks and 'river pigs' from Canada and the New England states migrated to this section of Wisconsin." These pre–Civil War loggers in Wisconsin were often educated men. In a St. Croix Valley camp where James Johnstone worked in 1856–1857, a copy of Sir Walter Scott's *Ivanhoe* was passed from logger to logger throughout the winter. Many years later, in contrast, he was forced to read aloud to his illiterate crew, who nevertheless enjoyed *Jane Eyre* enough to curse roundly or cheer aloud at appropriate moments.[2]

William Timlin worked as a logger in Michigan and Wisconsin shortly after the Civil War and described his co-workers on the Menominee River in 1871–1872 this way: "The work in the woods and on the river in those days was done by a drinking, reckless, and improvident class of men, for the most part. They were strong, generous, and bold, but not very sensible. Canadians, woodsmen from Maine and New Brunswick, and Irish boys from the farms of Wisconsin and Michigan formed the greater part of this class."[3]

By the early 1880s, immigrants from northern and eastern Europe were joining the logging workforce in increasing numbers; many of them had little or no knowledge of America, or even of logging. A sample from the 1880 census shows that almost 50 percent of Wisconsin woodsmen were from Canada, 10 percent from New York, 8 percent from Maine, 9 percent from Britain, 4 percent from Norway, and 2 percent each from Pennsylvania and Michigan. Four years later, Wisconsin officials who surveyed 3,810 "lumbermen, raftsmen, and woodchoppers" found that just under half had been born in the United States, a fourth in Canada, and 12 percent in Norway or Sweden; 7 percent were German, 6 percent British, and the rest from other countries.[4]

During the heyday of the lumber industry, between 1880 and 1910, logging camps were a multicultural, polyglot mix of laborers from many different places and backgrounds. Many Bunyan stories take clever advantage of this ethnic mix, contrasting cultural idiosyncrasies and poking fun at immigrants' accents. Loggers' countries of origin cannot always be traced in census records, but their race can, and the census shows that Wisconsin's lumberjacks were not all white.

As early as the late 1850s, bands of Ojibwe Indians, who for centuries had spread out each winter through the forests south of Lake Superior, began to winter alongside logging camps, where some joined the crews, and the presence of Indians around camps inspired at least one early Paul Bunyan story (appendix, no. 79). In the winter of 1877–1878, as soon as logging commenced around Rice Lake in Barron County, "an Indian village of sixty wigwams sprang up in a valley nearby" and some of the men worked as loggers. Knapp, Stout and Co. employed "four or five" Indian loggers in each of their camps around Chetek and Birch Lake, Wisconsin, during the 1890s. Many métis (mixed-race) descendants of white traders and Native American women also worked in the woods. Some métis woodsmen, such as James Bracklin, became well-respected foremen in part because they could supervise Native American loggers as effectively as white ones. Of the 5,600 people shown in the 1880 census as working in the woods, only 41 were identified as Indians. Most of these were loggers, but some performed chores around camps, and one, Alex Wilson of Oconto, was a timber cruiser.[5]

Until the mid-1880s, tribes in Wisconsin also managed their own logging operations on reservation lands. Despite pressure from white-owned lumber companies that wanted their timber, the Menominee and Ojibwe each employed Indian loggers and ran tribal sawmills that initially created jobs, training, and income on their reservations. But during the 1880s, the U.S. government imposed a policy called allotment on all reservations, which broke tribally owned lands into tiny fragments owned by individuals. When impoverished by an unusually hard winter or a bad wild rice season, tribal members had little choice but to sell their forest holdings. During the 1880s, white lumber companies made rapacious contracts with thousands of individuals that quickly stripped reservations of their pine.[6]

For example, during the 1880s white lumber companies rapidly clear-cut more than 400 million board feet from the Ojibwe reservations. The Oneida and Stockbridge-Munsee reservations were "almost completely denuded" of their trees during the 1880s. Government investigators concluded that the earlier policy of self-sufficient tribal lumbering

> had been perverted into a system under which greedy contractors have rushed upon the reservations; have aroused the desires of the Indians to obtain money without work; have made contracts practically unlimited as to the number of trees to be cut; have brought in swarms of white lumbermen to do the work; have already absolutely denuded the finest timber tracts, and are stripping the allotments so rapidly, that it is probable that within two or three years the pine lumber of the reservation will all be gone…

After 1889 contractors were required by law to hire Indian loggers "on equal terms, in preference to others, whenever suitable," and they remained part of the multicultural mix that made up the logging industry during the years when the Bunyan tales were being circulated.[7]

Native Americans were not the only woodsmen of color in Wisconsin. In 1880 there were also 219 African Americans in Wisconsin's northern counties, including residents of sawmill towns and logging camps. The number of black loggers rose steadily during the heyday of lumbering, until by 1910 it had about doubled, from 219 to 432. Black lumberjacks also served in the crews of rafts that brought finished lumber down Wisconsin rivers into the Mississippi. As the lumber industry moved west, so, presumably, did African American lumberjacks because by 1930 the number of black residents in thirty northern Wisconsin counties had fallen back to pre-logging levels.[8]

Racial tension often lurked just below the surface in logging camps, and it occasionally broke out. While returning up the Mississippi from a successful rafting trip to St. Louis in 1869, a group of drunken Wisconsin lumberjacks who stormed the steamboat's bar were halted by two black crew members ordered to block the stairwell. "Enraged by the thought of two 'niggers' barring their way, the raftsmen returned and mounted the stairs…," Harry Dyer recalled. "Bedlam followed, in the course of which 18 negroes were murdered." The Wisconsin loggers seized the pilot house, ran the steamboat aground, and escaped into the woods.[9]

The only black logger in Wisconsin of whom details have been discovered was "a Negro called 'Nigger Pete,'" according to William Alft of Antigo. "A man by the name of Peterson from Belle Plaine, Shawano County, who was in the Civil War, picked up this stray negro when he was about three years old, while he was in the South and brought him north after the war. He settled on a farm in Belle Plaine. The negro boy grew to manhood, always living with the Peterson family, and when old enough followed the work in the woods and river. He was a large, powerful man and it was claimed by all who knew him that he had the strength of four ordinary men. Peavie stocks that ordinary men could not break he would take one in each hand, hook them in a log, and break them with one hand."[10]

As with American Indians, black woodsmen appear in some of the most famous Paul Bunyan tales, where they are denigrated by the epithets and stereotypes one expects to find during the Jim Crow era (see appendix, no. 70, a motif that was widely repeated in later Bunyan collections). The early Bunyan tales, like mainstream American society at the time, were overtly racist, containing a broad spectrum of ethnic stereotypes that included ignorant "Scandihoovians," hard-drinking Irishmen, and crafty Yankees as well as inscrutable Indians and subservient African Americans.

As might be expected, few women worked in Wisconsin logging camps. Frank Cummings recalled, "My first experience in a lumber camp was, I believe, in the winter of 1874–75…My mother had been engaged by William, commonly called 'Bill,' Pond, to cook in a lumber camp some distance on the other side of Augusta…At that time there were a good many women cooks in camps, perhaps for two reasons: First, the crews were small as compared with those in later years, and second, there were fewer of the male sex who had learned the gentle art of cooking." Less than a decade later, however, the 1884 Bureau of Labor and Industrial Statistics found no women at all among the 3,810 woods workers. After 1900, women cooks began to cook in logging camps in significant numbers again.[11]

Occasionally other women came to logging camps. Foreman John Nelligan recalled the periodic visits of nuns deep in the woods:

> Catholic sisters often came to our camps collecting money for orphanages, and one could not help but admire their courage in going alone into the wilderness among the roughest of men without the slightest kind of protection. It is to the credit of those rough men that the sisters were almost invariably treated with courtesy and accorded the respect due them. Some there were, of course, who were always asking what business have they in the woods, but most of the lumberjacks respected them and their mission and gave freely and gladly to help them. It was through the humanitarian efforts of these women, they were well aware, that their illegitimate offspring, the unintended results of their wild revels, were reared in decency and given a chance in the world. When they came to our camps, we

always used them kindly and did our best to make them comfortable.

Nelligan concluded, "For all their rough edges, the lumberjacks were a chivalrous breed and the man who dared to be careless in his comments on respectable women was taking chances."[12]

Itinerant missionaries who occasionally made rounds through the forest were tolerated but not welcomed, especially when they came to preach on the Sabbath. Sunday was the only day that lumberjacks could mend clothes, relax, or hike to other camps for a social visit or a meal made by a rival cook; most preferred not to lose such opportunities to a sermon. John Fitzmaurice told of one missionary who berated a Michigan crew about their filthy appearance, profane language, hard drinking, and ungodly ways and then made rounds among his audience asking for a donation. Each man secretly picked some lice off himself and contributed them to a pillbox, which was dumped down the preacher's back the next morning. One Bunyan story from Wisconsin concerns a missionary's repeated attempts to convert the camp blacksmith; he is eventually stuffed up the forge chimney and emerges on the roof looking "more like the devil than a bush preacher" (appendix, no. 60).[13]

What was it like to work in a Wisconsin logging camp during the years when the Bunyan tales were created? Seventeen-year-old Joe Lucius spent the winter of 1888–1889 in the St. Croix River valley, where sleds carried loads weighing four and a half tons for eleven miles to reach the nearest riverbank. Each day began with a cook's assistant waking the crew of eighty to ninety men in the pre-dawn darkness in a "very distinct and loud voice. He would walk full length of the camp and say, 'Roll-ye-out. Roll-ye-out. Roll-ye-out and hear the little birds sing their praises to God-damn-you-get up!'"

Lucius noted that on Sundays "some wrote letters, but few could write except the Scandinavians, which were about ⅓ of the crew. About 5% French Canadian, Maine, Prince Edward Island, but

A Sunday morning shave in a bunkhouse near Chippewa Falls, Wisconsin, circa 1900 WHI IMAGE ID 1963

very few could read or write." For the literate few, the *Police Gazette* was the only reading matter available in camp. There was "no talking during meal time, no loud talking in camp, no quarreling. Fighting meant discharge." There was also "very little profanity in a lumber camp at that period. 'By the gee hovie' [Jehovah] and 'By the aternal Jasus.' I am spelling the last two just as they sounded…I never heard any singing in camp [in the evenings]. They just sat around, smoked, and visited, except on Saturday nights sometimes had a stag dance…Sundays patched clothes, darned socks, sometimes washed them."[14]

Henry Lueth recalled that in the Chippewa Valley, "All camps had their story-tellers and musicians, singers, and these would furnish all the entertainment to be obtained five nights of the seven.

A logging camp fiddler and dancer, Chippewa Valley, Wisconsin, circa 1913
PHOTO BY WILLLIAM BARTLETT, WHI IMAGE ID 55608

If we didn't have any entertainers in the camp we usually got all
the concerts we cared for from the wolves that roamed the whole
countryside in those days. They usually broadcasted their music on
the night air and it was very uncanny to hear it, too."[15]

A logger's reputation and self-worth were measured by how
much labor he could accomplish in a day; macho rivalry between

individuals, crews, and camps permeated all aspects of logging life. "There was competition in everything," recalled Thomas Pederson, who worked in the Chippewa Valley:

> The sawyers had to count the logs they sawed each day and report to the foreman every evening. So also the skidders who followed the sawyers with an ox team and hauled the logs out to the road where they were rolled up on a rollway ready for the teamsters to load on their sleds and take to the river here…it was a constant race every day, each gang striving to outdo the others in order to be able to report the greatest number of logs. It was a fine thing for the boss and also for the contractor, and we were all onto the game but we didn't care. Every gang strained itself to the uttermost to make the best showing. Another race that was more annoying was that the skidder always chased the sawyers in an attempt to put his chain around the end of a log before the sawyers had it cut off. It was considered a disgrace for the sawyers not to be able to keep out of the skidder's way.

John Fitzmaurice, who visited camps throughout Wisconsin and Michigan, believed this male competitiveness was the cause of most accidents and injuries in logging camps.[16]

"The woodsman knows," Fitzmaurice wrote in 1888, "when he goes out in the morning well and hearty, he may be brought in before night mutilated for life." After talking with loggers all across Wisconsin and Michigan, he concluded that "every lumber camp has its tragic story of disaster and death."[17]

Ax blades and saw teeth were always ready to rip open flesh or take off careless limbs. Piling massive tree trunks two-stories high on sleds, hauling them across uneven terrain, rolling them over stream banks, riding them downriver, and breaking up immense jams each offered many opportunities for death and mutilation, with the nearest doctors many miles away. Woodsmen who also worked in sawmills during the summer could lose a limb or sever an artery at any moment. The first safety guards on saws were not installed until 1891, and as late as 1907 almost 20 percent of Wisconsin's industrial accidents happened in logging camps or sawmills. "Those were the days when no pensions were paid to cripples," lumber raft pilot Matt Stapleton recalled. "[I]f the men were injured, they were left to shift for themselves and get along as best they could. There were no compensation laws in those days to protect the men when injured, and each fellow took a chance, and if he came out unhurt he was fortunate; if he was injured, he was out of luck."[18]

Injuries and illnesses were treated amateurishly by uneducated companions. Chippewa Valley camp cook F. E. Cummings recalled, "In earlier years when it meant perhaps a trip of twenty-five to fifty miles with a 'tote' team to the nearest railroad station, the sick or injured had to depend more on what care could be afforded them in camp, and they never lacked for any care their fellow workmen could give. Although not able to take advantage of hospital privilege as well as at present, nearly all woodsmen had hospital tickets. For a certain amount yearly the holder of such a ticket was entitled to free hospital treatment for sickness or injury serious enough to warrant it."[19]

"A Hospital ticket," recalled Otis Terpening, "That was what we called a Life Saver, The different hospital had agents visting the camps and selling them, They got a Per cent on ever one they sold, They cost ten dollars for a year, if you got hurt or sick they took care of you until you were well and that was all it cost you."[20]

It was common for loggers to pass the hat and collect a few dollars for an injured comrade. If he was among the literate minority, a disabled lumberjack might be employed by the company in an office job; if not, he might linger on doing light chores around camps. Many of the Bunyan stories feature a crippled woodsman whose deformity is the center around which a joke revolves, such as a limping man with one leg shorter than the other or a wooden-legged camp cook. But most injured lumberjacks were simply discarded by their employers like broken tools.

After evaluating statistics for 1910–1919, a state of Washington commission concluded that logging was "more deadly than war." Spring river drives claimed the most lives, as jams were broken and logs ridden through rapids and over falls. In 1905, eleven men died on a single day at the Little Falls Dam on the Chippewa River. When a logger was killed in the wilderness, his comrades typically buried him on the spot in a barrel or between two pieces of bark, and hung his spiked boots on a nearby tree as a grave marker. The shores beside some rapids became veritable cemeteries; one in Wisconsin claimed twenty-seven lives in a single year. On Christmas Day, Wisconsin lumberjacks greeted each other by saying, "I hope you live forever and I live to see you die." It was not an empty formality.[21]

The working life of loggers was also cut short by the brutality of the work. F. C. Leonard, who arrived in Eau Claire in 1874 and worked in the Chippewa Valley for the next thirty years, concluded that loggers "were rarely able to keep up the old pace of work and dissipation past the age of 50. Mr. Leonard's theory is that working in water did as much damage to their health as dissipation." Logging was consequently a young man's trade, and the grizzled veteran loggers who told Bunyan yarns in bunkhouses were a small and much-venerated segment of the lumberjack community.[22]

Wisconsin woodsmen such as Terpening, Cummings, Lucius, and Leonard were paid only modestly to take great risks and endure extreme hardship. Common laborers in the woods earned less than a dollar a day, plus their board; those with specialized skills or additional responsibilities might earn $30 to $50 per month; cooks and foremen, twice as much. Wages were written into a contract in the fall and paid in a lump sum in the spring. Only part of a woodsman's compensation was paid in cash; a substantial portion usually took the form of credit at the company store, where loggers could obtain necessities during the winter. If a worker left the woods for any reason before his contract was voided, he typically received severely reduced compensation for the weeks or months already worked. An early Paul Bunyan tale collected in Wisconsin ends with Bunyan tricking his crew out of their wages (appendix, no. 17).[23]

It's no surprise, then, that loggers were a transient labor force. One Wisconsin company's payroll ledgers from the 1860s reveal that most of its workers were entirely new each year; only a third carried over from the spring river drive to the following autumn's logging camps. Some were farmers who spent the months after harvest earning money in the woods, emerging in the spring in time to resume their planting with much-needed cash in hand. Others were rounded up in cities by "man catchers" through ethically dubious methods. In Chicago and Milwaukee, jails and taverns were sometimes cleaned out wholesale by lumber company recruiters, their broke and hungover occupants waking up the next day on trains rolling through northwoods forests en route to logging camps.[24]

W. G. Leonard, a lumberjack who worked in the Chippewa Valley, described the seasonal nature of logging to an interviewer in 1937:

> Each spring, after a winter in the woods, about 5,000 of these men descended on Eau Claire for a riot of drinking, fighting, gambling and women. In the matter of only two or three days a winter's pay would be gone. From then until drive time the men would be 'staked' by hotel and saloon keepers for rooms, drinks, meals and tobacco. After the drive was completed—usually early summer—another celebration was in order. Many of the men would go to Minnesota and the Dakotas for the harvest after which it would be time for another celebration; thence to the woods for fall and winter logging, and the cycle would be completed.[25]

The spring revels were an essential part of lumberjack life. At the end of the winter most woodsmen would collect their pay and head for the nearest town to celebrate until the water rose and the spring river drive started. Fresh from several months pent up in remote forests, thousands of dirty and bearded loggers burst with repressed desires into communities such as Ashland, Eau Claire, Marinette, and Rhinelander. In Superior, hundreds would link arms at one end of the main street and charge through the town, mowing down everyone in their path until they had cleared the streets. Fistfights were to loggers what gunfights were to cowboys; competitive combat was a rite of passage, and drunken brawls were commonplace.[26]

"I know you will think we were rather tough," Otis Terpening commented to Charles Brown, "But it seemed that when we had been in camp four or five months, we were so full of life and activity we just had to expand or die…One crew was always ready to fight any other crew, And when we was in some lumbering town it was sometimes rough."[27]

Edith Dodd Culver grew up in Ashland at the turn of the century, where "every spring, when the lumber camps broke up for the summer, our town was overrun with lumberjacks who flocked in with their winter's wages, bent on whooping it up in the saloons and brothels, not caring how they spent their money or who got it just so long as they could drink and revel while it lasted. Ten thousand loggers worked in the north woods in those days, and it was common to see the streets of Ashland crowded with these bearded, wool-shirted men."[28]

To small-town residents, it was like an invasion of Hell's Angels; to loggers, it was a time to prove their manhood. At the turn of the twentieth century, a Lake Superior logger named Bull Dog Regan, known for stomping on adversaries' faces with his steel-studded boots, was the acknowledged king of brawlers. Many woodsmen went through life with missing ears, smashed noses, or a mass of facial scars from defending their male honor in springtime fights.[29]

Although merchants in small towns deplored the loggers' violence, they also depended on the springtime influx of business and did everything in their power to rapidly separate the woodsmen from their wages. "The boys used to come down to Marinette for the drive," recalled James Brennan in 1929, speaking of the 1880s.

"They would all promenade up to the bar and get drinks six for a quarter, and the bartender took a drink. Then they would go out to Bill Diamond's, about a mile out in the woods from Marinette. Bill Diamond ran a dance hall. His lady used to tend bar. She would call out, 'One more big dance tonight: the last dance.' It was always the last dance; but it wasn't…The boys would blow all their money and then go back and drive logs down to the mill."[30]

"Dance" is, of course, a euphemism. Bill Diamond was a well-known brothel operator who opened his business near Marinette about 1877. Each spring he employed a woman named Mrs. Cassidy to hire prostitutes in Chicago and Milwaukee in time for the arrival of lumberjacks; some years he employed as many as sixty-five women. Diamond required that his customers lock up their earnings in his safe deposit vault, ostensibly for their own protection; loggers usually found, however, that a couple days later "when they wanted to leave, that it took nearly all of their winter's savings to pay the bill he would present."[31]

In the mid-1880s, rumors of kidnapping and violence at brothels in Marinette and Hurley reached Wisconsin governor Jeremiah Rusk. He sent an undercover agent to investigate the truth of the allegations and found that "the evidence fails to show that any innocent woman has ever been entrapped into these houses, or that any case of abduction has ever occurred. The inmates became so from choice." He blamed the rumors on sensationalist reporters from Chicago and St. Paul trying to distract readers from vice in their own communities. Rusk assured the public (with carefully crafted sarcasm, one assumes) that prostitution "will probably be eradicated fully as soon in Wisconsin as in any of the states."[32]

Marinette was by no means the only Wisconsin lumber town in which loggers found their desires easily accommodated. Green Bay, Peshtigo, Hurley, Ashland, Superior, and the mill towns of western Wisconsin all had flourishing red-light districts. "In all those towns along the [Chippewa] river there was whorehouses where the lumberjacks could go when they come to town," recalled Louis Blanchard, who logged in Wisconsin from 1886 to 1912. "They was run on a strict basis, and doctors looked the girls over every now and then…The houses had a bar and after you had a drink or two, you could hire a girl and go upstairs with her. You paid two dollars; the girls got one dollar and the house got the other dollar, and this is the way they made their living. Every house would have a half-dozen nice-looking girls to pick from."[33]

A 1913 state investigation discovered twenty-one brothels, employing more than two hundred prostitutes in Superior alone. The commission found that in most lumber towns "the world's oldest profession" was openly tolerated by the police and courts because it was essential to the local economy. Naturally, the annual spring bacchanalia produced epidemics of venereal disease. In Eau Claire, the commission traced eighty cases of gonorrhea back to a single source.[34]

Tales about Paul Bunyan's drunkenness and sexual prowess were once common but have not survived. Collectors of the stories after 1914 refer repeatedly to anecdotes "too coarse for publication," and the ex-loggers they interviewed often refused to share obscene Bunyan stories. Woodsmen's occasional references such as, "…Paul in 1911 while he was down at Woodruff on a drunk" hint at them, but the salacious and ribald stories of the oral tradition simply could not be put on paper. At the time, self-censorship kept loggers and interviewers from telling them or writing them down, and before the 1960s, no American publisher would have dared to brave prosecution and public condemnation by printing the dirty jokes of lumberjacks. Bunyan's exploits in mythical taverns and whorehouses consequently disappeared with the generation of loggers who invented them (see chapter 3).

The isolation, the danger, the male competitiveness, the brawling, and the revelry combined to create a unique lumberjack culture. After studying it in both the library and the field, folklorist Richard Dorson concluded that "the life of the jacks followed an unwritten creed, and he who violated its articles suffered dishonor and dismissal from a proud fraternity." The creed consisted first of "skill and superstamina," the ability to work superbly well from three o'clock a.m. to ten o'clock p.m. when the temperature was forty below zero. The two other supreme logger values were the courage to face any adversary in a brawl, and to get oneself and one's comrades insensibly drunk in the spring.[35]

These are, of course, core values of traditional masculinity not only in working-class occupations in the United States but across many nations and cultures. Physical strength, vocational skill, personal courage, and heavy drinking have always been the public measures of male worth, from the factory floor to the locker room.

This code may have seemed especially strong to Dorson's octogenarian informants in the 1940s—men who in their old age had lost the first three male virtues (vocational skill, super stamina, and pugilistic prowess) and retained only the last (heavy drinking). The stereotype of the supermasculine lumberjack also owed something to journalists who perpetuated it for commercial reasons. These writers, who would have been among the first to flee when the brawny woodsmen linked arms at the end of Superior's main street, romanticized the power and reckless abandonment of lumberjack legend in order to titillate middle-class readers in comfortable suburban parlors.

Any specific logger's life in 1890 was more nuanced than Dorson's code of values, journalistic hyperbole, or ex-loggers' nostalgia suggested. "Woodsmen are a good ways from being angels," wrote Chippewa Valley camp cook Frank Cummings,

> but the rip-roaring "lumber-jack" that we read about does not represent the great majority of the crew. A large proportion of the crews of my experience were made up from the men who worked in and around the saw mills during the summer, with a few mechanics whose regular employment might be slack in the winter season, also with a number of farmers, especially the younger ones, who had little farm work to do in winter and improved the opportunity to earn some money outside. Every crew would contain a number of veterans of the camps and river, and also a number of

new recruits. The great majority of the woodsmen were as sober and steady going men as one would find in any occupation. There were some among them who spent their winter's wages in the saloons soon after coming down from camp, but after giving the matter some thought, I would not place the proportion of that class higher than about one out of ten.[36]

After visiting hundreds of Michigan and Wisconsin camps between 1880 and 1888, hospital agent John Fitzmaurice concluded that the lumberjack character could be "briefly be summed up in a few terse sentences: Hard working, rough and ready, big hearted, generous, fraternal, impulsive, a hand for a friend, a foot for a foe, foolishly prodigal with his hard earned wealth, happy under very questionable conditions for joy, sensitive to the sorrows of others more than his own, and faithful to his engagements where he is used with even moderate consideration and kindness. This is the average shanty boy."[37]

Cummings agreed: "Physically a lumber camp crew would be hard to beat. It is no place for invalids or shirks, and that class would be 'shown the tote road' in short order. Even those addicted to drink when in town take on a healthy color after they have been a short time in camp. A more generous, kind hearted lot of men cannot be found anywhere than the average camp crew."[38]

Despite the brutality of their working conditions, Wisconsin's lumberjacks were slow to unionize. Although sawmill workers struck in support of a ten-hour day as early as the 1870s, loggers in the forest did not follow their example. This was due partly to the seasonal rhythms and transient nature of lumberjacks: they did not stay together as a group long enough to organize for concerted action. But it was also partly due to the culture of woods workers.

Loggers had no work "day." They signed on for an entire winter season and, being located many miles from any diversions, routinely worked twelve or fourteen hours every day, with cooks, teamsters, and some others working even longer. A lumberjack who could not finish his contract or failed to uphold his responsibilities was scorned and humiliated by his companions. In a culture whose virtues were braving frigid temperatures, felling massive trees with axes, hauling tons of unstable logs over icy roads, and risking death to break a logjam, advocating better working conditions was a sign of weakness.[39]

But as the logging industry expanded during the 1890s, the demand for more lumberjacks increased their bargaining power with employers, and radical ideas began to penetrate the forest. Charles Henry, a Chippewa Valley logging boss who first entered the woods just after the Civil War, recalled that during the nineties, "walking delegates, agitators, came in to make trouble between the employer and employed so that instead of men staying on the job until finished, as they used to, there usually is a crew going to camp, one there, and another leaving, looking for changed conditions. And, added to that disturbing element, a group of politicians...moved into all precincts to tell the masses that...all corporations were wicked robbers of the dear, unprotected people."[40]

In fact, by the 1890s new standards of social justice had sparked nationwide demonstrations and begun to improve working conditions throughout much of American industry. Progressive legislation passed between 1890 and 1914 regulated the actions of both business owners and workers, made corporations accountable to government, outlawed child labor, reduced the length of the workday, imposed safety measures, and protected workers in a wide range of industries. Henry simply resented that the Progressive movement, which was sweeping the rest of the nation, had finally reached deep into the woods.[41]

After 1900, logging grew steadily more mechanized. When railroads and trucks had replaced horses and rivers, pure brawn and reckless courage became less valuable; there were no logjams on a railroad spur. Logging camps and sawmills began to resemble conventional construction sites and factories, and lumberjacks gradually came to resemble other working-class laborers, with no unique culture of maxims, stories, and folklore spawned during long months of isolation in the wilderness. When telephones, newspapers, and radio penetrated logging camps in the 1920s, the nineteenth-century woodsmen's unique culture went the way of ox-drawn sleds, go-devils, and double-bladed axes.

By the mid-1920s, journalists and their readers were waxing nostalgic over the uncorrupted outdoor life of the hardy lumberjack, the ideal man who lived close to nature and earned his keep through honest manual labor. Their fantasies were fueled in part by fictional versions of the Bunyan stories in which the good-natured "American Hercules" and his crew of jovial misfits frolicked in an imaginary paradise. In these sanitized Bunyan stories, authors conveniently overlooked the frostbitten toes, amputated fingers, and crushed limbs found in every logging camp, along with the lice, filthy bodies, rancid odors, dirty clothes, oppressive boredom, petty cruelties, and repressed grief over killed and maimed comrades.

Many writers who celebrated the carefree lumberjack after 1925 had never met anyone who had actually harvested trees manually. Veteran woodsmen who had survived logging's supposedly "golden age" in Wisconsin were quick to emphasize how difficult and dangerous the work had really been, but the idealized caricature was too prevalent for their voices to be heard. Similarly, the original Bunyan stories told a half-century earlier in remote bunkhouses had been successfully colonized, harnessed by urban publishers seeking book sales or advertisers wanting to change lumbering's image. By 1925 the loggers' Paul Bunyan, like the life that gave him birth, was all but dead.

CHAPTER FOUR

How the Tales Were Told

*"The Bunyan stories are usually told in the evening
around the fires in the bunk-houses. The older narrators
speak in the French-Canadian dialect, and the stories
are often full of the technical jargon of the woods."*

FOLKLORE ARISES IN A COMMUNITY isolated somehow from mainstream culture, whose members all take for granted certain customs, beliefs, songs, sayings, and legends. Folklorist Richard Dorson contrasted it with learning: "Learning is handed on through books and teachers; it is precise, factual, intellectual. Lore survives in fireside talk; it is nourished by fears and fancies. Learning belongs to the individual, where lore clings to the group. We ask that lore live in people's mouths for at least several generations, that it be shared by many, that it bear the marks of much handling."[1]

By that definition, lumberjacks working together in the northern wilderness for months at a time certainly constitute a folk, and the Bunyan tales they told aloud meet the definition of folklore. Storytelling was a common pastime in logging camps, especially the sharing of tall tales that stretched both a speaker's skill at exaggerating and his listeners' gullibility. As a genre, the American tall tale reaches back into eighteenth-century New England, and some motifs used in the Bunyan stories were originally told about earlier characters around colonial hearths on the Atlantic seaboard.[2]

John Springer reported in 1851 that in Maine and New Brunswick logging camps, after work was finished, "The mine of song and story is opened, and the rarest specimens of match songs and 'stretched' stories are coined and made current by the members of the different crews."[3] Decades later, a Chippewa Valley logger told William Bartlett that lumberjacks were expected to be able to entertain one another: "A fiddler was just as necessary in camp as an ox-teamster. Dancing was not the only amusement. Each one had to contribute his part. He must sing a song, tell a story or whistle. If he could not do any of these, he must put a pound of tobacco in the 'poor box.' That pound was good for one month when he must put in another."[4] The Paul Bunyan stories were part of a cultural repertoire that saved loggers their pound of tobacco.

Until the tales were printed, though, Bunyan was not widely known, even in logging camps. Most Wisconsin woodsmen's memoirs from the period 1880–1910 fail to mention Bunyan even when they focus on lumberjack recreations. Timber cruisers John Nelligan and George Warren, who spent most of their careers in the Wisconsin and Minnesota woods between 1870 and 1910, each provided a wealth of specific detail about camp life without recording a single Bunyan story. By the time Nelligan wrote his memoir in 1927, the public had come to expect Bunyan stories from the woods, and his editor felt compelled to insert some into his manuscript anyway.[5]

Stewart Holbrook encountered the same ignorance of Bunyan when he traveled the lumber region between 1910 and 1923 to research his book about logging, *Holy Old Mackinac*. He later explained to Sterling North why it made no mention of Bunyan: "I ranged from Maine to Oregon, in all sorts of camps, and, during that time, I never heard a Paul Bunyan story told. I did hear his name mentioned—much as you would mention Joe Dokes, or George Spelvin, a sort of mythical character on which to hang a reference. Somebody might say: 'This snow ain't near so deep as the winter I was with Paul on Round River,' or something like that. Then a rash of Paul Bunyan books broke out, and are still coming out at the rate of one or two a year. I wanted to depict the logger as I thought he actually was. Hence, no reference to Paul in Holy Old Mack."[6]

Lumberjacks had other heroes besides Bunyan. Louis Blanchard, who logged in the Chippewa Valley from 1886 to 1912, said he heard very little about Bunyan but a great deal about a French-Canadian super-logger named Joe Muffreau, who performed some of the same exploits and was featured in some of the same plots as Bunyan. During the 1930s, Charles Deadman told WPA folklore collectors stories about a French-Canadian folk hero named Julius Naville, which employed the same motifs used in some Bunyan tales; in one of them, the Canadian trickster and his American counterpart meet (appendix, no. 13). Mary Agnes Starr, who heard tales about Canadian heroes Louis Cyr and Napoleon La Rue, concluded that "many an old French-Canadian-American lumberjack who could not recall a single Paul Bunyan tale could go on at length about Louis (Looie) Cyr."[7]

In practice, lumberjacks were much more likely to tell kinds of tales other than Bunyan stories. When Richard Dorson interviewed elderly loggers in the Upper Peninsula of Michigan in 1946, he found them telling "tales of toughness and brawling, cycles of anecdotes about colourful camp bosses, tall yarns framed by the white pines, and system-shocking remedies and cures"—but not Bunyan stories. "Lumberjacks sometimes tell Bunyan jokes," he wrote elsewhere, "including off color ones that don't get printed, but the major patterns of their storytelling, in my collecting experience in Michigan's Upper Peninsula, deal with vicious brawling fights, sly and ruthless camp bosses, and rough camp humor." The Bunyan tradition made up only a very small portion of all lumberjack lore.[8]

Besides being rare, the Bunyan tales did not last very long in oral form. They began to be told in lumber camps about 1885 and had largely died out by the 1920s. After World War I, lumbering was increasingly mechanized, and raw, physical strength was valued less than it had been a generation earlier. The hand tools and manual techniques of previous generations were obsolete, and the unique jargon of the trade had withered away. Instead of wintering together in remote forest shanties, loggers worked year-round and lived in permanent villages with their wives and children, who went to company schools. The stories lost their punch, and loggers lost interest in telling them. When James Stevens interviewed lumberjacks in Michigan about 1930, the majority could not tell him any Bunyan tales. By 1940, Carleton Ames found no one who could tell Bunyan stories among Upper Mississippi and St. Croix River valley loggers.[9]

But during the heyday of the lumber industry between 1885 and 1910, Bunyan tales were a unique, if small, feature of logging culture. There was no canon of Paul Bunyan stories, however; in oral form, they were not a stable collection of structured narratives like the Arthurian legends or the Arabian Nights tales. Generations of African American or Ojibwe families may have carefully preserved traditional tales about Brer Rabbit or Nanabohzo, but Paul Bunyan was not the hero of any stable narratives until he was fixed on paper.

Instead, nearly all evidence indicates that loggers' spoken references to Bunyan were fragmentary, impromptu, and created on the fly in a collaboration between the speaker and his audience. Parrish Lovejoy, who collected "an inexhaustible fund" of Bunyan tales from loggers between 1900 and 1920, explained, "The best audience included a few greenhorns, easy to string, who might be betrayed into asking guileless questions and who would be likely to accept or miss at least a few of the richer inventions." He tried to demonstrate this in a fictional account of a naive professor traveling through logging camps to research the life of Bunyan and who is ruthlessly (and amusingly) deceived again and again by his lumberjack hosts.[10]

Lovejoy corrected a correspondent who asked about the original, authentic versions of Bunyan narratives: "Chance for misunderstanding there, I judge. There were, no doubt, a set of 'standard' tales, references, allusions, etc., (which 'everybody' would be expected to know about, recognize etc) but woven all through, or adventitiously & anywhere or any time, there was apt to be some brand-new & original contribution &/or application—& this was to be expected…as part of the proper & accepted 'mode' or 'play.'" Lovejoy then went on to give this example from his own experience working with veteran loggers around the year 1900 in Michigan (eccentric spelling, parenthetical remarks, and ellipses occur in his original letter):

> One old-timer was so "good at it" that the rest of the crew kept egging him on, especially during the noon-lunch periods. The old-timer had told us about the time the ice-contractors near got stuck a-fillin of them big brewery ice-houses (which really used to line parts of Tawas Bay but how many summer visitors would know about that now?)
>
> "…so when the ice got too thick to handle good, four foot an' better & still freezing fast, they seen they was stuck, & them beer-factories had to git their ice put up—so they sent for Paul. Well Paul he looked things over & they was a big raft of logs as had got froze-in out in the middle the bay so Paul he said all right & had 'em fetch in 3–4 train-loads a-that big rope they anchors ore-boats with & run lines out ta that froze-in log-raft & tie on good…Then he had them ice-house fellers take off the fronts of all them ice-houses, & brace 'em up strong in-back, & when they had rigged like Paul he told to, they sent out word & Paul he brung in the Blue-ox team…Had 'em all fixed up good in time so he got back ta camp by noon & didn't hardly have ta lay off decking at all out at the roll-ways…Oh mebby lost time on decking up half a million foot-a logs or so & no time lost ta mention, hardly."
>
> (Story stops as tho all told. Ritualistic pause, waiting for some greenie to ask…If no actual greenie is present, some-

body pinch-hits for him & asks how the ice got packed away in the ice-houses etc…everybody understanding all the while that weeks of hard work would be involved in sawing the ice-blocks, getting them into place & insulated with saw-dust etc etc. Finally the (end-man?) pulls the trigger & asks the essential question, & the P-B-ist resumes…)

"Well th ox-team hadda strain some ta git it broke off & movin, but th way Paul done it was ta pull in all th ice on th bay at onct & leave them little contractors cut it up & pack it after Paul had it pulled inta them fronts-off houses so that practically they wasn't much ta do except shovel in th saw-dust & put them fronts back on."

It would go on like that, one incident merging into another & with local-adventitious integrating with the standard-items, for as long as that old-timer "wanted." He "made 'em up," in part or whole…& the way he braided it together—the "original" & his own "originations"—was (as I presume) a la Homer et al.[11]

Lovejoy's claim that Bunyan was rarely the center of a well-rounded, widely repeated story was confirmed by William Laughead, who worked in Minnesota and California logging camps between 1900 and 1908. He told an interviewer, "I never heard anyone in the camps or anywhere else mention Paul Bunyan in a narrative form, that is, start out to tell you a story about something Paul did…Any crews that I ever came in contact with in the woods, or any place else, wouldn't let any one man monopolize the conversation very long…He didn't just sit there and put in the evening just talking and everybody else in camp listening to him."

Interviewer: "You mean there wasn't any Homer in the logging camps?"

Laughead: "No, if there had been I don't think anybody would have listened to him. I've heard a lot of interesting things developed in the camps, but a man never told a continuous story; even if he had had an outstanding experience or been present at some

Loggers playing cards, location and date unknown WHI IMAGE ID 58513

big disaster or something of the kind. He didn't have a chance to tell that straight through. Somebody would say, 'Shorty, wasn't you at such and such a place at the time of the big flood?' 'Yeah, I was there.' And then they'd ask him some more questions, and he'd tell them some more…if there was a discussion about Paul Bunyan—it would wind up as an argument with each fellow trying to spring a gag that was a little bit bigger than the other one. I tell this, now you beat that, you know?"[12]

As Laughead indicated, narrators often deliberately left opportunities open for companions to step in and elaborate. "The stories are likely to contain occasional loose ends," Lovejoy informed Constance Rourke, "which appear from the fact that situations are described which their authors piously hope will be challenged, thus allowing a notable chance for expansion and further invention. If these openings are disregarded, the story stands as it is, and passes into currency unless some later story-teller elaborates it further."[13]

After talking with a number of retired loggers in 1938, newspaper editor H. J. Kent of Wautoma, Wisconsin, concluded, "Concerning these 'tall tales' about Paul Bunyan—or Bunion—I have always had a suspicion that they were never so tall or ingenious as some of those which have been given currency in recent years. Seasoned lumberjacks, moving westward and 'in the know,' would be likely to pass fragmentary remarks about Paul between themselves, like a hand-ball, for their effect upon the uninitiated. Casual remarks about 'snow snakes,' 'sliver cats,' 'side-hill gougers,' and 'triangulars' are, and have been, common for years."[14]

As Kent and Lovejoy pointed out, conversations about Bunyan were most often begun in order to test the gullibility of new recruits. In the Chippewa Valley, William Bartlett described how, "In every crew there would be, as a rule, those in camp for the first time, and it was for the benefit of these tenderfeet that the wonderful tales were related. A grizzled veteran would relate some astounding feat in, or associated with, logging operations, accompanied by the casual remark that this occurred the winter he worked in Paul Bunyan's camp. Some fellow-campmate would then recall having seen the first narrator in the aforesaid camp, where he also had worked, and would verify, amplify, and generally corroborate the story as told." An elderly logger told folklorist Rodney Loehr in the 1940s, "There was generally one or two good storytellers in a camp and any young fellow just starting sure got filled up on them. Some of the old timers would put in a whole week thinking up a good one to spring on a kid on Sunday morning."[15]

These new recruits were often farm boys, urban teenagers, or recent immigrants to whom the northern forest was especially intimidating. Many lumberjack yarns concerned mythical animals

Loggers in their bunkhouse, circa 1900, location unknown WHI IMAGE ID 4178

intended to frighten these innocents, and terrifying beasts appeared both as characters in the Paul Bunyan stories and in tales of their own. The fiercest of them all was the hodag, an alligator-sized monster with horns, sharp claws, vicious teeth, eyes that shot fire, and a terrifying howl. William Burtlett reported, "An old woodsman acquaintance said, that once he and some others in camp hired an Indian to go out into a swamp nearby and make the most blood-curdling noises. The tenderfeet in camp were then told this was a hodag wandering in his native wilds."[16]

New men who failed to uphold their end of the work were particularly susceptible to such treatment. Sometimes they were sent through the forest at night, fearing hodags and sidehill gougers all the way, in order to recover a piece of equipment that turned out to be imaginary. Otis Terpening, who worked in the Wisconsin and Michigan woods around 1890, described several such pranks to Charles Brown, including one that made an innocent new recruit "hit the tote road for mother and home" as soon as it was over.

Rhinelander promoter and Bunyan author Eugene Shepard made a reputation on such elaborate practical jokes, which he staged even after leaving the woods.[17]

But intimidating greenhorns was not the only reason loggers told Bunyan stories. Despite assurances to the contrary, there is also evidence that loggers did in fact sometimes tell complete stories about their hero. Some informants described bunkhouse competitions to see who could tell the yarn about Paul Bunyan that met with the best reception around the camp stove. Bernice Stewart, who traveled through Wisconsin camps during World War I to collect the stories, explained how they came up in conversation: "'That happened,' says the narrator, 'the year I went up for Paul Bunyan. Of course you have all heard of Paul.' And so the tale begins. It is matched by a bigger yarn, and the series grows."[18]

"The desire to play a joke, to make the best of an unlucky episode, to excite wonder or outdo a comrade would set someone going and others would follow," Marian McDonald wrote, after interviewing eight Wisconsin loggers in the 1920s. "Often two would put [pit?] themselves against each other to see who could tell the biggest yarn, and get the laugh on the other. As the men got interested, one after another would join. 'I can see old Gus Hendricks now' said one of them. 'He'd be lying quiet an' still in his bunk listenin.' By and by he'd raise up, "Did you every hear this one?" he'd say, and then he'd tell one to beat all the rest.'"[19]

Lovejoy "compare[d] the stories as they are told and counter-told to burling-matches, a sport of lumberjacks in which they try with deft turns of their pikes to upset each other's balance when poling rafts of logs along the rivers, a bold, continuous game that may last for hours...None of the old-timers ever laughs, either in telling or listening, and they often wrangle solemnly over details. 'That weren't the way I heern it,' one would say, and then would follow another version, whether traditional or improvised on the spot it is sometimes difficult to tell."[20]

The Bunyan anecdotes made up on the fly in damp, smoky rooms packed with tough lumberjacks possessed none of the cute sentimentality of later printed versions. "Their stories are raw and rugged, or when they tell tall tales, rapid and crisp," Richard Dorson commented after interviewing retired loggers. "The real folkstuff has bite and rawness." He found that some of the stories about Bunyan's immense size and strength included colorful ones about his private parts or sexual prowess that could not be printed.[21]

Bernice Stewart and Homer Watt had reported the same thing a generation earlier, though they recognized that having a young woman conduct the interviews may have eliminated many off-color Bunyan tales from their collection. "Some of these stories," they wrote, "as must be expected of any such series, are too coarse for publication. It has seemed to us, however, that for the most part the tales are quite wholesome; perhaps the circumstances under which they were collected have automatically excluded those of the rougher type."[22]

The scatological and salacious Bunyan tales did not survive the transition from oral tradition to print media because publishers would not risk offending middle-class readers or bringing down upon themselves obscenity prosecutions. By the time government bans and publishers' self-censorship had eased in the 1960s, all the loggers who once knew dirty Bunyan stories had carried them to their graves.

Chapter Five

The Earliest Surviving Versions

"…when he spoke, the limbs sometimes fell
from the trees."

THE BUNYAN STORIES progressed through four overlapping phases of transmission, starting with tales told aloud by semi-literate loggers in forest bunkhouses. These moved outward through newspapers and magazines published for educated, urban readers, ultimately morphing into picture book caricatures and cartoons aimed at children.

At the risk of oversimplifying a complex process, these four phases can be conceptualized this way:

1) **The oral tradition** (ca. 1885–1915): Bunyan tales told aloud in the years before they were widely published; by definition, none of these survive in print. These are discussed in this chapter and the next.
2) **The first printings** (ca. 1904–1916): tales gathered from living informants by collectors such as James Rockwell, P. S. Lovejoy, Charles Brown, Bernice Stewart, and Homer Watt, who heard them in oral settings and attempted to print them more or less accurately. These are discussed in chapters 7 through 9.

3) **Popularizations** (ca. 1914–1948): published versions in which the oral stories were deliberately embellished by professional writers to make them appeal to middle-class readers. These are discussed in chapter 10.

4) **Derivatives** (1925 and after): entirely new Bunyan stories invented by professional writers with little if any connection to the oral tradition. Most of these spun well-known motifs into fantastic tales through blatant hyperbole, mistaking exaggerated fantasies for legitimate tall tales. Some authors, such as James Stevens (discussed in chapter 10), used the oral tales merely as a launching point for entirely new fiction that became quite popular.

Determining which Bunyan tales lumberjacks actually told out loud between 1880 and 1910 is problematic. Although Stewart and Watt thought of carrying a Dictaphone into Wisconsin logging camps, no recordings of any field work on Bunyan have survived from before the 1930s. The unpublished correspondence of early Bunyan editors and dated interview notes by collectors both indicate tales that predated print, and careful mapping of motifs recorded in the earliest published versions add further evidence about the oral tradition.

Individual stories can also sometimes be dated by whether or not they contain characters and names invented by William Laughead. When Laughead prepared the first separate publication of the tales in 1914, he christened Bunyan's previously unnamed ox "Babe" and created other characters who were widely copied. Laughead explained to a correspondent in 1923 that, "When I see the names 'Babe,' 'Brimstone Bill,' 'Sourdough Sam,' 'Big Ole,' 'Johnny Inkslinger,' 'Shot Gunderson,' 'Tadpole River,' 'Benny the Little Blue Ox,' 'Big Joe, Paul's Cousin' and others, I can trace the writer's information to the advertising of The Red River Lumber Company." His names had become current by 1924, when George Laidlaw found that older loggers in Ontario generally reported that the ox had no name while young men just in from the woods always called it Babe.[1]

But this "Laughead test" does not always prove that a tale originated after 1914. Many later informants internalized Laughead's
names and used them unconsciously when recalling their youth;
some editors, such as the otherwise meticulous Charles Brown,
consciously inserted them in order to make the oral versions they
had collected live up to readers' expectations. In 1927, the editor
of logging foreman John Nelligan's memoir was so shocked to find
no mention of Bunyan that he felt "forced to take a few items out
of a book; for Bunyan stories belonged in the chapter on camp
recreation."[2]

By 1930, the authentic oral tales told in logging camps and later
popular versions created by professional writers had been woven
together into a tangled knot. In the memories of many elderly loggers, spoken versions from the 1890s and popular inventions from
the 1920s looped in and out of each other in hopeless confusion.
Editors of anthologies typically made no distinction between authentic oral tales collected in the field and absurd fictions invented
by novelists and children's authors. Most Bunyan editors before
1950 did not even cite their sources.

The only way to untangle this knot was to check the unpublished notes and letters of the earliest Bunyan editors to see how
they acquired their texts. Some of these archives did not survive, of
course, and others are clearly incomplete. But after examining the
manuscripts of all the important early Bunyan collectors and virtually all the published primary and secondary sources, I concluded
that the first reliably dated Paul Bunyan stories were told in northern Wisconsin about 1885.[3]

In 1938, retired logger Bert Taplin told newspaper publisher
H. J. Kent, of Wautoma:

> he first heard these yarns in the winter of '85 or '86, in the
> Manson camp north of Tomahawk…A cruiser by the name
> of Bill Mulhollen, in the employ of a lumber company at
> Turtle Lake, near Saginaw, Michigan, visited the Manson
> Camp on a trip from the Wisconsin Chippewa country,

and Mr. Taplin accompanied him on his search for good timber.

Mulhollen spent three nights in camp, and held Taplin's bunkmates spellbound with a steady flow of stories about the legendary lumberman...[appendix, no. 5] These yarns, says Mr. Taplin, were related with an air of authenticity, their "amperage" increasing with the cruiser's stay. Not until it was time to turn in on the last night did his bunk-mates realize how engagingly they had been taken for a "sleigh-ride," at which time they hurled overshoes and everything else that was handy at the story-teller.[4]

The man who told these stories, Bill Mulhollen, was a Wisconsin native (born in Fond du Lac County in 1849), had run off to the Civil War as a drummer boy, and soon after returning home went north to work in the Wisconsin pineries. He worked as a logger and a timber cruiser for the next several decades, eventually converting a Wausau barn into a home where he lived with his wife and a daughter when he wasn't in the woods. He ultimately followed the lumber industry to the Pacific Northwest, where he and his wife were living in 1910. At the time that he told these first Bunyan tales, he was thirty-seven years old, and the Manson Company was logging on the Rice and Tomahawk rivers north of Tomahawk in Oneida County.[5]

The logger who recalled hearing them, Bert Taplin (1857–1943), was born in Green Lake County and entered the woods at age fourteen, in 1871. He initially drove a tote team in the Tomahawk region and then worked for the next fourteen or fifteen years in the seasonal round of winter logging, spring river drives, and summer sawmill labor; after his marriage in 1886, he farmed in the summer and fall near Wautoma. As late as 1894 he was still working for the Manson logging company in camps between Tomahawk and Minocqua, but he ultimately settled in Wausau, where he died in 1943. His obituary reported, "Mr. Taplin always stoutly maintained that the greatest mythical lumber jack of all times, Paul Bunyon [*sic*], originated in the logging camps of northern Wisconsin."[6]

Taplin's account meets most of the standards for valid evidence that historians traditionally employ (see chapter 11). It is specific and detailed, and it possesses proximity in space; Taplin had lived in the same area where he heard Mulhollen during the intervening decades. He was known as a credible informant to local newspaperman H. J. Kent, and he had no obvious motive for fabricating his account. It's also plausible; similar accounts date from only a few years later, when Bunyan tales were known to be circulating in the vicinity.

Taplin's information is also independently corroborated by another logger who was in the same vicinity at the same time. "In the summer of 1886," Kent continued in his November 9, 1938, letter to Brown, "Jim McKeague of Wautoma worked on the road at Tomahawk, when there was barely a building there on the Fourth of July. When he returned in the winter, the town had built up with 17 saloons, 2 brothels, and several stores. He was a clerk in Jack Clark's double-front store, and heard Bunyan stories there." After talking with retired comrades, Kent concluded, "It also appears that Bunyan stories were not current in camps south of Marshfield, but were congenial to the regions of heavier pine, and probably travelled with choppers rather than mill workers."[7]

Just a few years after Taplin and McKeague heard the first Bunyan stories in the Wisconsin River valley, Charles Brown encountered them in Oshkosh, at the bottom of the Wolf River valley. "I think that I may truthfully state," he replied in 1934 to an inquiring graduate student, "that my own interest in the Paul Bunyan tales goes back to my young manhood in the nineties, when I heard some of the first of these from lumberjacks and men engaged in lumbering operations in the Wisconsin pineries. At lease one member of my relatives was engaged in this business." He later told W. W. Charters that this was "in the early nineties at Oshkosh by an uncle who was a lumber camp boss and also operator."[8]

Earwitness accounts of the oral tradition in Wisconsin multiply rapidly after those records from the mid-1880s and early 1890s. Bernice Stewart heard them in childhood visits to Wisconsin logging camps about 1903 and had no difficulty collecting them directly from veteran woodsmen in 1914–1916, and James Rockwell published a collection in Milwaukee in 1910. "In the past twenty years," Brown summarized in 1934, "I have [heard] these stories told over and over again by lumberjacks and others who came from lumbering regions all over northern Wisconsin and Michigan, also from Ontario, New Brunswick and other parts of Canada, from Maine and Minnesota."[9]

Another group of Wisconsin tales was gathered by Eau Claire historian William Bartlett (1861–1933) from loggers and lumbermen between 1913 and 1928. He identified his informants by name and published many of their memoirs in local newspapers and a book. Bartlett also communicated with all the other Wisconsin collectors of Bunyan lore. He died in 1933, struck down while crossing a Madison street on his way to participate in a program about Paul Bunyan.[10]

About 1927 Bartlett summarized what he had learned about the Bunyan tales in a seventeen-page manuscript he titled, "Paul Bunyan and Other Logging Camp Yarns," only a few paragraphs of which appeared in print. In it he deplored the popularization of the stories that was then sweeping the nation and went on to tell eleven Bunyan anecdotes and other tall tales in his own words; five of these had appeared nowhere else.[11]

Bartlett called characters by Laughead's names in 1927; apparently he adopted them himself because they were current, or his informants had internalized them after 1914. Bartlett also published the tales in newspapers before they had become widely known. In 1916 he printed in the *Eau Claire Telegram* Malloch and MacGillivray's 1914 "Round River" poem and excerpts from Stewart and Watt's 1916 collection under the titles "Logging Camp Yarns" and "Extracts from Paul Bunyan Yarns." Before his death, he also saw through the press dozens of short memoirs by lum-

berjacks, logging cooks, and raft pilots; described Shepard's hodag hoax; wrote historical articles of his own; and addressed local
groups on logging history, folklore, and customs.[12]

Different strains of the oral Bunyan tradition were also preserved
in three separate recensions from other Great Lakes states. In 1904,
the *Duluth News Tribune* briefly summarized four of the tales, presumably heard among loggers in northeastern Minnesota; this was
the first mention of Bunyan in print so far unearthed. In Michigan
in 1906, James MacGillivray published nine of the stories in a
small-town newspaper, the *Oscoda Press*. Then in 1914, William
Laughead of the Red River Lumber Company in Minneapolis
created a thirty-two-page booklet containing seventeen tales,
Introducing Mr. Paul Bunyan of Westwood, Cal., for the company's
customers as part of an advertising campaign. Unlike the earliest printings of Bunyan tales from Wisconsin, MacGillivray and
Laughead deliberately embellished the Michigan and Minnesota
stories for literary or advertising purposes.

The early Wisconsin Bunyan tales printed from 1910 to 1916 dif-
fer significantly from those assembled in Michigan by MacGillivray
and in Minnesota by Laughead (see chapter 7, Table 2). This might
suggest that different tales were popular in each state, but the seasonal mobility of loggers throughout the entire lumbering region
invalidates this conclusion. It is more likely that each editor simply
preferred some tales over others and chose to omit some that his
peers included.

The Bunyan tales told by loggers in Wisconsin between 1885
and 1915 share several features that distinguish them from the
better-known popularizations that followed.

First, Bunyan is portrayed in them as a lumberjack like his creators rather than as a fantastic superhero or magical demigod. He
is illiterate like most of his audience: "In the gentle art of writing
Bunyan had, however, no skill. He kept his men's time by cutting
notches in a stick of wood, and he ordered supplies for camp by
drawing pictures of what he wanted." He is a foreman rather than
a laborer, and he possesses unusual strength and skill, but he lives

in the same world as the men who invented and listened to the stories.[13]

Second, the earliest stories are laced with logging jargon that establishes both the speaker and listener as insiders, fellow members of a distinct community separate from mainstream society. Jokes such as, "Paul selected the famous 'round' forty, in section thirty-seven" and phrases such as, "That night Paul set the new man sprinkling the dry road," can be understood only by the initiated; the same is true of the frequent mentions of skidding tongs, peaveys, prune stones, sinkers, and other artifacts in the material culture of a logging camp. There are also routine references to rituals of lumberjack life, such as meals and the seasonal bacchanalia: "Paul Bunyan was a pioneer lumberjack, of French-Canadian birth, with a little Scotch in him. (Sometimes quite a lot, especially when his camp would break up in the spring.)"[14]

The earliest stories also play heavily on competitive masculine values such as physical strength, aggression, and drinking. "The lightest team in camp that winter weight 6,411 lbs," reported one informant, "and they just kept them in the cook camp to deck frid-cakes with." Bunyan himself "licked more men and got drunk in more new styles than any other knight of the peavie in those days." They also celebrate the virtues on which loggers prided themselves: "They were generous to a fault, give a 'twenty' to a bum, or clean out a bar-room and lick up all the rum."[15]

In all these ways the oral tales represented loggers' idealized version of themselves—massive in size, amazingly strong and clever, courageous in the face of adversity, capable in emergencies, and good-natured with comrades. As Daniel Hoffman suggested more than fifty years ago, the Bunyan stories enabled loggers to face their fears obliquely. They allowed men who endured hardship and risked death every day, but whose anxiety had to be repressed in the prevailing macho culture, to fantasize that things could be far worse and yet still come out right in the end. Bunyan showed them conquering their worst fears bravely, creatively, and successfully.

Many of the earliest stories recycle old motifs recorded long before Bunyan himself was invented. For example, in a story preserved by William Bartlett,

> it was necessary to build the camp on a high, rounding hill, far from water. A well thirty feet in diameter and 200 feet deep was dug. For curbing, timber piles were driven in around the well. The timber in that vicinity was soon cut and the camp dismantled. As the timber piling of the well was still sound and good, it was pulled out and sawed up into logs. Within a few years, the wind had blown the sand from around the old well, leaving the bare hole sticking up many feet in the air, and which may still be seen from miles around.

This projecting hole motif also appeared in the *Knickerbocker Magazine* in New York in 1850 (where bank swallow burrows are left protruding) and probably dates back much further. The stretching harness and lucky hunter Bunyan tales have similarly deep roots in American folk culture.[16]

Finally, although their creators were poorly educated, working-class men, the humor in many of the stories turns on logical paradoxes worthy of Lewis Carroll. After firing his gun, Bunyan "ran so rapidly that he outran the load and got the full charge of buckshot in the seat to his pants"; on another occasion, "It was so darn cold that the flame in Paul's big lantern froze." The famous Round River had no outlet but instead flowed in a closed circle; a particular crew member could leap even the widest river in only three jumps. The well-known pyramid forty was a hill "so very high that to see its peak took a week of steady looking." Bunyan "dragged a whole house up a hill with the help of his ox, and then, returning, he dragged the cellar up after the house." Such humor is not mere comic exaggeration but a sophisticated play on the basic conceptual categories with which we construct reality. Many other examples could be quoted from the surviving evidence of the oral tradition.[17]

The hero of these earliest Wisconsin Bunyan tales bears little resemblance to the jovial, working-class buffoon, the scheming middle manager, or the ultrapatriotic superhero that he would later become. Until the 1920s, loggers imagined Bunyan as one of themselves and defined him for their own purposes. But after the stories left the bunkhouses for the printed page and became a commodity to be sold to urban readers, he evolved into a symbol of national ideals and corporate values. By 1925, loggers had lost control of their representation of themselves, and Paul Bunyan had been appropriated by the mass media.

CHAPTER SIX

The Curious Claims of Gene Shepard

"I worked for Paul that winter. I was a young boy at that time and he put me wheeling prune stones away from the cook camp."

"**D**URING HIS ACTIVE YEARS," the local newspaper wrote when Gene Shepard died, "he spent virtually half his time in the open and was happiest when 'roughing it.' Mr. Shepard has cruised timber in the north, south and west. He engineered many timber deals for lumber concerns, in which vast sums were involved. Throughout the northwest he had a large acquaintance among lumbermen...He was one of the original Paul Bunyan boosters and his 'Round River Drive' [*sic*] is a clever oddity in verse...All told, Gene Shepard was in a class by himself and his memory will linger long. Woodsman, artist, nature lover, story teller and entertainer, he was undoubtedly one of the most unique personages to be found anywhere in the country."[1]

He also made two outrageous claims about the Bunyan tales that were often repeated. At least one of them was a lie.

Eugene S. Shepard (1854–1923) began cruising northern forests as a teenager in 1870. Over the next three decades he mapped and estimated the market value of vast holdings of lands owned by Cornell University, the Goodyear Company, and other clients, making and losing more than one fortune. He was equally at home with lumber barons and Ojibwe elders, and he was fluent in both of their languages. His plat books of Oneida, Vilas, and other northwoods counties were accepted as the official maps, and his son estimated that he named more than two hundred northern Wisconsin lakes. He was a first-class surveyor, upright businessman, and flawless cartographer who, paradoxically, never let the facts interfere with a good story.[2]

Though his timber estimates and survey notes were impeccably accurate, Shepard was best known as an imaginative liar, an enthusiastic practical joker, and a heavy drinker. His most famous prank was an 1896 claim, pulled off with help from his friend Luke Kearney, that he had captured a live hodag. Aided by creative taxidermy, clever ventriloquism, dim lighting, and pulleys and wires, Shepard convinced hundreds of visitors to the Oneida County Fair that the ferocious beast was real. The story was picked up in the press and reported as scientific fact across the nation. After the truth was known, customers continued to pay to see his fake hodag, not because it was a new scientific discovery but because it was the greatest hoax of the century. In later years he also led guests at his resort into the forest to find "perfumed moss" (which he had scented the previous night from a jar) and enticed anglers onto the lake by making mechanical fish jump in the distance.[3]

Like other timber cruisers, Shepard bivouacked in logging camps when in the woods and socialized with lumberjacks when they came into Rhinelander each spring. He was a friend to everyone and a charismatic talker, with countless acquaintances throughout the Wisconsin and Minnesota logging regions; his biographer called him the region's most famous timber cruiser. Joe Lucius arrived in Superior in 1887 and worked as a logger or forester all over northern Wisconsin for the next several decades. He remembered Shepard as "a tall and very homely man generally wearing, when in his home town, a straw hat, overhauls, and rubbers. When he

Eugene Shepard driving his favorite horse,
Getaway, circa 1900

FROM *PAUL BUNYAN, HIS CAMP AND WIFE,* 1929

was about there was al-
ways 'something doing.'
He knew everyone, and
almost everybody knew
Gene…He was a good
story teller widely known
for his tall tales."[4]

"He had a sense of
showmanship," his son
recalled in 1963, "and
a showman is what he
should have been…in those days, people may not have known who
the President of the United States was, but they all knew who Gene
Shepard was. He was very welcome wherever he went, and he went
into some of the damnedest places."[5] Wherever Shepard went, he
told stories about Paul Bunyan, with whom he claimed to have
worked in his youth.

A fellow timber cruiser, Martin Fitzgerald, specifically recalled
how Shepard told the Bunyan stories:

> As the lumberjacks sat around the bunkhouse evenings, lis-
> tening to stories, "Gene" Shepard was their conception of
> Paul Bunyan. I can see him now sitting in the chair, with
> one leg crossed over the other, with the upright foot tossing
> back and forth as he talked…Gene was a heavy man with a
> happy round face which reflected his thoughts as he related
> his yarns. I have heard him repeat stories, but they were
> never the same as the original telling. Always he added new
> particulars and amplified with greater details of astonish-
> ment the story at each unfolding. I think more fascinat-
> ing episodes in Bunyan tales originated with Gene Shepard
> than in any other mind…Shepard may have obtained the
> original idea from some other lumberjack, but the listener
> would never recognize the creation after Shepard's second
> telling, so marvelous were the circumstances supplied.[6]

Shepard even said that he had invented Paul Bunyan. He told Charles Brown that this had happened "about 45 miles west of Rhinelander," a story that Brown repeated more than once. Fred Holmes reported in 1938 that, "This view of the authorship of the Bunyan stories was confirmed by many personal acquaintances of Shepard who enjoyed his companionship in logging operations in Northern Wisconsin." In October 1920, Gifford Pinchot, chief of the U.S. Forest Service, 1905–1910, stopped in Rhinelander and called on Shepard, "who claims to be the originator of Paul Bunyan." Pinchot wrote to P. S. Lovejoy that Shepard "says he has been telling Paul Bunyan stories for fifty years" and was "one of the queerest geniuses I have ever met."[7]

Shepard lied for dramatic effect so often about so many things that claims by him must always be considered false until confirmed by outside evidence. At the time he met Pinchot, for example, he was suffering from both physical and mental illnesses, and if he had been telling Bunyan stories for fifty years (since 1870), he must have made them up as a teenager as soon as he entered the woods.

But two pieces of circumstantial evidence lend some credence to his claim to having created Bunyan.

First, in the fall of 1882, Shepard set up a logging camp outside Rhinelander, where he harvested pine until the following March; he had many opportunities that winter to tell Bunyan tales among the men who worked for him. Only three winters later, Bill Mulhollen told the first documented Bunyan tales just a few miles away, near Tomahawk (see previous chapter). No documents have been found to connect Shepard and Mulhollen, but during the early 1880s the two moved in the same limited social circle in upper Wisconsin River lumber towns. The proximity of the two earliest documented Bunyan raconteurs is suggestive, even if no conclusive proof validates Shepard's claim to being the person who invented the lumberjack hero.[8]

Second, Mulhollen's only surviving tale described Bunyan harnessing a moose to pull a sled (appendix, no. 5); Mulhollen told about it, but Shepard actually did it. In 1896, he imported a pair of moose from Minnesota, trained them to pull his two-wheeled trap, and made postcards of himself driving it. In typical fashion, Shepard claimed they could outrun any team of horses, though apparently no one ever saw them move faster than a gentle trot. Of course, Shepard may have taken the idea from a tale that was circulating orally rather than being the inspiration for the story; or he could have thought it up independently.[9]

What *can* be known for certain is that Shepard was in the right place at the right time to have invented Bunyan, that he circulated the stories throughout the logging region long before they appeared in print, and that he played a central role in popularizing them during the heyday of Great Lakes lumbering. William Laughead knew about Shepard when he compiled the first Bunyan book in 1914: "There was a man named Shepard—he was no relation to the Esther Shephard that later wrote the Paul Bunyan stories. He lived in Rhinelander, Wisconsin, and he was a noted a wit and was quite a character. He had told a lot of Paul Bunyan stories. I think some of them were probably told in Wisconsin papers, and had gotten into print that way [none have been found], but they hadn't reached beyond that territory. I had never seen any of his stories, and I don't know that any of them were ever illustrated."[10] By the time the Bunyan tales were first set in type, Shepard had been telling them for nearly a generation.

We don't know which stories made up his oral repertoire because little or no documentation survives. He had received only a rudimentary education in a rural schoolhouse, and putting words on paper was probably more difficult for him than speaking off-the-cuff. His first venture into publishing Bunyan tales was outright plagiarism, his second was heavily dependent on previous versions, and the third was dramatically recast after his death by his widow. These three problematic publications are the only record of what Shepard was saying about Bunyan in logging camps in the late nineteenth century.

The first of these publications involved Shepard's second outrageous claim. On April 25, 1914, James MacGillivray and Douglas

Malloch published their poem "Round River Drive" anonymously in the *American Lumberman,* and within two weeks Shepard was claiming he had written it himself. In a letter to a client on May 10 Shepard wrote, "I will send you some anecdotes and observations made during one winters logging 40 or 50 years ago in Paul Bunyans camp on Round River, as soon as I have them in printed form." He ran off a number of broadsides whose Round River text was identical to Malloch and MacGillivray's word-for-word, except that he replaced the original Michigan place names with Wisconsin ones. These broadsides were signed "E. S. Shepard And American Lumberman"; when they were exhausted, Shepard shamelessly reprinted the text as a trifold pamphlet issued by the C. C. Collins Lumber Company of Rhinelander.[11]

When William Bartlett wanted to reprint the poem in 1917, he contacted Shepard, who embellished his lie by insisting "it must go in just as it reads including my signature and the name of the American Lumberman as it is copyrighted." This prompted Bartlett to contact Malloch, who told him, "Needless to say, it was written by myself. I cannot understand what Mr. Shepard means by sending out the poem in the shape he did as it certainly creates a false impression. I assume it was an inadvertence on his part." Charles Brown thought that Shepard probably considered it just another practical joke. To someone who had hoodwinked the nation's press with the hodag hoax and collected fees from hundreds of tourists to smell scented moss, lifting another writer's work probably seemed a minor matter.[12]

In any event, Shepard passed off "Round River Drive" as his own for the next several years. Less than a year before his death, he referred to it publicly as, "the story the *American Lumberman* poet helped me get into rhyme." Wisconsin authorities continued to mistakenly cite him as its author for several decades. In 1938 Malloch, its true author, and his wife stopped in Rhinelander at a logging museum and bought a printed copy for 25 cents, only to discover that it was credited to Shepard. Malloch told Charles Brown that "it was the first time that he had ever paid for a copy of his own verses."[13]

Shepard's second Bunyan publication was less controversial. On May 11, 1922, after both his mental and physical health had greatly deteriorated, he published in the Rhinelander newspaper a letter reminiscing about his days working for Paul Bunyan back in 1862. In only three paragraphs, he introduced ten jokes. Seven of these had previously appeared in other publications, including, of course, MacGillivray's and Malloch's "Round River" poem.

Three of the stories were new, however. Those concerned wild black potatoes that caused the Irish loggers to riot, passing mention of a character called Finn Lawler (the name of an actual timber cruiser who had worked in Vilas and Oneida counties), and Paul's wife cleaning him up before Shepard drew his portrait: "I am inclosing…a picture I made of Paul in 1911 while he was down at Woodruff on a drunk. His wife had just come to town after him with some Indians. She consented to my sketch of him when she had made him presentable by parting his hair with a hand axe and combing it with a piece of old crosscut saw." This hair-combed-with-ax-and-saw motif was repeated later the same year, credited to Shepard, in the Red River Company's pamphlet *The Marvelous Exploits of Paul Bunyan* and went on to be widely anthologized for several decades.[14]

Portrait of Paul Bunyan, by Eugene Shepard, circa 1916

WHI IMAGE ID 57974

The portrait of Bunyan that accompanied the piece stands in stark contrast to the happy-go-lucky, French-Canadian lumberjack made famous by Laughead, or the sleek, muscular giant of Rockwell Kent. In Shepard's portrait, Bunyan looks like a person who has actually spent several months in the woods and, despite the careful grooming with ax and saw, resembles a Sasquatch more than the Bunyan of Disney cartoons and amusement parks. Gifford Pinchot told P. S. Lovejoy that it resembled, "the earliest type of known man."[15]

Shepard sent the Bunyan drawing and broadside to Bartlett on March 30, 1917, with the comment, "This is only about ¹⁄₁₀ the stuff I have on the history of this now famous old devil. I will write you some more of the stuff along the same lines some day when it rains or school don't keep and send it to you. I am so busy now that I have no time but will try and remember you." Sickness, marital problems, legal controversies, and financial reversals all appear to have kept him from sending anything more. Shepard's earlier books and files had become the property of his first wife in a 1911 divorce settlement, and when he died in 1923 his remaining papers, presumably including any later Bunyan material, passed into the care of his second wife, Karretta. Neither group of manuscripts has ever been located.[16]

His country seat, a drawing used by Eugene Shepard on his business card, circa 1916

After Bunyan became a national icon in the late 1920s, Shepard's widow collected many of the Bunyan stories he had told, put them into amateurish verse, and printed them as *Paul Bunyan: His Camp and Wife.* Karretta Shepard explained to W. W. Charters that the poems had not been written by her husband ("had he written them they would have been told better and much more interesting as he was an exceptionally good story teller while I am simply no good at it") and described the book's origin: "a friend of Mr. Shepard's, Judge Eastman's wife, of Chicago, insisted that I write them, so I tried to tell them as I remembered them, even to the explanation of the origin of the hodag." Although the words in the poems are hers, the tales and motifs are those that she could recall Shepard telling and retelling over the years.[17]

The book is illustrated with eleven of Shepard's original drawings of Bunyan and northwoods life, as well as photographs of his home and of the hodag. Conspicuously absent from the collection is "Round River Drive," perhaps because Karretta Shepard knew he was not its author. By the time the book was printed in 1929, Bunyan stories were sweeping the nation and few of the book's jokes, motifs, or characters were entirely new. The best-known ones, such as the pyramid forty, the

SKIDDERS AHEAD OF THE SAW.

Skidders getting ahead of the saw, by Eugene Shepard FROM *PAUL BUNYAN, HIS CAMP AND WIFE*, 1929

round river, the winter of the blue snow, the ham-skating cooks, and the stretching harness, are included, and the sidehill gouger and the hodag make predictable appearances. The only original anecdote in the book describes Bunyan shooting five thousand deer with bullets made from morphine pills; these "were put to sleep and stacked like hay" (appendix, no. 75).[18]

Shepard's published versions of the Bunyan tales did not reach a wide audience. His ephemeral "Round River" plagiarism quickly disappeared, and *Paul Bunyan: His Camp and Wife* died on publication; only six libraries in the world own it today. He did not live long enough to see himself cited as a source by the editors whose Bunyan books reached exponentially more readers than his own. Shepard's legacy lay in having told Bunyan tales aloud so well and so often during his cruising career, between 1885 and his retirement about 1905, that they lodged forever in the memories of hundreds if not thousands of lumberjacks. There they took on a life of their own, circulating around camp stoves in smoky bunkhouses for a generation before finding their way into print.

Chapter Seven

Out of the Woods and Onto the Page

"In the gentle art of writing Bunyan had, however, no skill. He kept his men's time by cutting notches in a stick of wood."

LOGGERS TOLD STORIES ABOUT BUNYAN deep in the forest for nearly thirty years before the outside world caught wind of him. Woodsmen invented him, swapped tall tales about his exploits, inserted caricatures of themselves onto his crew, and used him to express their ideals and their apprehensions. For the whole time Great Lakes forests were being cleared by hand, Bunyan was the private possession of the lumberjacks and existed only in their imaginations. But about 1910, all that began to change.

The name "Paul Bunyan" appears to have been printed for the first time on August 4, 1904, in the *Duluth News Tribune*. The paper's daily gossip column, "Caught on the Run," outlined four of the tales without giving a full version of any of them. Here is the earliest article about Paul Bunyan in its entirety:

In spite of a great deal of talk about the decline of the great American Lumber 'Jack he remains the same jolly picturesque individual that he was in days gone by. His language, his jokes and his apparel are a never ending source of amusement to those who have not grown accustomed to his ways.

If the firm for which he works fails to suit his taste in the matter of food, blankets or length of the work day, the luckless capitalists are immediately classified as being "gunnysack," "haywire," or "lard can."

His pet joke and the one with which the green horn at the camp is sure to be tried, consisted of a series of imaginative tales about the year Paul Bunyan lumbered in North Dakota. The great Paul is represented as getting out countless millions of timber in the year of the "blue snow." The men's shanty in his camp covered half a section, and the mess camp was a stupendous affair. The range on which an army of cookees prepared the beans and "red horse" was so long that when the cook wanted to grease it up for the purpose of baking the wheat cakes in the morning, they strapped two large hams to his feet and started him running up and down a half mile of black glistening stove top.[1]

This, the earliest printed evidence of the oral tales, contains the heart of the entire Bunyan tradition. The motif of his great size and power is basic, of course. The opening jokes about his crew having cleared North Dakota of its forests and the "year of blue snow" recur in most of the later collections, as does the anecdote about his enormous stove being greased by cooks skating on hams. This short paragraph, however, gives only seeds of the tales; they sprouted in the articles that followed.

The first printing of any Bunyan stories in fuller form occurred two years later, when the unsigned article "Round River" was printed in the *Oscoda* (Michigan) *Press* on August 10, 1906. It was written for a special commemorative edition of the paper and told about a dozen Bunyan anecdotes in a linked sequence. Although it was unsigned, the piece was drafted by lumberman James MacGillivray for his brother William, editor of the newspaper. The brothers had grown up in Oscoda and had worked in the lumber industry throughout the Great Lakes and Pacific Northwest. Many of their 1906 stories, such as the title tale in which Bunyan's loggers encounter a river that flowed in a circle with no outlet, were repeated for decades by other Bunyan editors.[2]

James MacGillivray gave conflicting accounts of where the stories came from. In 1948 he told the *Milwaukee Journal* that he had first heard about Paul Bunyan in 1887 near Grayling, Michigan, as a thirteen-year-old chore boy at a camp on the Au Sable River: "Hardly an evening went by that some lumberjack

CAUGHT ON THE RUN.

* * *

In spite of a great deal of talk about the decline of the great American Lumber Jack he remains much the same jolly picturesque individual that he was in days gone by. His language, his jokes and his apparel are a never ending source of amusement to those who have not grown accustomed to his ways.

If the firm for which he works fails to suit his taste in the matter of food, blankets or length of the work day, the luckless capitalists are immediately classified as being "gunnysack," haywire" or "lard can."

His pet joke and the one with which the green horn at the camp is sure to be tried, consists of a series of imaginative tales about the year Paul Bunyan lumbered in North Dakota. The great Paul is represented as getting out countless millions of timber in the year of the "blue snow." The men's shanty in his camp covered a half section, and the mess camp was a stupendous affair. The range on which an army of cookees prepared the beans and "red horse" was so long that when the cook wanted to grease it up for the purpose of baking the wheat cakes in the morning, they strapped two large hams to his feet and started him running up and down a half mile of black glistening stove top.

* * *

The first mention of Bunyan in print occurred in the Duluth News Tribune, *August 4, 1904*

did not bring out some new angle on the prowess of a mythical 'Paul Bunyan.' I had never heard the name before, despite the fact that I had lived in the renowned lumber mill area of Oscoda–Au Sable, twin towns that led the world in saw mill production in the eighties."[3]

But three years later the aging MacGillivray told the Library of Congress that he first heard the stories from Jimmy Conn (1870–1940), "a little, wizened, log-jobbing Irishman" who would have been only a teenager in 1887. Conn was Michigan's version of Gene Shepard, "rearranging, augmenting or subduing the fabulous feats of one, Paul Bunyan, that were circulating through the Michigan lumberwoods…He soon grew renowned through the Great lakes timber country as a super tale teller."[4]

These two earliest publications of Bunyan tales (Duluth 1904 and Oscoda 1906) did not overlap at all; the 1906 Michigan text does not contain any motifs printed in the 1904 Minnesota article. This suggests that MacGillivray had not seen the group printed in Duluth two years earlier.

The two inaugural printings of Bunyan stories also did nothing to make the lumberjacks' hero better known. The two newspapers reached only local audiences in lumber towns: the *Duluth News Tribune* had a circulation of only fourteen thousand and the *Oscoda Press* just nine hundred. In each paper the Bunyan material was presented as an inside joke aimed at readers already familiar with logging, rather than as stories intended for outsiders. The general public was not alerted to the Bunyan tales until six years later when, in February 1910, a national magazine based in Milwaukee collected the largest group gathered to date and sent them to readers all around the country.

The article, "Some Lumberjack Myths," appeared in the February 1910 issue of *Outer's Book*, a Milwaukee nature magazine.[5] Although edited and published in Wisconsin, *Outer's Book* reached a national audience of forty-one thousand readers with articles about hunting, fishing, and camping. The article's author, James Evan Rockwell (1883–1953), was a reporter for the *Duluth Herald* who had grown up in Ontario. Starting as a cub reporter on the *Herald* in 1903, he eventually rose to be its city editor and later went on to publish newspapers across the Midwest.[6] In his 1910 *Outer's Book* piece, Rockwell told seventeen Bunyan tales. He expanded all but one of those found in the 1904 *Duluth News Tribune* into complete stories and added several new ones (appendix, nos. 2, 20, 21, 30, 35, 70, 74, 81, 82, 84, and 88).

Rockwell did not identify his sources beyond saying,

> The old stories told around many a roaring log stove are likely to be forgotten unless an effort is made to preserve them in print. The old time lumberjacks were French Canadians—Maine men, men from the big woods of Michigan,

specialists in their line. They were big, red-blooded, courageous men, who followed the woods as a profession, and
an interesting, dangerous profession it was. They were men
of nerve, imagination, and great physical strength…in the
camps of Northern Minnesota, men may yet be found who
have logged in Maine, ridden the rapids of the Ottawa,
helped strip Michigan of her forests, and who are now beat-
ing down the last stand of the white pine in the North.
These are the men who will tell you of Paul Bunyan…[7]

Rockwell provided his own photographs of logging camps to
illustrate the piece, and he had obviously been in the forest listening to woodsmen talk about Bunyan. Gene Shepard also turns up
in Rockwell's article, just when the Bunyan tales reach a national
audience for the first time.

Shepard had passed through Duluth regularly since 1891 to
survey Minnesota lands and to establish a lumber town in the
Boundary Waters. "Mr. Shepard is one of the best known and most
popular men in Northern Wisconsin," the Duluth press reported
in 1901, "and he has a name as well all over Northern Minnesota."
Between 1892 and 1905 the Duluth papers reported on Shepard's
activities several times, printing his opinions about the lumber industry and even interviewing him when he stopped in the city in
1901. That he told tall tales on these visits is confirmed in the 1901
interview, in which he claimed that he had successfully bred a captured hodag that produced nineteen "puppies" the size of summer
squash.[8]

In his *Outer's Book* article, Rockwell did not explicitly attribute
any of the tales to Shepard but described him in words that suggest a personal acquaintance: "Not many years ago 'Gene' Shepard,
the famous Wisconsin woodsman-joker, hoaxed the whole scientific
world with a photograph of a Hodag, caught in his lair. Among other
things Gene had learned taxidermy, and at some expense and no end
of labor, he transformed a peculiarly shaped log into as ferocious an
animal in appearance as ever a Jack saw in his wildest nightmare."[9]

SOME LUMBERJACK MYTHS

By J. E. ROCKWELL

WITH ILLUSTRATIONS FROM PHOTOGRAPHS BY THE AUTHOR

 N O region is richer in myths than the northern Minnesota lumber woods, but with the passing of the old time "lumberjack" and the coming of the modern woodsman, the myths are rapidly being lost. The old stories told around many a camp had its own set of stories, and the men, in traveling from camp to camp— for the old time lumberjack was a rover— swapped these yarns in the long winter evenings, when the steaming socks were hung over the roaring sheet iron stove. It would be impossible to collect them all, but some of the best known exploits of this famous character will be related:

Bunyan first reached a national audience through the Milwaukee nature magazine, Outer's Book, *in February 1910.*

The two men certainly could have met before Rockwell's 1910 article and, given Shepard's widely praised talents as a raconteur, the old woodsman might have entertained the young reporter with Bunyan stories just as he had regaled Rockwell's colleagues in 1901 with his hodag puppies. But, as with Shepard's claims to having invented Bunyan, there is no proof that he actually supplied Rockwell with stories. Once again, he was in the right place at the right time: the author who first brought the tales to national attention knew about Shepard, and Shepard was in a position to have shared his Bunyan stories.

On February 6, 1910, Rockwell's *Outer's Book* article was reprinted in the *Washington Post* (25,000 readers); the *Wisconsin State Journal* (circulation 4,900) also printed it on May 23. Each newspaper told Rockwell's Bunyan stories and discussed Shepard's 1896 hodag hoax, repeating the *Outer's Book* text almost verbatim. With seventeen of his stories circulated to more than 70,000 readers around the country in 1910, James Rockwell must be credited as the writer who first brought Paul Bunyan out of the northwoods and into mainstream American media.[10]

Over in Michigan, editor William MacGillivray was probably among Rockwell's readers; he appropriated two of the *Outer's Book* stories when he reprinted the Round River sequence in Detroit a few months later. That MacGillivray was indebted to Rockwell is suggested by the incident of the ham-skating assistant cooks.

In the first-recorded version of this tale (Duluth 1904), the ham skaters' racial identity is not mentioned. But the next time it appears in print, in Rockwell's 1910 *Outer's Book* collection and its reprint the same month in Washington, DC, the skaters are called African-American. Six months afterward, MacGillivray repeated the motif of the black assistant cooks, which had previously appeared only in Rockwell's article (see Table 2).

In nearly all the published versions after 1910, the ham skaters are described in the racist language one expects from American popular culture in the first half of the twentieth century. Racial stereotypes were a staple feature of the Bunyan stories: the buffoonish French Canadian, the stern Yankee, and the ignorant Scandinavian joined the hapless African-American in a smorgasbord of offensive caricatures. A particularly extreme example is this 1914 description of Bunyan's cook shanty, which was staffed by "...two niggers with hams strapped on their feet skating around the griddle to grease it...while three Chinamen on roller skates were carrying the cakes from the griddle to the table, and it took two Dagos on bicycles running around the griddle to put the batter on." Other characters in this text (from the national trade journal *American Lumberman*) include Oscar the Turk and Big Charley the Swede.[11]

MacGillivray expanded Rockwell's motif of black ham skaters by making an assistant cook accidentally use blasting powder instead of baking powder when making pancakes; the resulting explosion sent the two assistant cooks through the roof. This motif also became a staple of later collections (appendix, no. 69).

MacGillivray's 1910 *Detroit News* version of Round River was the largest printing of Bunyan tales yet, as the paper was delivered to 122,000 readers in Detroit and the surrounding area. This Michigan recension finally found a nationwide audience on April 25, 1914, when Round River was retold in verse in the *American Lumberman*, a trade journal published in Chicago that reached 13,000 professionals in the lumber industry. Six weeks later its authors were revealed in the *Oscoda Press*: James McGillivray, who had drafted the 1906 newspaper version, and Douglas Malloch, a poet whose work often appeared in the *American Lumberman*, had collaborated on turning the prose tales into light verse.[12]

Most of the stories in the first three collections—the 1904 column from Duluth, Rockwell's 1910 article in Milwaukee,

Table 1: *Publication of the Bunyan Tales in Periodicals, 1904–1917*

DATE	AUTHOR TITLE	PUBLISHER PLACE	# OF COPIES # OF MOTIFS
August 4, 1904	Unknown "Caught on the Run"	*Duluth News Tribune* Duluth, MN	14,000 4
August 10, 1906	MacGillivray "Round River"	*Oscoda Press* Oscoda, MI	900 9
February 1, 1910	Rockwell "Some Lumberjack Myths"	*Outer's Book* Milwaukee, WI	41,000 17
February 6, 1910	Rockwell "Frozen Snakes Used as Skids"	*Washington Post* Washington, DC	25,000 17
May 23, 1910	Rockwell "North Woods Myths Passing"	*Wisconsin State Journal* Madison, WI	4,900 17
July 24, 1910	MacGillivray "Round River Drive" [prose]	*Detroit News* Detroit, MI	122,000 11
April 25, 1914	MacGillivray & Malloch "Round River Drive" [verse]	*American Lumberman* Chicago, IL	13,000 13
June 1916–June 1918	Lovejoy "Chronicle of Life and Works of Mr. Paul Bunyan"	*American Lumberman* Chicago, IL	13,000 40
March 1917	Stewart & Watt "Legends of Paul Bunyan, Lumberjack"	*Transactions of the Wisconsin Academy* Madison, WI	250? 32

and MacGillivray's 1906–1910 "Round River" sequence from Michigan—were unique; the contents of the three hardly over-lapped (see Table 2). Most of the tales in William Laughead's 1914 booklet from Minnesota, which ultimately spawned the national Bunyan craze, were also unique. The only motifs common to both the 1906 Michigan text and Rockwell's 1910 Milwaukee text were the giant ox (which had no name) and snow so deep the trees were cut off forty feet above ground; in 1910 MacGillivray also appro-priated Rockwell's ham-skating stove greasers. Their other twenty-two anecdotes did not overlap, as if Rockwell and MacGillivray had access to, or at least chose to print, separate bodies of sto-ries that revolved around different motifs. Together, Rockwell and MacGillivray brought twenty-six Bunyan anecdotes out of the woods and onto the printed page.

The majority of the earliest printed Bunyan tales were entirely new; none of the collections repeated many traditional folk stories that had already circulated. Of the twenty-six first printed between 1904 and 1910 in Duluth, Milwaukee, or Oscoda, only five are closely related to tall tales that predate Bunyan. Both MacGillivray and Rockwell described snow as deep as treetops; this had been, in many previous New York and New England jokes, as deep as chim-neys or church steeples. Two of MacGillivray's Round River anec-dotes had already circulated in the East: the stretchable harness had been published in nearly identical form in 1833, and the tree so big that loggers cut from both sides unbeknownst to one another had appeared in 1841. Rockwell also repeated two well-known jokes: a shouter's voice breaking limbs from trees was a motif preceded by a New Englander's voice that blew out windows in houses across a river, and loggers had been talking about the mysterious hodag at least since 1870.[13]

James Rockwell never received credit for bringing Paul Bunyan into mainstream American culture. He left Duluth in the spring of 1917 to edit the Fargo, North Dakota *Forum*, and then he served in World War I. He returned to Minnesota to publish the *Duluth News Tribune*, worked in New York in the 1920s as a newspaper

Table 2: *The First Bunyan Motifs to Be Printed, 1904–1914*[14]

MOTIF	DULUTH 1904	MICH. 1906	WIS. 1910	MINN. 1914
axes ground on stones rolling downhill		X		
beans cause Mt. Lassen volcano				X
beans fall through ice, cooked in lake			X	X
Big Onion River camp described				X
bird lays square eggs on hillsides			X	
buckskin harness stretched in rain		X		
bunkhouse covered half a section	X			
Bunyan cleared North Dakota of trees	X		X	X
Bunyan drove logs to Gulf of Mexico				X
Bunyan dug Great Lakes				X
Bunyan was eight feet tall, three hundred pounds			X	
Bunyan's pipe held bushel of tobacco			X	
Bunyan's pipe loaded with shovel			X	
Bunyan's voice blew limbs off trees			X	
Bunyan's wife described			X	
burst water tank for ox started Mississippi				X
dinner horn blew down trees				X
dinner horn caused tornado				X
donut holes punched by blacksmith				X
griddle greased by ham-skating assistant cook	X		X	X
hodag described			X	
loggers cut from opposite sides, unknown to one another		X		
logs driven back upstream			X	
ox described (but not named)		X	X	
ox hauled forty-acre section at once				X

Table 2: *continued*

MOTIF	DULUTH 1904	MICH. 1906	WIS. 1910	MINN. 1914
ox hoofprints created lakes				X
ox is named Babe				X
peas cooked in hot springs		X		
pyramid forty described		X		
railroad needed to serve meals in cook shanty				X
Round River, which flowed in a circle		X		
sidehill gouger with uneven legs described			X	
sleepwalker eats grindstone		X		
snow as deep as treetops		X	X	
snow snakes used as skids			X	
soup fermented by ugly man's looks		X		
waiters ran on tabletops				X
whirligig fish described			X	
winter of the blue snow	X		X	X

broker, and finally settled down outside St. Louis in 1929 to edit and publish the *Murphysboro* (Illinois) *Independent* until 1945. He died in 1953 at age seventy on his hobby farm in the Chicago suburbs, having watched Paul Bunyan rise from obscurity to worldwide fame. No evidence has been found that he ever wrote about the lumberjack hero after his 1910 Milwaukee *Outer's Book* article.[15]

The MacGillivray brothers' Round River stories became the heart of the Bunyan canon as editors reprinted and expanded them again and again in subsequent decades. William MacGillivray joined the *Detroit News* in 1907 but left in 1911 to work for the Michigan Conservation Commission. He eventually retired to his childhood home of Oscoda, where his Bunyan stories had begun, and he died there in 1952 at the age of seventy-nine.[16]

Printing the Bunyan stories for the first time between 1904 and 1914 inevitably altered them in important ways (Table 3). In logging camp bunkhouses, most references to Bunyan were transitory quips, improvised on the spot, to tease new recruits. When told aloud at greater length, they were still created on the fly as banter bounced back and forth in impromptu lying contests.

All this changed when editors printed the tales on paper. Although Rockwell and the anonymous Duluth editor did not intentionally embellish the stories, moving them from live speech to printed text nevertheless significantly altered their form and content. Other editors, including MacGillivray, Laughead, and most of their successors, went even further by deliberately enhancing the tales in order to meet readers' expectations.

As long as the stories were created orally in groups of men conversing together, they could not take the shape of conventional narratives. Any story's plot, characters, figures of speech, and length would change every time it was told. There was not even a definable body of tales that constituted the official canon of Bunyan legends. When a correspondent asked in the 1940s about the original, authentic Bunyan stories, Michigan forester P. S. Lovejoy replied, "that the chronicle kept growing, & that nobody ever 'knew all—or most?—of it,' and that there never was any sharply definable block of 'original material.'"[17] In an oral setting, any specific tale was short-lived. Once a story had been improvised, it vanished and might never again be told the same way, even by the same speaker. The tales moved from camp to camp and region to region, changing in each new context to take the shape of the new situation.

But when they were published, the Bunyan stories had to be deliberately planned and firmly fixed before they could be consumed by readers. And once the ink was dry on the page, a tale was permanently frozen in black and white, stabilized in a way that the spontaneous collaborative versions spoken aloud in logging camps could never be. Extemporaneous conversations became concrete artifacts.

Printing also changed the authorship of Bunyan tales. In the forest, the stories belonged to an isolated community of semiliterate, working-class men who shared specific skills, jargon, customs, values, challenges, and risks that the outside world hardly knew existed. The line between creator and audience was vague and ever shifting, and every logger was expected to play either role as needed, to keep the stories constantly evolving in unpredictable ways.

But articles in a newspaper or magazine possessed a single author, such as Rockwell or MacGillivray, who intentionally shaped them in specific ways to appeal to certain readers. In print media, the power to determine the stories' content and permanently fix it was not shared but was tightly concentrated in editorial offices. Plots, motifs, values, and even specific words were chosen by middle-class, educated professionals with commercial ends in mind. Creator and consumer, author and audience were separated in a way they could never have been around bunkhouse stoves. Although printing enabled the tales to be distributed much more broadly, it passed the power to portray logging life—its hardships, its fears, and its heroes—from isolated lumberjacks into the hands of urban publishers.

The audience for the Bunyan tales changed as dramatically as their authorship, and this, too, significantly altered the stories. Instead of being aimed at uneducated lumberjacks joking around their bunkhouse, the printed tales were intended for affluent, middle-class readers who expected them to have a clear beginning, middle, and end. In order to meet those expectations, editors had to expand passing quips about Bunyan into full-fledged narratives. Laughead explained in 1923 that, "...most of them have been built up from very scanty sources. Often a single phrase has been expanded into a story and supplied with a cast of characters." In the 1910 reissue of "Round River," MacGillivray even added nine paragraphs of introductory matter to help his urban audience unfamiliar with logging life get the jokes.[18]

Magazine subscribers wanted traditional short fiction in conventional formats, and book readers expected sequential chapters that

Table 3: *How Printing Changed the Bunyan Tales*

ORAL TRADITION	PRINTED TEXTS
created by semiliterate manual laborers	created by professional writers & editors
created collaboratively in groups	created privately by a single author
creator & audience intimately overlapped	creator & audience distantly separated
lumberjacks controlled production	publishers controlled production
common possession available for free	private commodity offered for sale
privately circulated among loggers	publicly available to all readers
shared for personal reasons	shared for commercial reasons
spontaneously improvised	carefully planned & edited
fluid & changing whenever told	fixed on paper
short-lived utterances	permanently preserved texts
brief, transient quips & allusions	lengthy & complex narratives
often depended on technical knowledge	technical knowledge stripped out
aimed only at working-class adults	aimed often at middle-class children
uncensored	censored

advanced a unified theme, such as Bunyan's entire life story. This opened the door for wholesale invention by professional writers who had never been anywhere near a logging camp.

The resulting fictions led William Bartlett to comment about 1927 that, "Most of the more lengthy recitals are extremely tiresome, containing, as they do, so little of the original, genuine material and so much of the musings and imaginations of their authors." A decade later, when the Bunyan craze was reaching its height, Charles Brown told a correspondent, "...the trouble with most Bunyan writers is that they invent Bunyan lore that no lumberjack ever told and tell the stories in such literary language that no logger ever employed. Witness James Stevens book."[19]

The Bunyan stories were also censored for the first time when they moved into print. Originally told aloud in a competitive, exclusively male environment resembling a locker room, many of the oral tales and jokes concerned Bunyan's sexual prowess and private parts (which one presumes were in proportion to the rest of his physique). None of these could be put on paper and delivered to suburban living rooms or bookshops. The Federal Anti-Obscenity Act, or Comstock law, was being used in 1915 to prosecute publishers of birth control instructions; no sane publisher would have dared to print the dirty jokes of lumberjacks. For her 1925 anthology, Esther Shephard collected the stories in logging camps throughout the Pacific Northwest. She reported that, "Many of the Paul Bunyan tales are very vulgar and obscene and obviously cannot be included in a volume of this kind." Not until the 1960s did such assumptions change, and by then both the salacious tales about Bunyan and the men who told them had passed away.[20]

The 1904–1910 articles were just the first steps in a process that transformed Paul Bunyan from the private hero of loggers into a national icon. The inevitable effect of printing the tales was that they were polished and cleaned up, like a lumberjack who washed, shaved, cut his hair, and put on new clothes when he went into town in the spring. After Bunyan left the woods for the printed page, he was never the same again. Luckily, just as the tales emerged from the forest, two Wisconsin researchers set out to collect and preserve them directly from the mouths of loggers.

CHAPTER EIGHT

Stewart and Watt, the First Careful Collectors

"...a little collection of these tales made in the lumber-camps by Miss Stewart..."

DURING THE ACADEMIC YEAR 1912–1913, a University of Wisconsin freshman told English professor Homer A. Watt (1884–1948) about the Paul Bunyan stories she had heard since childhood. Watt not only suggested that she pursue the topic further but became excited about it himself. Together, they would become the first serious researchers to deliberately gather Bunyan stories directly from lumberjacks.[1]

The student, K. Bernice Stewart (1894–1975), had grown up in sawmill towns spread across far northern Wisconsin and Michigan as her father, a timber cruiser, moved from place to place. He traveled extensively through the logging region, sometimes taking his young daughter into the woods with him. She also grew up with literary ambitions. In 1909, as a high school junior at Antigo, Wisconsin, her story "Final Thirteen" placed second in a statewide essay contest sponsored by *Outer's Book* magazine (her story ran in the issue preceding Rockwell's Bunyan tales). When she arrived in Madison, Stewart joined the staff of the *Daily Cardinal*, the student newspaper, where she was a reporter from 1914 to 1916. She

Bernice Stewart, when she was collecting Bunyan tales in the field, circa 1916

Homer Watt, circa 1940
COURTESY OF BARBARA FRIEND

was also active in women's sports and elected to Phi Beta Kappa shortly before she graduated in 1916.[2]

Homer Watt was a recently married English professor who had graduated from Cornell in 1906 and won a fellowship at Wisconsin the following year. After earning his doctorate in 1909, he joined the Madison English faculty. He wrote about the Elizabethan dramatists, prepared a guide to all of Shakespeare's plays, compiled a *Dictionary of English Literature*, and was also an innovative teacher and generous mentor. He encouraged students to write about their personal experiences and urged faculty to give a more sympathetic reception to student writings, "which are too often only riddled by an ogre with a blue pencil."[3]

After reading Stewart's freshman paper on the Bunyan tales, Watt encouraged her to research them in greater depth, and by 1914 both student and professor were systematically collecting the stories. In the summer of 1915 they gave a preliminary oral report on their work to the Wisconsin Academy of Sciences, Arts, and Letters, which spawned much discussion. No records of the presentation or conversation survive, but Stewart was asked back in 1916 and 1917 to update the academy on their project.[4]

Watt described it this way to a colleague: "...with the active assistance of one of my students, Miss Stewart, who has lived all her life in the woods of Wisconsin and Michigan, I have been for two years collecting lumberjack tales and legends...Miss Stewart is especially well equipped to gather the materials; not only has she lived for years in the north woods, but her father is an old lumber cruiser and her circle of acquaintances is wide." He explained that "Miss Stewart leaves for the Eau Claire and Chippewa River districts as soon as Commencement is over (she graduates this year) and will engage in a month's study of the early days of lumbering and of lumber-camp tales and songs. Although our plans are not yet completed for this trip we have been thinking of using a dictaphone on the visits to old lumber men so that an actual record in dialect may be made of some of the tales and songs."[5]

No recordings or formal interview notes have survived, but in 1941 Watt came across a box of file cards "left over from the days when Miss Stewart and I were projecting a book on Bunyan." These contained the motifs they had heard in the field or collected from correspondents, and when Watt had them typed up, the list filled six pages with more than seventy motifs. This list, the only surviving notes from the earliest scholars to collect Bunyan stories, is given at the end of the appendix.[6]

While in the Chippewa Valley at the end of June 1916, Stewart visited William Bartlett. "She called at our home," Bartlett recalled, "and I was much impressed by her apparent fitness for the work undertaken." In the local paper he wrote, "Miss Stewart is no novice in matters pertaining to logging camp life. Her father was a timber cruiser in northern Wisconsin and Michigan and as a young girl she herself spent several winters in camp. Becoming interested in the yarns which the typical old time woodsmen were accustomed to relate for the benefit of any tenderfoot who might be present, Miss Stewart has for some years past been making a careful study of the subject."[7]

Although Watt may have joined Stewart on some collecting trips, she is more often mentioned as the person with connections to lumberjacks and was probably the chief fieldworker. He, on the other hand, probably provided the critical and analytical text that accompanied the stories (which he repeated in slightly different form two decades later) and was probably the conduit through which their work reached a scholarly journal in 1916.[8]

In that publication, Stewart and Watt summarized their research methods this way:

> The following study of lumberjack legends has grown out of a little collection of these tales made in the lumber-camps by Miss Stewart, who for years has heard the stories told by the lumberjacks of Wisconsin and Michigan. Recently by corresponding with and interviewing lumbermen and others who are or who have been intimately connected with the lumber-camps we have added to the original collection a considerable number of new legends, besides many different versions of stories already in our collection, and a great deal of miscellaneous information about the hero, Paul Bunyan, and his blue ox. Some of these stories, as must be expected of any such series, are too coarse for publication. It has seemed to us, however, that for the most part the tales are quite wholesome; perhaps the circumstances under which they were collected have automatically excluded those of the rougher type.

They published acknowledgments to "Mr. B. R. Taylor, Mr. M. W. Sergeant, and Mr. Harold Stark, students in the University who have recently lived in the lumber districts of northern Wisconsin, and who have heard Paul Bunyan tales from boyhood, to Mr. Douglas Malloch of Chicago for a copy of his poem, The Round River Drive, a metrical version of some of the tales which was published in the *American Lumberman* for April 25, 1914, to the Red River Lumber Company of Minneapolis, Minnesota, and to lumbermen and others who have sent us material from the lumber districts."[9]

They did not acknowledge Eugene Shepard. Stewart must have known about Shepard. As a teenager, she lived only thirty miles away from him in Antigo, and he was a well-known celebrity who worked in the same profession as her father. It's possible that they considered him an unreliable source due to his reputation for exaggeration, heavy drinking, and deliberate deceptions.

It's harder to explain how they could have ignored Charles Brown, whom they both knew personally and whose building they entered nearly every day (the Wisconsin Historical Society headquarters housed the university library at the time). The most likely explanation is that in 1916 he had little to add to the tales they had gathered in the field; when Brown published his first collection six years later, it was heavily dependent on their texts.[10]

Stewart and Watt also relied very little on James Rockwell's or William Bartlett's Bunyan material. Stewart may have known about Rockwell's February 1910 *Outer's Book* collection, as her award-winning high school essay was published in the previous issue, but only nine of his motifs appeared in their collection; his other nine did not. They also make no mention of William Bartlett, suggesting that Stewart visited him in Eau Claire only after their collection had gone to press; they included only two motifs preserved separately by Bartlett. It appears, therefore, that Stewart and Watt owed little if anything to the other Wisconsin Bunyan collectors. Their tales came from an independent culling of oral sources, supplemented by the printed ones they acknowledged.

Watt told Wisconsin Historical Society director Milo Quaife in 1916, "We are expecting finally to get out a little volume to set forth our discoveries, if there are any." He had already "compared many of them with the French legends from Rabelais and other writers with a view of discovering whether or not the French-Canadian lumbermen brought the tales from the Old World." Stewart, at the same time, was "trying to work out the philosophical significance of these stories and has no interest whatever in pinning them down to a given locality or in the question of their truth." As late as 1920, after Watt and Stewart had both left Wisconsin, they were still planning "a little book on lumberjack life and lore" to be illustrated with photographs that Stewart's father had collected; by then they had more than doubled the number of tales they printed in 1916, through correspondence.[11]

But no book ever appeared. In the summer of 1916, Watt was offered a position at New York University, and though he continued to collect Bunyan stories with an eye toward publication, his new responsibilities precluded it. "I wish I could say that I have carried out my intentions of some twenty-five years ago to continue to gather Bunyan material and put it into a book form," he told W. W. Charters in 1941, "but, alas, I have allowed other interests to distract me from Bunyan and Bunyanism, and I have little more on hand now than I had when I left Wisconsin in 1916." Watt became chair of the NYU English department and a mentor to novelist Thomas Wolfe.[12]

Bernice Stewart, meanwhile, carried on their research for another year, corresponding with Archie Walker at the Red River Lumber Company and with Douglas Malloch at the *American Lumberman*. She allowed Bartlett to print some of their material in Eau Claire newspapers in 1917 (including a photo of herself, at his request) and commissioned illustrations for the projected book from a friend. But after graduating in 1916, she took a job in the university press office, which kept her so busy that she had "almost been obliged to forget Paul Bunyan." She moved to Washington in 1918 to nurse returning American soldiers, and then she moved to New York in 1919, where she married one of them (insurance executive Alexander C. Campbell, 1887–1975) and reared a family in the suburbs.[13]

Their seminal, thirteen-page article, however, preserved more than thirty Bunyan tales and had a lasting influence. Because Stewart and Watt were the earliest academic researchers to gather the stories directly from lumberjacks, their short text has long been considered the most reliable version of Paul Bunyan.

Before Watt left Madison in the summer of 1916, he gave the manuscript of this article to Arthur Beatty, an English department colleague who edited the *Transactions of the Wisconsin Academy of Arts, Letters, and Sciences*. Beatty had it set in type by early June, but difficulties with the state printer delayed its publication for almost a year. In March of 1917 their stories and analysis finally appeared under the title "Legends of Paul Bunyan, Lumberjack" in the 1916 volume of *Transactions of the Wisconsin Academy of Arts, Letters, and Sciences*.[14]

Just over half of the tales were previously uncollected: twenty-five of the forty-eight Bunyan motifs in their article had never been recorded before. These came from Wisconsin's Langlade County and logging camps along the Flambeau and Wisconsin rivers (presumably through interviews), from the Upper Peninsula of Michigan (possibly from interviews), from the Saginaw Valley in its southern peninsula (the "Round River" poem), from northern Minnesota (Laughead's 1914 Red River Company pamphlet), and from camps as far west as Oregon, Washington, and British Columbia (from correspondence). They concluded, "It is quite apparent that the lumberjacks in their slow migration westward have carried the tales freely from camp to camp into all of the lumbering states of the North and into the forests of Canada."[15]

Stewart and Watt were the first to record two motifs about Bunyan and his crew that were widely repeated afterward. They learned that the great ox was so strong that "on one occasion Paul dragged a whole house up a hill with the help of his ox, and then, returning, he dragged the cellar up after the house." In another classic anecdote, Paul is illiterate: "In the gentle art of writing Bunyan had, however, no skill. He kept his men's time by cutting notches in a stick of wood, and he ordered supplies for camp by drawing pictures of what he wanted. On one occasion only did his ingenuity fail; he ordered grindstones and got cheeses."[16]

The latter joke may be traceable to a real Wisconsin lumberjack. Bruno Vinette, who arrived in the Chippewa Valley in 1855, recalled it being told about a foreman named Peter Legault: "Like many others of the Canadian French, including myself, this young Peter Legault could not read or write, but he made up for this lack by the use of drawings or pictures...The story about him most frequently told was that, when foreman in a logging camp, when ordering supplies he wished to include a grindstone and drew a circle on paper to denote same. When the supplies arrived, he found a cheese but no grindstone, at which he exclaimed, 'I no order cheese. I order grindstone. Oh, I for got de hole!' " This is presumably the same French-Canadian logger about whom Stewart and Watt recorded, "When Joe Mufferon died, the sad news was carried back to camp. Pete Legout said, 'Hum? Joe dead? Dat's funny. He never done dat before.' "[17]

Another unique story that Stewart and Watt discovered depicts Paul Bunyan as a scheming camp boss: "Discovering in the spring that he had no money on hand, Bunyan suddenly rushed into camp shouting that they had been cutting government pine and were all to be arrested. Each man thereupon seized what camp property lay nearest his hand and made off, no two men taking the same direction. Thus Bunyan cleared his camp without paying his men a cent for their labor." This is the only occurrence in all the many collections of the tales where Bunyan cheated his crew.[18]

Although Stewart and Watt's article reached only a tiny audience, it was a well-connected one. Because the Wisconsin Academy's archives for 1916–1917 have not survived, precisely how many copies were printed or how they were made public are not known. At the time, the academy had roughly two hundred members receiving its *Transactions*, but these included nearly every prominent scholar in the state and many others around the nation. It also exchanged its publications with peer institutions and mailed them to library subscribers. In addition, Stewart and Watt distributed off-prints to personal contacts (Watt sent one to P. S. Lovejoy in 1920), and the academy sold copies to inquirers (Esther Shephard, who published the first retail book of Bunyan tales in 1924, purchased a copy in January of 1922).[19]

Through these routes Stewart and Watt's stories were preserved in the country's libraries where future editors could easily find them. This is in direct contrast to the fate of Rockwell's mass-market 1910 article, which appeared in a popular magazine ignored by contemporary libraries and soon disappeared (only one U.S. library now appears to own the February 1910 *Outer's Book*). Stewart and Watt's collection was also preserved more successfully than the Michigan Round River tales, which were printed only in daily newspapers (soon discarded) and a trade journal aimed at the lumber industry; it was rediscovered only in the 1940s. The impact of Stewart and Watt's work derives therefore not just from their careful research methods but also from their publication methods, which ensured their tales would be acquired, preserved, and cataloged in trusted institutions. Their means of production moved Bunyan out of the northwoods and into libraries for the first time.

Their work was not limited exclusively to scholarly publications. Their tales were reprinted nearly verbatim by Bartlett in the *Eau Claire Telegram* on April 20, 1917, and in the *Vilas County News* on December 21, 1921. Over the next decade, during the beginning of the Bunyan craze, they were cited more often by compilers than any other source, in part because their collection was acquired, cataloged, and preserved in libraries.

Stewart and Watt also attempted the first serious analysis of the Paul Bunyan phenomenon. Unlike later editors, they made no attempt to identify where the tales had originated or whether Paul Bunyan had ever existed, though they speculated that there had probably once been a real-life model for the lumberjack hero:

> We have found in several localities characters still living about whose prowess as lumbermen exaggerated stories are already being told; it is probable that the tales will continue to be told, with additions, after these local heroes have died. In a similar manner, we believe, did Paul Bunyan come into existence. He was probably some swamper or shacker or lumberjack more skilful and more clever than average,

about whose exploits grew a series of stories; after his death his fame probably spread from camp to camp, more tales were added to those told about him, and thus, gradually, he became in time an exaggerated type of the lumberjack, and the hero of more exploits than he could possibly have carried out in his life-time.[20]

Neither Watt nor Stewart was a specialist in folklore, but they adopted the standards and embraced the concerns most prominent in the discipline at the time. One of these was to trace American folktales back to Europe:

It seems certain, too, that many of the tales now included in the Bunyan cycle were narrated long before Bunyan became the lumberman hero. Similar tales, lacking, of course, the local color of the Bunyan yarns, are to be found in the extravagant stories of Baron Munchausen and of Rabelais as well as in folk-tales from more settled parts of the United States of America. An extremely interesting study, so complex, however, that we have not yet completed it, is the tracing of the old world originals of the Bunyan stories to determine just to what extent the American tales are new and to what extent they were brought from France and England by early pioneers.[21]

Stewart and Watt concluded that the Bunyan stories they had collected resembled traditional European folktales in three ways. "The tendency to group the tales about one hero is universal in legend," they wrote, "as is illustrated by the Arthurian and Robin Hood cycles, and less completely by the folk tales of Riibezahl, the spirit of the Riesengebirge of Germany, Puck, or Robin Goodfellow, and the strong man, Tom Hickathrift, of England. Moreover, like other legend groups, the Bunyan stories tend to be concerned with a single locality, Round River or Big Onion River. Finally, many of the legends are more or less closely connected with a single exploit, the clearing of the pyramid forty, in much the same way, to compare the little with the great, that Greek legends center in the Argonautic Expedition and the Trojan War, and Arthurian legends in the search for the Holy Grail."[22] These comparisons probably owe much to discussions with their colleague and editor Arthur Beatty, who was a specialist in European folk literature, but they also reflect the widespread preoccupation of academic folklorists at the time with possible European origins of American folktales.[23]

Despite the stories' superficial resemblances to European myths, Watt and Stewart were quick to identify their uniquely American feature, "the remarkable quality of the exaggeration in the Bunyan legends. This quality is worth analysis not only because it shows universal tendencies, but because it is the basis of what has come to be known as typical American humor." They argued that American comic hyperbole

> is really only a natural development of the attempt to "boom" new sections of the country by representing conditions as superior to what they actually are. It is but one aspect of the cheerful, rose-colored, but quite distorted optimism which aroused the disgust of Dickens and other Englishmen (see Martin Chuzzlewit) and has earned for Americans among Europeans whose boom days are over the name of braggart. It is this quality of humorous exaggeration, then, and the idea of a contest in lying, which makes the Bunyan legend cycle typically American, or, it might be better to say, typically pioneer, in spirit. And the reader does not have to look far for American parallels. Mark Twain's books are full of tales of the same stamp...[24]

Stewart and Watt noted the origins of many Bunyan motifs in American folklore that predated the lumber industry, suggesting that "the majority of the Bunyan legends are very likely adaptations of tales which have elsewhere an existence in some form." But they also pointed out that others are indeed unique to logging culture:

"To Professor [William B.] Cairns of the Department of English at Wisconsin we are indebted for an ingenious explanation of the possible origin of the tale of the pyramid forty and its prodigious supply of timber. In the early days of lumbering in the North more than one man staked out a claim on a single forty and, ignoring section lines, cut 'government pine' for miles around, securing, it was humorously reported by those who knew but winked at the robbery, a great deal of timber from one forty." This widespread practice not only gave rise to Bunyan tales of vast harvests from a single section but also to the woodsmen's term "round forty"—a section where logging companies took so many trees beyond the surveyed boundaries that the parcel resembled a circle rather than a square.[25]

In 1918, Bernice Stewart left Madison for Washington, where she met returning soldier and Yale graduate Alexander Campbell. They were married at the end of 1919 and moved to Manhattan, where he rose to the top of the Metropolitan Life Insurance Company. She was active in the New York City club of University of Wisconsin alumni, moved to Westchester County during the 1920s, and raised two children. When her husband retired in 1953, they moved to San Diego, where she died in 1975 a week shy of her eighty-first birthday. She appears never to have written about Bunyan after 1916.[26]

Homer Watt, on the other hand, maintained his interest in the lumberjack hero throughout his career. He was appointed chair of the English department at NYU's Washington Square campus in 1918, his English literature textbooks were used throughout the country, and he held visiting appointments at universities in Virginia, Colorado, and California.[27]

During the 1930s, at the height of Bunyan's popularity, he wrote two groups of tales for different audiences. The first was five pages of Bunyan material contributed to Lewis Wann's 1933 textbook, *The Rise of Realism*. For an undergraduate audience, he created a narrator named Rockin' Horse (with one leg shorter than the other from having worked on the pyramid forty) situated in a fictional bunkhouse with a new recruit. Watt gave the tales largely as he and Stewart had collected them nearly twenty years before, apart from the frame and using characters' names made popular by others. He repeated more than twenty well-known motifs, only two of which were not found in his and Stewart's 1916 article.[28]

In a footnote to this 1933 piece, Watt warned, "In collections of Paul Bunyan yarns it is not always possible, unfortunately, to separate those which belong to the legitimate Bunyan cycle from those which have been added from other sources or even invented by the compilers. Compilers have, moreover, sometimes destroyed the mood and flavor of the Bunyan tales by sentimentalizing or otherwise distorting them."[29]

In 1936 Watt made a second selection, "a sort of bed-time story or series of stories in a frame" under the title "When Gran'pa Logged for Paul," which he contributed to a high school literature textbook. The grandfather in the piece is called Gran'pa Stewart, and the little boy to whom he tells the tales is Harry Stewart—the name of Bernice's father. At the time, she had children of the right age to encounter the textbook in their own classrooms, and it is tempting to imagine that they had stayed in contact after both moved to metropolitan New York (no evidence has been found, however). When he died at age sixty-four in 1948, it was not only Watt's many academic honors and accomplishments that the *New York Times* highlighted in his obituary. It devoted two full paragraphs to the Bunyan research he had done with Bernice Stewart in Wisconsin thirty years before.[30]

In the intervening decades, Bunyan had become an icon of America's national character and a ubiquitous symbol of strength and ingenuity. By the time Bernice Stewart died in 1975, he had grown into a crude caricature of the authentic folk character she knew as a Wisconsin girl, a cutesy buffoon to amuse children instead of a homegrown hero to inspire lumberjacks.

Chapter Nine

Charles Brown Gets Caught in the Middle

"The cook one day made such hard doughnuts that
the blacksmith had to put the holes in them.
Paul said they were all right but would taste better
if the holes were larger."

SQUEEZING THE ORAL BUNYAN TRADITION into the conventions of print gave the tales new shapes and sizes. Even careful collectors such as Stewart and Watt had to expand loggers' passing remarks into well-rounded anecdotes, as is shown by comparing their brief notes (appendix, no. 100) to their finished 1916 text (appendix, nos. 1, 4, 17, 23, 41, 43, 44, 53, 62, 69, 80, and 96).

When the Bunyan craze began in 1922, this problem was compounded by the desire of publishers and marketers to appeal to a broad audience and led to entirely new fabrications projecting the fantasies of literary professionals onto an ersatz Bunyan. During the height of the Bunyan craze, 1925–1950, serious collectors of the tales fought a losing battle to separate the wheat from the chaff, to preserve and promote the authentic folklore of woods workers. Charles Brown personifies that struggle.

Brown (1872–1946) was an unlikely scholar. Nothing in his childhood suggested he would become a leading archaeologist, university instructor, and author of dozens of academic articles. Or that he would preserve more authentic Bunyan stories than anyone else.

While growing up in Milwaukee, Brown was more interested in natural history than in baseball or girls, and he spent many hours on Saturdays at the new Milwaukee Public Museum. Lacking funds to go to college, he initially found work in the shops of the Chicago, Milwaukee, St. Paul & Pacific Railroad and about 1891 joined the staff of a Milwaukee building contractor as a draftsman.[1]

Although drafting enabled Brown to support himself and his widowed mother, his true love was museum work. When the Milwaukee Public Museum moved in 1898 to a grand, new building, he landed a job there as an "attendant," which meant doing everything from mounting specimens to guiding tours. At the time, the institution had only eleven employees, and the appointment, humble though it was, gave Brown daily contact with the only people in the city who shared his passions for natural history and archaeology, and he gradually rose through the museum's ranks.[2]

His professional successes caught the eye of Reuben Gold Thwaites, director of the Wisconsin Historical Society in Madison. The Historical Society, like the Milwaukee Public Museum, had just opened an elegant new building with much-expanded exhibit space. Thwaites persuaded Brown to become the first director of its museum, a position he held from February 1908 until June 1944. During his career, Brown transformed the historical museum from an attic stuffed with bric-a-brac into a rich collection documenting the state's material culture. Collecting trips across Wisconsin kept him in constant contact with local leaders and pioneer settlers who were intimate with the history and traditions of their communities.[3]

By the time Brown arrived in Madison in 1908, he was already fascinated by Paul Bunyan. He had first heard the stories in the early 1890s in Oshkosh from an uncle and never lost interest in lumberjacks and their folklore. "Years ago, when a boy," he recalled in 1931, "I happened to be in Oshkosh when the Wolf River crews came in off the drive and were 'running the town.' They were a real wild lot and fights were a quite common sight. One night I went to the opera house which was filled with lumberjacks. After the regular performance had been finished, a big woodman chucked his hat up on the stage and challenged any man in the house to a wrestling match. He did not have to wait long for an opponent...Altho rough they were a jovial crew and the police generally let them pretty well alone." In 1906 he began collecting Bunyan tales from sailors on the Milwaukee waterfront, men who had started their careers in the woods, and never gave up the pursuit.[4]

In 1913 Brown began teaching folklore at the University of Wisconsin's summer session. This program had started in 1885 as a way for the university to reach nontraditional students, especially public school teachers. Its enrollment grew from under two thousand when Brown first joined the staff to more than five thousand during the 1920s; Wisconsin's was the third-largest summer program in the nation in 1925. Between 1913 and 1945 he gave lectures, mounted exhibits, led field excursions to archaeological sites around Madison's lakes, and conducted weekly folklore meetings that featured Paul Bunyan. In 1927, when the Hearst Newspaper Corporation devoted a full-page spread to the Bunyan phenomenon, it singled out Brown for legitimizing the tales in his University of Wisconsin courses.[5]

For his 1922 folklore summer course, Brown printed up a small collection of Bunyan tales for his students. It was called *American Folk Lore / Paul Bunyan Tales / Prepared for the Use of Students of the / University of Wisconsin / Summer Session.* The eight-page booklet contained thirty-one anecdotes, some very brief and others drawn out at length. It was the first in Brown's long series of ephemeral publications preserving Bunyan stories from Wisconsin.

This first—1922—collection drew largely on other publications. For example, all the motifs used by Rockwell in the *Outer's Book* back in 1910 appeared. Brown also knew Bernice Stewart and

Homer Watt personally, and about two-thirds of his stories came from their 1916 article. He was acquainted with Gene Shepard, who had given the Historical Society one of his "Round River" forgeries. Brown also corresponded with Laughead and Lovejoy (though the now-vanished letters may not have dated from this period), and he cited Esther Shephard's December 1921 *Pacific Review* article, "The Tall Tale in American Literature." The only motifs introduced for the first time in Brown's 1922 booklet were two passing references to mythical forest creatures. He reported that "the upland trout built its nest in tall trees and was very difficult to catch" and mentioned the "rumptifusel" which, like the hodag, was a beast of "great ferocity."[6]

The number of copies Brown printed in 1922 is not known, but probably no more than a few dozen people would have enrolled in his course. The booklets nevertheless lasted until 1927, when a reprint was called for; this suggests an edition of a few hundred copies, at most. The 1927 reprint, identified on its cover as "second issue," merely contains the same texts arranged in a different layout. It listed as additional sources the 1922–1925 anthologies by W. B. Laughead, Esther Shephard, and James Stevens, although Brown used no tales from any of the three.

Even before popularizers began to distort the Bunyan tradition in the mid-1920s, Brown decided to collect them as they had originally circulated in Wisconsin logging camps. Soon after issuing his first collection in 1922, he tried to locate people who had known Bunyan stories in the woods and to gather every publication about Bunyan that could be found.

Among his first informants was Colonel George E. Laidlaw (1860–1927) of Bexley, Ontario, an amateur archaeologist and folklorist. Brown, suspecting the tales may have started in French Canada, asked Laidlaw to look for any actual loggers named Paul Bunyan and to send any tales he could find. Between February and June of 1924, Laidlaw canvassed the old-timers in his vicinity and interrogated young loggers returning from the woods. His informants had logged not only in Ontario but also in Michigan and northwest of Lake Superior. One of them had left the woods in the mid-1880s to work on Great Lakes ships and had heard Bunyan stories throughout the entire region ever since (but not before). During 1924, Laidlaw kept up a steady stream of letters to Madison, sometimes writing to Brown three times a week.[7] In all, he supplied Brown with more than thirty Bunyan anecdotes or brief references from Canada during 1924 and 1925. Brown had used only six of these tales in his 1922 collection; six others found their way into his later booklets, but some never appeared in print.[8]

For the next several years, Brown corresponded with veteran Wisconsin woodsmen, sent questionnaires to retired lumberjacks, visited them on his travels through the north, and interviewed those who came to Madison. He asked about their jobs, beliefs, values, customs, maxims, sayings, tales, and songs, and especially if they remembered any Bunyan stories. "In the past twenty years," he told a correspondent in 1934, "I have heard these stories told over and over again by lumberjacks and others who came from lumbering regions all over northern Wisconsin and Michigan, also from Ontario, New Brunswick and other parts of Canada, from Maine and Minnesota."[9]

The richest harvest that Brown gathered was a stream of long, intimate letters from Otis Terpening (dates unknown), who logged in Wisconsin for several years around 1890. "You will have to excuse mistakes," Terpening wrote in an early letter, "as my hands are more used to a Peavey stock. I am nothing but a Lumberjack, I worked all over the Northern part of your State, drove the Brule an St. Croix, the Eagle, an rafted on Lake Supeerior, worked on Madline Island, got my education following the Lumber Camps an River trails from Michigan to the Red Waters of Minn."[10]

Between 1929 and 1932, Terpening sent Brown a series of densely packed, single-spaced letters totaling more than thirty pages; other letters between them have not survived. Terpening described many details of logging camp life, shared moving personal reflections, and offered Brown several pages of Bunyan stories that he recalled

hearing in the woods. Brown used about half of these in his publications (appendix, nos. 22, 34, 42, 45, 83, and 98).[11]

Brown gathered tales from at least twelve other informants during
the early 1930s. Retired logger John Carney of Wausau, Wisconsin,
told him a series of stories about mythical fish that Bunyan's crew
caught. A. P. Jones of Black River Falls sent in a Wisconsin version
of "Round River" that he had heard from an old-timer in which
the loggers persist for forty years, until the logs are worn down to
the diameter of fish poles. Two informants gave him versions of
the giant mosquitoes story, in which Bunyan's attempt to route the
troublesome pests by introducing giant bees goes awry when the
two species breed, producing giant insects with stingers at both
ends (all given in the appendix).[12]

He also collected tales from Madison residents who had heard
them during their childhoods in the northwoods. For example,
attorney James J. McDonald was the son of a camp foreman;
born in Hayward in 1886, he grew up in St. Croix Falls and New
Richmond. Madison veterinarian Charles Deadman (1881–1948)
was raised in Michigan's Upper Peninsula in a family from eastern
Ontario. Both had listened to the stories in their childhood and
remained lifelong Bunyan fans; in 1931 McDonald contributed a
long selection of the tales to the Wisconsin Blue Book.[13]

Between 1922 and 1937, Brown put many of their tales into
six more Bunyan pamphlets. In these privately printed collections
Brown capitalized on the wave of public enthusiasm while at the
same time trying to preserve the authentic oral tradition. It was
an awkward balancing act, at best. For example, he felt compelled
to use the names for characters, such as Babe the Blue Ox, that
Laughead and James Stevens had made common in their well-
known books; to have insisted that the ox had no name would
have puzzled his readers. On the other hand, he refused to invent
from scratch entirely new stories, or to reprint ersatz ones whose
authenticity he rejected (such as Stevens's).

Brown thought of compiling all his tales into a single book, but
he soon gave up the idea: "There are several Bunyan books now on

Four of Charles Brown's privately printed Bunyan pamphlets, 1922–1937

the market," he told a correspondent in 1928, "hence it seemed useless to print another." Instead, he concentrated on publishing the tales in inexpensive pamphlets designed to be read aloud in educational settings. "At the present time," he told a another inquirer in 1934, "my interest in them has been largely devoted to making small selections, particularly of the Wisconsin myths, useful to storytellers at Boy and Girl Scout, Campfire Girl and other vacation camps. There they have become very popular and my leaflets and booklets have been called for from almost every state and province in the U.S. and Canada."[14]

In the mid-1930s, Brown's folklore-collecting efforts received an unexpected boost when the Roosevelt administration inaugurated the Works Progress Administration. About 10 percent of WPA funds enabled states to hire authors, researchers, and clerical workers for historical and literary work. Brown immediately went after federal funds to collect and preserve Wisconsin folklore, in addition to writing a guide to the state and surveying its historic records. He was appointed director of the Wisconsin Writers' Program in October 1935, ostensibly providing only general oversight while middle managers executed the work. He was nevertheless quickly burdened with administrative red tape and ultimately embroiled in political turmoil.[15]

In December 1935, Brown set up a folklore section within the Writers' Program and hired as its supervisor thirty-nine-year-old Dorothy Moulding Miller, a single mother of three who had been active in Madison literary circles and worked in advertising and radio. Over the next three years she directed several field interviewers, two clerk typists who transcribed their notes, and about a dozen volunteers. Following the death of Brown's first wife early in 1937, she and her boss were married. For the next several years, Dorothy and Charles Brown made a systematic survey of the state's folklore together, gave lectures, wrote articles, and traveled to professional conferences.[16]

Dorothy and her staff began by scouring printed sources for folklore hidden in obscure books, pamphlets, and newspapers. They then interviewed local residents in Shawano, Rice Lake, La Crosse, Prairie du Chien, and Dane County. In two years they conducted more than six hundred interviews and collected "5,000 stories-songs-rhymes-riddles-epitaphs; 8,000 games, superstitions, customs, weather lore & sayings; and made 6 folklife maps." From Washington, folklorist John Lomax congratulated them on collecting "an amazing amount of good material...The work has been carefully and thoroughly done." National magazines wanted stories based on the growing collection, and Dorothy made broadcasts and traveled as far as New Orleans to give lectures based on them.[17]

The Wisconsin Folklore Project's archives eventually totaled almost five thousand pages. They contain a singular omission, however—only a handful mention Paul Bunyan. When he spoke with the press in 1937, Charles Brown used Bunyan as an example of the folklore they were seeking, and the project's informants and correspondents included many longtime residents of the northwoods. It is very strange, then, that almost nothing about the lumberjack hero survived in the project's records.[18]

The only interesting Bunyan material preserved in the WPA project's files came from Charles A. Deadman (1881–1948), who made the following claim for the French-Canadian origin of the tales (in the words of collector Jane Olson):

The start of the Paul Bunyon [*sic*] stories as explained by Mr. Deadman is that during the year 1835 [*sic*] the French people in Quebec revolted against the English and were successful. The leader of the French contingent was an officer by the name of Paul Bon Jean. The American version entered into the stories in this way:

The American lumberjacks of years ago used to haul their logs [recorder's error for "supplies"?] on flat boats up the river by means of a windlass and cable. If at any time the men operating the windlass wanted to rest they would place a gadget called the "paul" [pawl] in the steering wheel and hold the boat in a stationary position. The American lumberjacks would tell just how much this "paul" could endure in weight or pressure while in operation.

The French and Americans would meet in their different travels and the French heard the Americans telling about what wonderful feats their "paul" could accomplish, and, they not understanding the full meaning, began telling what wonderful things their Paul Bon Jean had accomplished, and from then on the stories grew rapidly in size, both in Canada and the United States. The "Blue Ox" stories originated with the Irish people.[19]

Deadman's opening paragraph merely repeats Stevens's erroneous 1925 genealogy of Bunyan (see chapter 11). His etymology of "Paul" from "pawl" was echoed by Bunyan collector George Slecht ("Cal Crosshaul") in a 1943 interview but has been found nowhere else. Deadman also told several stories about a French-Canadian strongman named Julius Naville, some of which (such as the reversible dog and the "frozen sounds that thaw in spring") are well known from much earlier folktales. In one of these, Naville meets Bunyan (appendix, no. 13).[20]

Beyond Deadman's few pages, hardly any Bunyan material survives in the Wisconsin Folklore Project archives. There is a wealth of information about logging, lumbering, river rafting, lumberjack life, loggers' superstitions, and local characters such as Bruno Vinette and Louis Blanchard, yet hardly anything about Bunyan. Interviewers surely must have asked about and informants talked about him. The project must have generated hundreds of pages about Bunyan, and yet fewer than twenty survive in its files. What became of the Wisconsin Writers' Program files on Bunyan?

The solution to this mystery lies in a 1930s political controversy. The creation of government jobs during a period of high unemployment led to close scrutiny of hiring practices. In 1936, although he violated no laws or government regulations, Brown was accused of nepotism by a disgruntled administrator when he temporarily hired his son as a fieldworker and then married Dorothy Miller, a member of his staff. His superiors found it hard to justify three federal relief positions going to a single family at the height of the Depression and refused to stand up for him. The public embarrassment, added to the burden of running the program on top of his full-time museum job, prompted him to step down in the fall of 1937. "Heading a Federal Writers Program in Wisconsin," he wrote to a friend, "as I did for two years much against my own wishes and in addition to my other work and at a real monetary loss to myself, was a very ungrateful undertaking not properly or fully appreciated here or in Washington. After two years of devoted and unselfish service I resigned the position. Some day I will tell you the whole story."[21]

On top of his personal struggle, Brown's project was facing its own trials as conservative lawmakers attacked Roosevelt's social programs throughout 1939. Funding for the Federal Writers' Program as a whole was finally killed by congressional opponents effective September 1, 1939, and the various states scrambled to find new resources. Harold Miner, assistant director of the Wisconsin Writers' Program, recalled that Brown's staff had "acquired a splendid esprit de corps…There existed among them a gay, almost tender fellow-feeling which I find it impossible to define or describe…They were truly a family." After 1939, spurned by their government sponsors, criticized by the conservative press, and laid off from their jobs, a number of staff simply carried away records of their work because they feared what might happen to them in the hands of political opponents.[22]

Charles and Dorothy Brown seem to have joined their colleagues in privately retaining large portions of the Wisconsin Folklore Project's files. When the Madison office finally closed for good in the summer of 1941, Charles Brown told W. W. Charters, "the Wis. Folklore Society [a private group] has a new lot of Paul Bunyan manuscript material." Over the next decade, the Folklore Society (whose mailing address was the same as Charles and Dorothy Brown's home) issued twenty publications whose topics and arrangement directly mirror the WPA Folklore Project's records. After Brown died in 1946, Dorothy published several pamphlets directly based on WPA materials while living in California. A substantial number of Bunyan manuscripts closely resembling WPA-collected folklore records on other topics are among the papers she donated to the Children's Literature Research Collection at the University of Minnesota in the 1960s. There can be little doubt that the Browns carried off the Bunyan portion of the federal records series.[23]

Between 1935 and 1939, the WPA project kindled widespread public interest in Wisconsin folk traditions. Shortly after Brown resigned, a group of supporters gathered around him to form the Wisconsin Folklore Society. In a 1943 article, Brown described the group this way:

> The Wisconsin Folklore Society was organized in 1938. Its purpose is to encourage the collection, preservation and the use of Wisconsin folklore in educational work. The large amount of valuable material which its members have collected has already found great use in story telling, writing, music, drama, pageantry, festivals, art (paintings, murals, pictorial maps), decorative art, and recreation. One of our active members has lectured throughout the state and in adjoining states on folklore. Another has organized folk festivals and organized and conducted Wisconsin groups

participating in the annual National Folk Festival. A University student group has prepared a series of Wisconsin Indian pictorial folklore maps. Wisconsin mural painters have made use of the Society's material in preparing murals for Wisconsin state and federal buildings. Vacation camps make use of similar material in story-telling and other activities. Two summers ago the School of Music of the University engaged in the recording of folksongs throughout the state. Commercial advertising has benefited by the use of some of our Paul Bunyan material. Meetings of the Wisconsin Society are held at the University during the winter and spring months. An annual joint meeting is held with the Wisconsin Academy of Sciences, the Wisconsin Archeological Society and the Wisconsin Museums Conference in different cities of the state.[24]

By then, Wisconsin was exhibiting as many symptoms of the Bunyan mania as any other state. Lecturers such as Cal Crosshaul (whose real name was George Slecht, of Hudson, Wisconsin) dressed up as lumberjacks of the 1880s and recited the stories. Reunions, festivals, celebrations, jamborees, and pageants were organized around Bunyan themes, schoolchildren enacted plays and wrote reports about him, and artists painted murals depicting his exploits.[25]

Brown was caught in the middle between his scholarly standards and the nationwide Bunyan obsession. Although he was committed to unearthing the authentic folk tradition, he could not escape the cultural representations that surrounded him. At the same time, he didn't entirely shun the popularizers. He delighted in collecting the mass-market books and magazine articles at the same time that he denounced their authenticity. Although he was scrupulously accurate in his archaeological and editorial work, he was sometimes happy to ride the Bunyan wave just for the fun of it.

For example, when a rivalry broke out between promoters in Michigan and Wisconsin over Bunyan's origin, Brown wrote to a Madison newspaper, as if it were historical fact, that, "The testimony of 'Gene' Shepard of Rhinelander, bosom friend and henchman of Paul's, on this point has never been successfully controverted. The place of [Bunyan's] birth has been definitely fixed as in the former great white pine forests not far from Gene's home town." In two of his Bunyan pamphlets he identified this as, "45 miles west of Rhinelander. The late Gene Shepard identified the location by means of the perfumed moss which grew abundantly on the site of the old camp buildings." Brown fought

Charles Brown, when he was issuing privately printed Bunyan pamphlets, circa 1940 WHI IMAGE ID 62838

to maintain a balance between a scholarly effort to collect reliable evidence about the folktales' origins, on the one hand, and his boyish desire to join in the popular enthusiasm, on the other.[26]

Toward the end of his life, the Wisconsin Folklore Society became Brown's front for publishing Bunyan stories. Operating out of the Browns' home, it issued twenty booklets between 1940 and 1947, including collections of Native American folktales, lore about steamboats, stories about hermits and lost treasures, Cornish immigrant and local history tales, legends of ghosts and hauntings, and eight Bunyan pamphlets. Much of this material appears to have come from the missing WPA Wisconsin Folklore Project files.

Paul Bunyan was the centerpiece in all this activity. Although they reprinted a few stories collected by others, the great bulk of the Browns' 1940s tales came from correspondence or interviews they conducted between 1906 and 1946. In all, more than fifty informants supplied Bunyan tales for their collections; those who can be identified were the following:[27]

Balch, James (merely described as "a South Carolinian" in Brown's notes)

Barrett, W. W. (unidentified; supplied one story in 1932)

Bordner, John S. (1877–1959; director of the Wisconsin Land Economic Inventory survey in the 1930s; sent two stories in 1931)

Bowman, James Cloyd (Marquette, Michigan; author of 1927 children's version of the tales)

Briggs, Professor Harry Russell (ca. 1896–1968; University of Wisconsin professor)

Burnham, E. H. (a retired lumberjack of Holcombe and Green Bay, Wisconsin; knew Gene Shepard and corresponded with Brown in 1930)

Carney, John (retired logger of Wausau, Wisconsin, interviewed by Brown)

Chetlain, John Francis (of Chicago; sent one story in 1928)

Clark, Gregory (Canadian journalist who wrote about Bunyan in the *Toronto Star Weekly* in 1924)

Clark, John (1861–1938; ex-logger and teamster of Washburn who entered logging camps in 1880s, according to the *Washburn Times*, February 10, 1938)

Coyle, Patrick (of Eagle River, Wisconsin)

Deadman, Dr. C. A. (1881–1948; Madison veterinarian from northern Michigan)

Dobre, Frank (untraced)

Dyer, Harry G. (1864–1950; retired logger and raft pilot who settled in Madison)

Foote, Justine (untraced)

Gardner, Sheldon (untraced; sent oral tales to Brown in 1943)

Gleason, Edward (published one story in the *Capital Times*, Madison, Wisconsin, April 17, 1936, about snow snakes)

Hobbs, George (retired logger interviewed at Pelican Lake, Wisconsin, 1930)

Holman, Earle G. (1887–1984; newspaper editor in Antigo, Wisconsin; sent one Bunyan story, 1944)

Johnson, R. P. A. (untraced)

Jones, A. P. (of Black River Falls, Wisconsin)

Jones, Professor Edward Richard (University of Wisconsin professor of soils science and author of Bunyan pamphlets in the early 1930s)

Kaufman, Elmer (of Antigo, Wisconsin)

Kearney, Luke S. (logger, close friend of Gene Shepard, and author of *The Hodag*, which he sent to Brown in 1930; interviewed by Brown December 15, 1930)

Kent, H. J. (Wautoma, Wisconsin, newspaper editor who gathered tales for Brown in 1938–1941)

Kerst, Richard W. (supplied one story, 1932)

Kiethly, Enos (of Dixon, Illinois)

Laidlaw, Colonel G. E. (1860–1927; Ontario amateur archaeologist who supplied tales 1924–1925)

Lucius, Joseph (born 1871; retired logger of Solon Springs, Wisconsin; acquaintance of Gene Shepard whom Brown interviewed)

Maier, Louis A. (northern Wisconsin banker whom Brown interviewed during the 1930s)

Martin, Joe (Ontario logger who supplied tales through Laidlaw, 1924)

Mathie, Karl (of Wausau, Wisconsin; sent one story in 1929)

McCann, Robert (retired logger interviewed by Brown in 1934)

McDonald, James J. (born 1881; son of a St. Croix River valley camp foreman; became a Madison attorney and friend of Brown)

Owen, Professor Ray S. (ca. 1893–1967; University of Wisconsin professor of engineering)

Pond, Alonzo W. (1894–1986; Beloit College archaeologist)

Rayford, Julian R. (of Mobile, Alabama; sent one story in 1946)

Schmidt, E. E. (Milwaukee paper company executive who sent a story to Brown in 1929)

Shay, Frank (1888–1954; author of *Here's Audacity! American Legendary Heroes*, New York: Macaulay Co., 1930)

Shepard, Eugene S. (1854–1923; see chapter 6; his second wife, Karretta, also supplied one tale to Brown in the 1930s)

Slecht, George ("Cal Crosshaul"; Brown called him the state's foremost Bunyan expert during 1930s)

Stapleton, Matt R. (1856–1941; ex-lumberjack and raft pilot from Rhinelander, Wisconsin; wrote many letters to Brown in the early 1930s)

Sugden, Earl (Cazenovia, Wisconsin; author of Bunyan verse during 1940s)

Taplin, Bert (1857–1943; logger who supplied the earliest documented Bunyan story in 1938)

Terpening, Otis W. (retired logger of Ithaca, Michigan, who worked in Wisconsin ca. 1890 and supplied many tales to Brown, 1929–1932)

Twenhofel, Professor W. H. (1876–1957; University of Wisconsin professor of geology, 1916–1945)

Valiquette, Henry C. (retired Mississippi River steamboat cook interviewed by Brown in La Crosse, June 1940)

Wadsworth, B. (of Madison, untraced)

Whelan, R. B. (supplied one story, 1935)

This list is necessarily incomplete. Many stories recorded in Brown's unpublished papers are unattributed, and because his manuscript collections are scattered, it is impossible to know how many other people may have sent stories to him over the decades.

Brown's eight Bunyan publications from the 1940s contain some overlapping content, but each revolved around a distinct topic, such as cooking and eating, or a particular character, such as Brimstone Bill or Johnny Inkslinger. Six of the eight appeared after Brown retired from the Wisconsin Historical Museum in June

1944 and had more leisure time to edit them. His health began to fail early in 1945, and his correspondence with W. W. Charters suggests that he was rushing them through the press during the rest of that year.

On July 27, 1945, Brown wrote Charters that *Ole Olson* and *Shanty Boy* were at the printer; on November 7, *Bunkhouse Yarns* had just been published, and *Sourdough Sam* appeared on December 5, just a few weeks before his death. Each of these productions was only a few pages in length, issued in what Brown called "very limited" editions, and sold for 25 cents. The six-page *Paul Bunyan Classics: Authentic Original Stories Told in the Old Time Logging Camps of the Wisconsin Pineries...*, issued in 1945, can be considered Brown's last selection of the best Wisconsin stories about Bunyan.

Taken as a whole, Brown's 1940s pamphlets preserved more than 180 Bunyan motifs.[28] Almost a third of these—52 of 183—had not been printed in any of his earlier booklets. While a few had appeared in other people's publications, the vast majority of the new stories were drawn from the cache of WPA Wisconsin Folklore Project files or informants with whom he corresponded. Nearly all of the 1940s tales were also used by Brown's widow in her 1948 book *What Say You of Paul?* Unfortunately, that book, which was meant to be the crown jewel in their career, was hastily assembled and deeply flawed.

About a year after her husband's death, Dorothy Brown was asked to re-issue their Bunyan material in a format for use by schools during the state's 1948 centennial year. She had moved to California in October of 1946 with their eight-year-old daughter and was working as a freelance journalist and children's author, using the collection of Wisconsin folklore files that she had taken with her for raw material. Dorothy accepted the Bunyan offer, in part because she still had some manuscript tales that had never been printed. She was also working on manuscripts of circus lore, herb and flower lore, and Indian place name legends, all topics on which the Wisconsin Folklore Project had accumulated files under her direction. She moved back to Madison in January 1948, found work at the

Wisconsin Historical Society among her husband's old colleagues, and by mid-March had a manuscript ready for the typist.[29]

Dorothy described the book this way in March 1948: "I have taken the very best of the classic tales as written by C. E. and myself, (these have appeared in print in early folklore booklets by C. E. B.), then I am adding some very rich material that we have gathered from reliable original sources which I think are just too good and should be interesting to P's [Paul Bunyan's] enthusiasts." Six weeks later her manuscript was at the printer and she was waiting for the forward by Professor W. W. Charters to arrive. The book was finally published at the end of July 1948, just in time for the official Centennial Exposition the next month. Two decades later she donated her surviving Bunyan files to the Children's Literature Research Collection at the University of Minnesota.[30]

Despite Dorothy's high hopes and best intentions, *What Say You of Paul?* was a slipshod production. No story's source was cited. Original anecdotes published for the first time from living informants were mixed haphazardly among tales taken from earlier publications. The text was laced with important errors; she acknowledged, for example, "Bernice K. Stuart Campbell" (K. Bernice Stewart Campbell) and omitted William Laughead and the Red River Company from her acknowledgments, even though Laughead's Red River trademark was used on the cover and his names for characters appear throughout her text. Following nearly seventy-five pages of Bunyan tales she inserted a section of lumberjack superstitions and jargon (a topic covered in detail by the WPA Folklore Project) and thirty pages of very bad verse by Wisconsin poet Earl Sugden. The whole production was wrapped in simple card-stock covers and bound with staples.

The little book died quickly and quietly, probably because it appeared within months of Harold Felton's sumptuous anthology of Bunyan tales, which reviewers considered the capstone on the entire Bunyan enterprise. The number of copies Dorothy printed is not known, but *What Say You of Paul?* has become a rare book. It was never reprinted, and only forty-four libraries worldwide possess copies (compared to the many thousands that own various editions of Esther Shephard's and James Stevens's Bunyan books). It did almost nothing to make the decades of important work by her husband and herself better known.

After Charles Brown died on February 15, 1946, W. W. Charters wrote to Dorothy, "I feel a kind of loneliness when I am thinking about Paul Bunyan and suddenly remember that Mr. Brown is no longer actively working in Madison. I appreciated all that he did for me in furthering my Bunyan hobby, but I particularly loved his good will, his kindliness, and charm. I am sure that you miss him a great deal from day to day."[31]

Brown's personality was key to his success as a collector and publisher. Although his Bunyan booklets reached very small audiences when compared to commercial popularizations, he was in personal contact with virtually every serious student of Bunyan and shared his research openly with them. He knew or corresponded with Gene Shepard, Bernice Stewart, Homer Watt, Douglas Malloch, P. S. Lovejoy, Ida V. Turney, and Harold Felton. He counted William Bartlett, Gladys Haney, W. W. Charters, and Richard Dorson among his personal friends.

Anthropologist Nancy Lurie, who interned under Brown at the Wisconsin Historical Museum in 1941, recalled him as "a kindly, humorous man, skinny, balding, and probably nowhere near as old as I thought he was when I was seventeen." When he retired in 1944, his colleagues celebrated that "throughout the state, Badgers in all walks of life came to know 'Charlie' Brown and to treasure his friendly interest in their varied hobbies." They commented at his retirement party on his "little black pipe, his right-angled bow, his enthusiasm for Indians, and his many stories." His reputation for infectious enthusiasm and good-humored energy still survives in Madison, where the local chapter of the Wisconsin Archeological Society is named for him.[32]

CHAPTER TEN

Bunyan Becomes a Celebrity

*"…we have added to the original collection a
considerable number of new legends, besides many
different versions of stories already in our collection,
and a great deal of miscellaneous information about the
hero, Paul Bunyan, and his blue ox."*

"ALL I EVER WANTED TO DO," recalled Archie Walker of the Red
River Lumber Company, "was to sell lumber."[1]

In 1914, when Charles Brown was just beginning to teach folk-
lore and Bernice Stewart to collect Bunyan tales, Red River Lumber
Company needed to expand or die. Walker could see that the
Minnesota pineries would soon be exhausted and so had bought
timber lands in northern California and put up a gigantic sawmill.
He also needed to expand sales beyond his traditional customers in
the Upper Midwest, and that meant more and better advertising.
As he was pondering this problem, his thirty-two-year-old cousin,
William Laughead (1882–1958), came through the door.

Laughead had once worked for the family concern as a cruiser and
a lumberjack, but recently he had been struggling to make ends meet
as a freelance graphic designer. "I went in and saw Archie Walker," he

said later. "Archie was an officer of the Red River Lumber Company. He said that an idea he wanted to get over was that 'we're operating in a big way out here…That's the idea we've got to sell—not only to our old customers in the Mississippi Valley but the new territory we've got to break into, east on the Atlantic seaboard'…So I said to him, 'That's kind of a big message to get over in a short time…' Archie says, 'Say, you've heard a lot of this Paul Bunyan stuff in the camps, haven't you?…There must be an angle there…You go ahead and write up something and let me see it.'"[2]

Back in 1901, when Laughead had been cruising land for the company in northern California, he stayed with three brothers named Eastman in a logging camp. They had come out from Michigan in 1884 and entertained him with tales about a clever lumberjack named Paul Bunyan. When he got back, he heard more about Bunyan while working in camps around Brainerd, Bemidji, and Akeley, Minnesota, between 1901 and 1908.[3]

Laughead drew up a thirty-six-page brochure called, *Introducing Mr. Paul Bunyan, of Westwood, California*. Interspersed between photographs and descriptions of the Red River Lumber Company's products were a handful of Paul Bunyan stories he had dressed up in marketing language and carefully shaped to fit between the advertisements. The company printed five thousand of these in 1914 and mailed them to Red River customers in the Mississippi Valley and eastern states, mostly managers in urban lumber yards, sash and door factories, and other buyers of finished lumber. This was the first "book" about Paul Bunyan.

Red River salesmen in the field quickly sent back bad news. "The thing wasn't going over very well…,'" Laughead remembered. "There were even a lot of people in the logging business who had never heard of Paul Bunyan, and when it got to the sawmill and then to the wholesaler and the lumber dealer and the manufacturer who was buying the lumber for factory purposes, they didn't know anything about Paul Bunyan. There was all kinds of confusion."[4]

Laughead and Walker had faith in their idea, though, so they took out weekly advertisements in trade journals, calling their product, "Paul Bunyan's Pine." Laughead drew a portrait of Bunyan and trademarked it as the Red River Lumber Company's logo. For the next three decades, the slogan and trademark were stamped on every board they sold and printed on every piece of paper they sent out.

In 1916 Laughead reprinted the booklet, with the same stories in different format, and sent another five thousand copies to their customer list. "We never sent books to anybody that wasn't connected with the lumber industry until after this Paul Bunyan thing developed from other sources and people got interested and began asking for books." Neither Laughead nor the Red River Company ever copyrighted their text, either, thinking that widespread copying by others would only promote their brand.[5]

Laughead's 1914 and 1916 texts of the tales came from his memory of hearing them in Minnesota and California camps between 1901 and 1908. His portrait of Bunyan, an image that be-

came known worldwide thanks to the company logo, "was a memory of a face of a logging contractor in Minnesota, Pete Dick, one of the greatest fellows that ever lived. The mustache that stuck out sideways—I knew a loud-mouthed French cook in the camps by the name of Charlie Revoir, and he had a mustache like that. I kind of stuck the two of them together."[6]

Laughead made up names and invented personalities for a supporting cast who became permanent fixtures in the Bunyan canon. "I had never heard the names of any characters in connection with Paul Bunyan, except Paul himself," he later recalled. "I was making a picture of this big ox, and I thought he ought to have a name. About as cute a name as you could get for a great big ox would be Babe, and that's where he got his name."[7]

Portrait of Paul Bunyan, by William Laughead FROM THE MARVELOUS EXPLOITS OF PAUL BUNYAN, 1922

Many years later he offered this explanation for the origins of the other main characters in the Bunyan tales:

> Johnny Inkslinger was a natural. Camp clerks were called Ink Slingers, and to provide a character to save Paul's ink I added the "Johnny." Names like "Shot Gunderson" and "Chris Crosshaul" were always floating around to make fun of the Scandinavians with, so I picked them up for a couple of foremen...It was fun to mimic the French-Canadians with story clichés like..."The two Joe Mufraws, one named Pete" and "The Habitant that wore out six pairs of shoepacs looking for a man to lick." That is the source of "Big Ole" and the bully who wanted to fight Paul Bunyan...Sourdough Sam came from a reference to a cook whose sourdough barrel blew up and took off an arm and a leg. The Sourdough Lake incident was an elaboration inspired by a lake of that name in Minnesota...they were derived from memories.

Laughead also insisted that he never had any interest in creating literature or folklore: "At that time it was just another advertising job. It never occurred to me it was 'Folk Lore' or anything that would interest a critic. I had made no research or attempt to document sources."[8]

Laughead embellished his memories to make the tales more readable and amusing, infusing Bunyan and his crew with qualities they did not have in the oral tradition. Some of the oral tales showed Bunyan as a particularly strong and ingenious lumberjack working among his peers, but Laughead consistently cast him as a foreman seeking the sort of efficiencies that any small-business manager wanted. Both heroes reflected the values of their creators—loggers invented an ideal woodsman and Laughead an ideal manager—in a process that would be repeated again and again for the next several decades.[9]

Over the next few years, only a handful of other Bunyan publications appeared. Watt and Stewart's short collection was printed in a scholarly journal in the spring of 1917 (see chapter 7), a long series by Michigan forester P. S. Lovejoy (using the pseudonym Charles Albright) ran in the *American Lumberman* throughout 1916–1918, a few soldiers' stories appeared in *Stars and Stripes* at the end of the war, a group ran in the *Seattle Star* in the autumn of 1920, and Constance Rourke included some examples when she wrote about Lovejoy in the *New Republic* the same year.[10]

Then, in 1922, the Red River Company issued the pamphlet that launched Bunyan on the road to fame. This third, much expanded, edition of Laughead's stories was entitled *The Marvelous Exploits of Paul Bunyan: as told in the camps of the white pine lumbermen...*; it is also sometimes cited under its cover title, "Paul Bunyan and His Big Blue Ox."

Laughead's sources for the 1922 booklet included, of course, the stories he'd recalled in 1914 and 1916. But he also referred to recent publications by Esther Shephard, Ida Turney, and Constance Rourke; quoted several western informants; and thanked two Wisconsin natives, Richard R. Fenska (1884–1966) and Eugene Shepard (Laughead paraphrased Shepard's May 1922 newspaper article closely, giving full credit to the author).[11]

Fenska was a forester who grew up in Shepard's hometown of Rhinelander, Wisconsin, and told W. W. Charters in 1941 that he had been collecting the tales "for nearly 50 years": "Ever since the days of the logging camps in northern Wisconsin during the early Nineties 'Paul' has been a good pal of mine. Of course at first I believed in him like the small boy who believes in Santa Claus. Later, however, I got a great 'kick' out of passing on the achievements of 'Paul' to the uninitiated."[12]

Fenska went on to earn degrees from Beloit College in 1911 and Yale in 1912, worked for the Wisconsin Forestry Board in 1913–1914, and taught at the University of Wisconsin in 1913–1915. Laughead quoted him in 1922 that, "The origin of Paul is as much a myth as the legend itself. There are some who feel that he was known in the Northeastern forest back in the early 19th century but the best available evidence points to the pineries of the Lake

States as the 'Mother' of Paul Bunyan. It is certain that he developed to the zenith of his powers in that region during the '80s and '90s." The stories Fenska supplied for Laughead's booklet, like Shepard's, must have had strong Wisconsin roots.[13]

A copy of this third edition of Laughead's booklet found its way to the *Kansas City Star*, which ran a five-column article about Bunyan on August 21, 1922. It repeated many of the tales and praised the Red River Lumber Company for preserving them. "The public's reception of our advertising brochure as a 'book' caught us by surprise," Laughead later recalled. "It was the circulation of the *Kansas City Star* that brought it to the attention of outsiders and then we began to get requests from everybody...We even got requests from book dealers who wanted to stock the book and sell it but we never filled any orders like that. We weren't in the publishing business; we were selling lumber. After the 1922 edition, first printing, we printed the books in our own print shop at the Westwood office." They had printed ten thousand copies initially but had to reprint another five thousand to keep up with the demand following the *Kansas City Star* article.[14]

Over the next twenty-two years, the *Marvelous Exploits of Paul Bunyan* went through ten more editions, making thirteen in all, 1914–1944. The editorial matter and the advertising changed slightly with each edition, but the stories remained largely the same. "Our booklet 'Paul Bunyan and His Big Blue Ox,'" Laughead explained to Dorothy Brown in 1942, "has gone through a number of printings and some changes in format. These changes did not effect [*sic*] the story copy and illustrations so we have not preserved the old issues. All the material in our older booklets was included in this one. We have regretted, before this, that we did not think about it from the standpoint of the collector." He assured Esther Shepard that the choice of new tales in each edition was made carefully: "...it has never been my intention or the policy of this company to foist anything spurious on our readers. We exclude a great deal of available material because it is entirely modern invention and not in harmony with the period of the old White Pine logger."[15]

Although Red River trademarked their logo, they deliberately chose not to register copyright for the books, because spreading Bunyan tales meant publicizing their name and brand. Unfortunately, it also allowed Laughead's creative work to be exploited by unscrupulous imitators.

A few months after the *Kansas City Star* praised Laughead's Bunyan stories, a writer named Hubert Langerock blatantly plagiarized them in a leading literary journal. Langerock was a radical activist who had attended the first International Socialist Congress in Paris in 1889 and more recently helped organize loggers with the International Workers of the World.[16] His eleven-page article reprinted more than fifty of Laughead's tales almost verbatim, without any acknowledgment, in *The Century Magazine*, a leading New York journal aimed at the country's intellectual elite. It was the first publication to put the Bunyan tales in front of influential East Coast writers, artists, editors, and publishers.

Every Bunyan anecdote in Langerock's article was taken directly out of Laughead's 1922 pamphlet, many of them in exactly the same language. Bunyan researcher Esther Shepard immediately recognized the resemblance and wrote to Laughead, asking if he was writing under a pseudonym. "No, I am not 'Hubert Langerock,' alleged author," he quickly assured her,

and never saw the article in question until your letter reached me yesterday and I bought the magazine. Writing and picturing Paul is all in my day's work and part of the job. It has been our policy, not to copyright our material and to encourage it's use by writers. We have believed that a wide circulation of the legends in all classes of publications was beneficial publicity for us and our Paul Bunyan trademark. At the same time, if magazines are giving out checks for Paul Bunyan stories, we would rather see the money go to a "regular guy." The tenderfoot who sold the "Century" article did not have brains enough even to turn a few sentences around backward to hide his tracks. It is a shame that such a boob could slip one over on the editor of "Century."[17]

The only original parts of Langerock's article were its introduction and conclusion, which ended with the reflection that Bunyan was "so far as can now be discovered, a wholly American mythical figure, if not the only one. Robert Frost's poem, 'Paul's Wife,' in *The Century Magazine* for November 1921, made use of Paul; and he has been the subject of magazine articles and a chap-book; but except for that, he still awaits adequate treatment at the hands of literature."[18]

He didn't have to wait long. Soon, two New York publishing houses were going head-to-head with rival Bunyan collections.

"Strangely enough, I first read them in *Century* magazine either very early in 1923 or 1922," recalled James Stevens. "Here was this story or article about Paul Bunyan and his Big Blue Ox. It filled up a number of pages. And I recognized the name of the writer as one who was notorious in the I.W.W. movement out West, both in California and the Northwest, and I wondered what his stuff could be."[19]

James Stevens was a lumberjack with literary ambitions. Born in Iowa in 1892, he had grown up in Idaho, where he was expelled from school in the ninth grade for chewing tobacco. He never went back. Instead, he started working in lumber camps at age fifteen as a chore boy and teamster. He wandered across the West from camp to camp between 1908 and 1917, went to France with the AEF in 1918, and returned to work in western lumber towns in the early 1920s. Everywhere he went he heard references to Paul Bunyan.[20]

Stevens had always wanted to be a writer. He admired the work of H. L. Mencken, and, while working in a sawmill at Bend, Oregon, in the fall of 1923, he wrote to Mencken. "In my letter I'd simply told him that since 1910 I'd been a reader of his, and that I'd worked since [age] 13 around logging camps...I got a letter back from him telling me that the *American Mercury* was to be started, the first issue of January 1924." Mencken encouraged Stevens to submit a story, and three months later his first fiction was accepted for publication.[21]

Recalling that the *Saturday Evening Post* had printed a reference to Bunyan in a story in 1922 and having just seen *The Century* collection, Stevens realized there might be a market for the tales he had heard in logging camps. He went to work at his typewriter and sent Mencken a Bunyan story, "The Black Duck Dinner," in February 1924. "I heard an old Minnesota lumberjack tell it at the Brooks-Scanlon sawmill in Bend, Oregon, while I was working there. I worked there for two years, 1922, 1923, and up to March 1924." Mencken loved it and put his own publisher, Alfred Knopf, in touch with Stevens. Mencken and Knopf asked, "if I were sure that it hadn't been published before and if there had been anything that I knew of published on Paul Bunyan, and that if not, Knopf was interested in publishing a dozen stories like this one, making them all into a book. Well, that lit me up sky high."[22]

"I wrote to the Red River Lumber company," Stevens continued, "to make sure that I was free to use those stories in my first Paul Bunyan book...the response I got...was written to me by Bill Laughead. I'd made some statement that this article in *Century Magazine* was the only place I'd seen Paul Bunyan stories in print before I wrote my 'Black Duck Dinner' for the *American Mercury*. Then he told me that this was a complete plagiarism, that without his knowledge or consent this man had simply taken the booklet and typed it over and submitted it as an article."[23]

Stevens had no desire to plagiarize or even to reprint Laughead's tales. He wanted to use the Bunyan stories as kernels around which he would create entirely new fiction. "I was using them as a sort of pattern, or as material to use in creating my own literary work. I didn't give a hoot about advertising loggers' folklore or promoting it...And I didn't give a hoot about how much good it might do the lumber industry." He also claimed that "there was no thought in my mind, no pretension that I was a folklore collector, that I was a researcher or that I had an academic or scientific interest in the loggers' lore of Paul Bunyan. To me, it was natural material for the creative artist to use, and that's the only way I thought of myself and my art."[24]

Stevens began his Bunyan book for Knopf in the fall of 1924. "I was too green to ask for an advance. In fact, the idea that the publishing firm of Alfred A. Knopf, the publishers of Thomas Mann, H. L. Mencken and so many other great writers, would want to publish a book by me—why, they could have had my stuff for nothing." Still, Stevens was a working man and needed to eat somehow while writing. "I wanted to have enough money so I could feel secure in taking five months to write it," he recalled, "and I didn't have much savings. I had a Ford sedan which I had sold for $450...I wrote the 1925 Paul Bunyan in Tacoma and found lots of old-timers there, old Minnesota men with the great St. Paul and Tacoma Lumber Company which had Minnesota origins, as did Weyerhaeuser and others of the area." Knopf was delighted when he received the manuscript: "...the 12 stories of my first book were just taken and put into type, and the next thing I knew I received the galleys."[25]

Stevens later said that he

> took Bill Laughead's Sourdough Sam and MacGillivray's Pea Soup Shorty as patterns and invented Creampuff Fatty and Hot Biscuit Slim. I invented Hels Helson, the bull of the woods, who was a sort of offshoot of Bill Laughead's Big Ole, the Blacksmith. I used all of Laughead's principal characters. I thought up a number of rivers, then John Shears, the boss farmer, Shanty Boy, and the Iron Man of the Saginaw, Joe Fournier, Little Meery, Mark Beaucoup—invented in France, 1918—Jonah Wiles, who was the enemy of Sourdough Sam...Every story that I did was around some original bit of folklore, which was simply an anecdote in the first place—or a "gag," as Bill Laughead says.[26]

But just as Stevens was settling in Tacoma to write his tales for Mencken and Knopf, a University of Washington English instructor named Esther Shephard (1891–1975) was already bringing out the first book of Bunyan tales.

She had grown up in Minneapolis at the height of the lumber industry and gone out to Seattle to study. While researching her master's thesis on American frontier literature, she came across Constance Rourke's 1920 *New Republic* article about Lovejoy and his collection of Bunyan tales. She wrote Lovejoy asking for more information, dug stories out of newspapers in the Pacific Northwest, and began talking with local loggers herself.[27]

After an excerpt from her thesis appeared in *Pacific Review* in 1921, she decided to compile an anthology of the Bunyan tales. She ordered a copy of Stewart and Watt's pamphlet from Wisconsin, obtained copies of Laughead's booklet and one made as a class project by teacher Ida V. Turney, and set off on the road to interview as many loggers as she could find.[28]

In December of 1924, Shephard and her husband Ellis published *Paul Bunyan* themselves through a private press they set up. It sold so well that a second printing was needed in February 1925, and later that year they sold the rights to Alfred Harcourt, who issued a slightly larger and more attractive edition. Harcourt reprinted this several times during the height of Bunyan's popularity, including a very successful 1941 edition designed and illustrated by Rockwell Kent.

Harcourt had been interested in publishing a Bunyan anthology for five years. In April of 1920, freelance writer Constance Rourke heard about Lovejoy's repertoire and proposed publishing an article in the *New Republic*; she interviewed him in May 1920. When her article appeared a few weeks later, Lovejoy called it, "the first-such even approximately non-putrid version." It brought awareness of the stories into the mainstream for the first time and, in Lovejoy's words, "fetched on so much kindly-send-on-everything-right-away correspondence" from Bunyan enthusiasts. This response led Rourke to approach Harcourt, but disruptions in her and Lovejoy's personal lives eventually stifled the book project. Then in 1925 Harcourt found Esther Shephard.[29]

The books by William Laughead, Esther Shephard, and James Stevens that made Bunyan famous during the 1920s

Shephard assembled the tales that she had collected from western informants with those already printed by Stewart and Watt, Laughead, and Turney, arranging them as a conventional biography of Bunyan that she phrased in loggers' jargon. Although this device pleased her readers, it dramatically altered the tales and distorted the context in which they had been created. Like Stevens, she used the names for characters that Laughead had invented, including Babe the Blue Ox. She also failed to identify her sources, and she mixed authentic tales from oral sources with fanciful inventions such as one in which Bunyan conducts logging operations from an airplane in Alaska.[30]

Bunyan's emergence into the mass media during the 1920s is chronicled in Tables 4 and 5.

Shephard's and Stevens's books were immediate successes with the reading public. By 1925, after making a decisive difference in the "Great War," Americans were eager to embrace a national icon who symbolized their pride in the country's strength and ingenuity. In addition, most adults in the 1920s had grown up in rural

Table 4: *Publication of the Bunyan Tales in Major Periodicals, 1918–1927*

DATE	AUTHOR TITLE	JOURNAL LOCATION	NOTE
May 23, 1919	Cummings "All Together, Boys"	*Stars and Stripes* Paris, France	Tales from Minnesota
June 13, 1919	Jenderny "That Lumber Camp"	*Stars and Stripes* Paris, France	Tales from Wisconsin
July 7, 1920	Rourke "Paul Bunyon"	*New Republic* New York, NY	Prints stories from Lovejoy's collection
November 1921	Frost "Paul's Wife"	*Century Magazine* New York, NY	Poem
1921	Shephard "The Tall Tale in American Literature."	*Pacific Review* Seattle, WA	Includes several tales collected in the Northwest
August 21, 1922	unsigned "Paul Bunyan and His Big Blue Ox"	Kansas City Star Kansas City, MO	From Laughead
May 1923	Langerock "Wonderful Life and Deeds of Paul Bunyon"	*Century Magazine* New York, NY	Plagiarizes Laughead
April 1924	Hader "A Gallery of American Myths"	*Century Magazine* New York, NY	Compares Bunyan to European myths
June 1924	Stevens "Black Duck Dinner"	*American Mercury* New York, NY	Stevens's first publication
January 21, 1925	Littell "Paul Bunyan"	*New Republic* New York, NY	Favorable review of Shephard
June 1925	Mackaye "A Homer of the Logging Camps"	*Bookman* New York, NY	Compares Stevens and Shephard
June 1925	Van Doren "Document and Work of Art"	*Century Magazine* New York, NY	Compares Stevens and Shephard

Table 4: *continued*

DATE	AUTHOR TITLE	JOURNAL LOCATION	NOTE
July 8, 1925	Chase "Paul Bunyan"	*New Republic* New York, NY	Favorable review of Stevens
August 26, 1925	Dobie "Paul Bunyan"	*Nation* New York, NY	Compares Stevens and Shephard
August 29, 1925	Rourke "The Making of an Epic"	*Saturday Review of Literature* New York, NY	Compares Stevens and Shephard
October 30, 1927	"America's Only Folk-Lore Character"	*The American Weekly* New York, NY	Full-page printing of many tales, in Hearst Sunday supplement

areas, and, although they had migrated into cities, they found that the Bunyan tales evoked nostalgia for the frontier America of their childhoods. Book sales were also fueled because two of the nation's most creative young publishers had launched competing products into the market.

For decades, staid Victorian publishers such as Harper Brothers and Scribner's had dominated the book trade. But in the 1910s Alfred Harcourt and Alfred Knopf each broke away from established firms in order to publish the voices of a new generation. By 1925, their new books were eagerly anticipated each season by thousands of booksellers and readers. Harcourt, acting apparently on his own instincts, had seen the potential in Bunyan back in 1920 when he read Constance Rourke's summary of Lovejoy's collection; after their book project failed, he was delighted to discover Esther Shephard in 1925. Knopf, meanwhile, was led to Bunyan by Mencken, who had stumbled upon lumberjack-author James Stevens in 1924. By 1925, the stage was set for a contest between two competing versions of Bunyan.

Table 5: *Publication of the Bunyan Tales in Books and Pamphlets, 1914–1927*

DATE	AUTHOR TITLE	PUBLISHER LOCATION	# OF PAGES # OF COPIES
1914	Laughead *Introducing Mr. Paul Bunyan*	Red River Lumber Company Minneapolis, MN	16 5,000
1916	Laughead *Tales about Paul Bunyan, vol. II*	Red River Lumber Company Minneapolis, MN	33 5,000
1919	Turney *Paul Bunyan Comes West*	University of Oregon Eugene, OR	34 Very few
1922	Laughead *Marvelous Exploits of Paul Bunyan*	Red River Lumber Company Minneapolis, MN	36 10,000
1922	Brown *Paul Bunyan Tales*	Author Madison, WI	7 Very few
1924	Shephard *Paul Bunyan*	Harcourt Brace New York, NY	235 unknown
1925, April	Stevens *Paul Bunyan*	Alfred Knopf New York, NY	245 unknown
1926	Wadsworth *Paul Bunyan and His Great Blue Ox*	Doubleday & Doran New York, NY	238 unknown
1927	Bowman *Adventures of Paul Bunyan*	Century Company New York, NY	302 unknown

Shephard's book purported to have been collected in the field directly from the mouths of loggers. In fact, she acknowledged in her introduction dependence upon the previous collections by Stewart and Watt and Laughead, as well as newspaper printings of the stories; she also individually thanked P. S. Lovejoy, with whom she had corresponded, and Eugene Shepard, in Rhinelander. Stevens, in contrast, acknowledged no one other than his "old camp comrades" in logging shanties and lumber mills, and Mencken. Shephard, the English scholar, tried to present the spirit of the stories faithfully and dress them in loggers' dialect. Stevens, the self-educated lumberjack-hobo, transformed them into his own creative works of fiction and tried to dress them in polished prose.

The first of several reviews comparing the two books appeared in June 1925, and four more followed during the course of the summer. Some of New York's leading critics, such as Percy Mackaye, Carl Van Doren, and Stuart Chase (see Table 4), offered opinions. On April 12 the *New York Times* gave Stevens nearly an entire page, including reproductions of three of his book's woodcuts. On June 28 the *Los Angeles Times* not only ran a review but also gave space for Stevens himself to tell how he had heard the tales in camp and came to write the book. The *Chicago Tribune* compared Stevens and Shephard briefly on November 21, and papers in a dozen smaller cities from Fresno, California, to Middletown, New York, also ran reviews, including the press in small towns such as Galveston, Texas; Lincoln, Nebraska; and Sheboygan, Wisconsin.[31]

For the next eight decades, Shephard's and Stevens's books of Bunyan tales fought for the attention (and dollars) of readers. Each was reprinted several times during the 1930s and 1940s as Knopf and Harcourt rode the Bunyan wave. Stevens told an interviewer in 1963 that, "as close as I can calculate, the 1925 *Paul Bunyan* has sold 252,000 copies, first at $2.50, then in the dollar edition [Garden City Publishing Company's "Star Books" issue], and now in the $3.00 edition…140,000 of that 252,000 were in the pocket books that were sold in the post exchanges during World War II [the paperback Armed Service Edition]." Harcourt commissioned artist Rockwell Kent to design and illustrate his 1941 edition of Shephard's anthology; the sizes of its various editions and reprintings have not been discovered, but Shephard's collection has never been out of print since it first appeared in 1924.[32]

Throughout this battle of the books, the Red River Lumber Company continued to mail a free copy of Laughead's stories to anyone who asked. Laughead later estimated that, "We distributed, free of charge, about 110,000 or 125,000 copies." The number of copies that Harcourt published is not known, but if Shephard's books sold roughly the same number as Stevens's, then American readers bought more than 600,000 Paul Bunyan books between 1925 and 1950. In comparison, the most important American book of 1925, F. Scott Fitzgerald's *The Great Gatsby*, sold a mere 30,000 copies between 1925 and 1940.[33]

With the nation's most important newspapers and literary journals running stories about Bunyan books in the summer of 1925, many enterprising writers jumped on the bandwagon. The first Bunyan children's book, by Wallace Wadsworth, appeared in 1926; the first graduate thesis in 1927; and the first encyclopedia article in 1929 (*Encyclopædia Britannica*). The high point in this initial wave of Bunyan popularity was probably reached on October 30, 1927, when nearly five million readers of Hearst newspapers around the nation opened their Sunday supplements to find a full-page article about Bunyan, "America's Only Folk-Lore Character."[34]

But that was just the start. Over the next two decades, more than one hundred books about Bunyan appeared, and since then the stream of publications, which included at least nineteen piracies of Stevens's stories, has never ceased. People had always been free to elaborate on a folktale—indeed, lumberjacks had been expected to outdo one another at it—so publishers didn't hesitate to make up new Bunyans to suit their needs. Perhaps the most ridiculous early example of this was Michigan children's author James Bowman's version, which had anthropomorphic trees exclaim, when they learned they would soon be cut down and sawed into lumber, "Won't it be wonderful! To be free! To travel and see the great wide world and to meet all our distant cousins!" The Bunyan wave crested with the 1947 anthology, *Legends of Paul Bunyan*, edited by Harold Felton, whose lavish exterior concealed a hodgepodge of authentic oral tales mixed indiscriminately with some of the worst of the popularizations.[35]

The midcentury Bunyan mania went far beyond books and magazines into many other expressions of the nation's culture. During the 1930s local business leaders and northwoods chambers of commerce across the nation seized upon Bunyan in order to promote tourism. A prime example of these efforts was the Mystic Knights of the Blue Ox, formed in Bayfield, Wisconsin, in 1932 as "a Fraternity of the Followers of Paul Bunyan, Legendary hero of the American Lumberjack, Organized for the Purpose of Perpetuating His Memory for Posterity by the Erection of a Statue of the Mighty Paul and the Establishment of a Museum of Bunyan Relics at Bayfield, Wis." One of its founders, J. P. O'Malley, told Dorothy Brown, "It was more or less an advertising stunt, and to get people to come to Bayfield to enjoy a 'dinner out' as Mr. Weber called it...Camp No. 1 was the Bayfield Camp, The next one was Superior No. 7. Paul couldn't count very well and thought 7 came after 1. Minong was number 13. Mr. Maier organized another camp in Taylor County a few years later."[36] In January of 1933 they held their first "lumberjack dinner," which, according to the press,

> was planned largely as a lark by a group of Bayfield live-wires, headed by Gus Weber, former lumber camp cook, who served a real old-time, open-air lumber camp dinner, with all its great variety of robust, masculine dishes...From all the communities of the bay region, and from other parts of northern Wisconsin to Feldmaier woodlot north of Bayfield came scores of men, many of them former lumber workers, all dressed in rough, outdoor clothes, all ripe and ready for a real frolic in the great outdoors. The total attendance was over 200. They engaged in lumberjack sports and all sorts of rough and tumble horseplay in the snow, listened to a program of logging reminiscences from old-timers of the region, ate a hearty meal of well-cooked lumberjack fare, and went home after one of the most enjoyable days many of them had ever spent.[37]

OUT OF THE NORTHWOODS

When the Mystic Knights held their second event two years later, nearly five hundred people gathered outside Bayfield, and annual events followed for several years, all with the purpose of raising funds for a Bunyan statue and museum to be located in Bayfield. Apart from the convivial gatherings, though, the group produced nothing significant. About 1941 the reins were handed over to Louis Maier, a retired forester who kept it afloat on paper in Milwaukee until at least 1944, but no Bunyan statue or museum ever materialized in Bayfield.[38]

More successful promotional efforts started about the same time in Brainerd and Bemidji, Minnesota, and became staples of the local tourist industry. Robert Walls has described at great length the Bunyan pageants, festivals, and tourist destinations, as well as the effect of the Bunyan stereotype on actual woods workers. John Harty recently explained the extent and effect of Bunyan-based tourism on the American landscape.[39]

Throughout the Bunyan craze, William Laughead continued to work in the Red River Lumber Company advertising department. James Stevens became public relations counsel for the West Coast Lumbermen's Association and wrote fiction. Esther Shephard and her husband ran the McNeil Press until his death in 1938, when she took a faculty position at San Jose State College.[40]

Just as Bunyan had been the lumberjack's idealized version of himself, he quickly came to represent an idealized version of the American national character—an ingenious, good-natured, and virtually omnipotent father figure who transformed useless wilderness into valuable retail commodities. As the country entered World War II, he came especially to symbolize the nation's size, strength, and power. Rockwell Kent's illustrations to Shephard's text showed a sleek, strong-jawed, muscular Bunyan ready to take on the fascists, while Stevens's armed forces editions of the tales were carried to the front in soldiers' shirt pockets and knapsacks.

But Bunyan's appeal couldn't last forever. P. S. Lovejoy, who told Bunyan stories for live audiences around the time of World War I, predicted its decline in a 1941 letter to W. W. Charters:

The vocabulary & every-day experiences of the land-clearing & lumbering days have been shrinking so fast even during the last 2–3 decades, that for some years I've been finding fewer & smaller audiences at all worth trying P-B stuff on. They "get" less & less of the "feel & flavor." Only the cruder phases "register" with people who have not lived & worked on farms & in the logging camps. Since that gap is due to increase rapidly from now on, if the "original feel & flavor" is to be at all retained or recorded, the footnote annotations must evidently become longer & longer, I take it; with the "available" or "effective" incidents with still "register" at all as per deacon-seat renditions presently too few to bother with. Nothing left except some raw hyperbole?[41]

The next year Homer Watt suggested to Lovejoy that after the original audience for Bunyan tales had passed away, raw hyperbole would appeal only to the very young "and that only in children's stories will he remain, like Jack the Giant Killer. There is no reason why America should not ultimately develop its traditions of the nursery just as Old England has done." He even prepared a manuscript of the tales for his grandchildren, but World War II and unexpected family responsibilities kept it from being published.[42]

During the 1950s, Bunyan evolved from a patriotic icon into a fairy-tale hero, his rugged masculinity softened into a buffoonish charm and the tales' sharp-edged wit smoothed into cutesy sentiment. By then the loggers who had invented him were long dead, and the editors who had popularized him gradually followed them to the grave. Lovejoy, Brown, and Watt died in the 1940s; MacGillivray, Rockwell, and Laughead in the 1950s; and Stevens, Shephard, and Stewart in the 1970s. Bunyan himself lived on, of course, and since 1975 new publications about him have appeared at the rate of one every three weeks—more than six hundred in all—and his name still populates the nation's landscape on storefronts, billboards, and other advertisements from Maine to California.

Chapter Eleven

Competing Claims to Fame

"In these degenerate days, there are young fellows who would not know a peavey from a grade stick, or a round turn from a cross haul, yet they will lay claim to having worked in Paul Bunyan's camps. No credence can be placed on what such irresponsibles have to say."

O NCE BUNYAN'S NAME AND FACE had become valuable commodities in the 1920s, everyone wanted a piece of the action. During the Depression, impoverished Great Lakes communities devastated by the departure of the lumber industry tried especially hard to lure sportsmen to a nostalgic, Bunyanesque northwoods. A common tactic in towns all across the northern United States was claiming to be Bunyan's birthplace. Bangor, Maine; Oscoda, Michigan; Rhinelander, Wisconsin ("45 miles west" of it, to be precise); Akeley and Brainerd, Minnesota; and Westwood, California, have all publicly claimed the honor. At the same time, a good-natured rivalry prompted several states to announce that the Bunyan tales, if not the hero himself, had actually been born within their borders. Because so many of these dubious claims have been widely repeated, it's worthwhile to examine the surviving evidence for and against them. Where, after considering the surviving evidence, did the Bunyan tales originate?

None of the accounts dating Bunyan tales before the mid-1880s holds up well when measured against the standards with which historians usually assess claims about the past:

- **Specificity**: how clear and precise is the evidence?
- **Proximity**: how close, in space and time, was the witness to the event?
- **Gedibility**: how trustworthy is the witness who made the record?
- **Bias**: did the witness have an interest in any specific outcome?
- **Plausibility**: how likely is the claim, given what else is known?
- **Corroboration** is there supporting evidence from other sources?

Only a handful of accounts survive from people who said they heard Bunyan stories before the mid-1880s. Those claims and their supporting evidence are given here in chronological order, each followed by an assessment of its reliability.

1837, Quebec: James Stevens, already mistakenly convinced that Bunyan came from Canada, traced him back to the Papineau Rebellion of 1837 in which French-speaking residents tried to throw off the yoke of English domination. "I questioned many old time French-Canadian loggers before I found genuine proof...," he wrote at the start of his 1925 anthology. "Z. Berneche, a snowy-maned, shining-eyed, keen-minded veteran logger of ninety years, told me about the original hero. His uncle, Coller Bellaine, fought by the side of Paul Bunyon, and later worked two seasons for him."[1] As discussed in chapter 2, the records of the Papineau Rebellion (created as English authorities put down and punished the rebels) do not contain anyone whose name resembled Bunyan, and no mention of him can be found in French-Canadian folklore. Either Stevens invented this story as a literary device, Berneche was sincerely misinformed, or the canny old woodsman imposed upon Stevens's credibility.

1850s, New York or Pennsylvania: On May 1, 1940, William Laughead wrote in the Bemidji (Minnesota) *Daily Pioneer*, "In 1920, Mr. Henry Neall, then well along in years, wrote to The Red River Lumber Company that he had heard Paul Bunyan stories when a boy in his grandfather's camps in Pennsylvania and that his grandfather referred to them as old traditions." In the eleventh (1940) edition of the company's Bunyan tales he also reported, "One of our correspondents, a man of advanced years, wrote us in 1922 that he had heard some of the stories when a boy in his grandfather's logging camps in New York, and that they were supposed to be old at that time." This is the only report dated earlier than the mid-1880s that Laughead ever received: "I regret that I can add no conclusive evidence [to the question of Bunyan's origins] but none has come my way in 25 years of contact and correspondence with students of the Paul Bunyan myth."[2]

Laughead's account of Neall's report is too vague to carry much weight. Neall may have heard classic folk tales with motifs that later appeared in the Bunyan canon, but there is no clear evidence that Paul Bunyan was the hero of them. This is most likely an example of an informant's memory conflating the early use of motifs with the later hero (see chapter 1). Neall's report is also uncorroborated: if he did hear tales about Paul Bunyan in the 1850s in New York, he is the only person on record who did. Richard Dorson, in his survey of nineteenth-century tall tales from the Northeast, combed the local press meticulously without finding any mention of Bunyan that would validate Neall's recollection.[3]

1866, Michigan: James Stevens wrote in 1948, "In 1930 the president of one of Michigan's largest banks recited to me his memories of the Paul Bunyan tales he had first heard as a twelve-year-old in the shanty camps. That was in the winter of 1866–1867. I credited the account not only because of the character and reputation of the man who gave it, but also for its accordance with what I'd heard from so many others."[4]

This sounds plausible but lacks specificity and corroboration. One wishes that Stevens had identified his informant, related some of the tales, or given examples of what he'd heard "from so many others." Even Stevens himself admitted it had no supporting corroboration: in 1930–1931, he and his wife spent several months in Bay City, Michigan, talking to retired loggers and searching library collections for original stories about Bunyan. "We just found nothing of that kind," he told an interviewer, "...nothing on Paul Bunyan until 1914."[5]

1869, Minnesota: Fred Staples of Lakeland, Minnesota, who was born in 1853 and started logging as a teenager, wrote in 1940, "I was fifty years in the woods and can't remember a time when I didn't know about Paul Bunyan. I started driving a team for Uncle Isaac [Staples, founder of Stillwater, Minnesota] when I was sixteen years old and I heard about Paul Bunyan the very first winter I was in the woods."[6]

This is the most compelling report of Bunyan prior to the 1880s. It is precisely located in time and place, and its creator had no obvious bias. Staples's uncle Isaac and his father, Winslow Staples, are well documented in late-nineteenth-century records. Its major weakness is that it is entirely uncorroborated, despite exhaustive research among elderly Minnesota loggers by the state's two most prominent historians, who concluded in the 1930s that there was no oral tradition of Bunyan in Minnesota before Laughead.

Professor Theodore Blegen (1891–1969), superintendent of the Minnesota Historical Society from 1931–1939, began interviewing loggers in the 1920s; forty years later he concluded: "there is scarcely a shred of evidence that the lumberjacks were familiar with Paul Bunyan, told stories about him, or indeed had ever heard of him." Minnesota lumber historian Agnes Larson (1892–1967) carefully investigated primary sources on the state's lumber industry from 1931 to 1949. After extensive interviewing, she "failed to uncover a single person who during the time he had worked in the Minnesota lumber camps had heard of Paul." If Fred Staples accurately recalled hearing about Bunyan in the 1870s, he was apparently alone among his contemporaries in doing so.[7]

1870, Wisconsin: Eugene Shepard told Gifford Pinchot in the fall of 1920 that he "had been telling Paul Bunyan stories for fifty years." For this to be strictly true, Shepard would have had to have told the stories as a boy of sixteen, when he first entered the woods as an apprentice timber cruiser. There is no reliable corroborating mention of Bunyan that early, and, given Shepard's penchant for lying, we can safely dismiss this claim as mere hyperbole. By 1920 Shepard had, indeed, been telling Bunyan stories for decades, but when and where he first did so is unknown. Certainly it was not as early as 1870, when Shepard himself was a greenhorn.[8]

1873, Minnesota: The only other early account from Minnesota comes through James Stevens and is open to the same objections as the preceding ones. He wrote in the introduction to his 1925 book:

> Perhaps the Paul Bunyan narrator who won most lasting fame was Len Day, whose firm of Len Day & Son was one of the largest lumber concerns of Minneapolis in the sixties. I had often heard of him; and lately Mr. Michael Christopher Quinn, yard superintendent for the North-western Lumber Company, of Hoquiam, Washington, for twenty-two years, gave me a first-hand account of him. In 1873 Mr. Quinn was working in a great log drive down the Mississippi; his camp was at Haney Landing, Minnesota. Len Day was then eighty-five, a prosperous and influential lumberman. But the lure of the drive and of camp life still stirred the true logger's soul of him, and he came to the camp each spring. Every night the gang gathered in the cookhouse to hear the old camp bard declaim a canto of the Paul Bunyan epic. "Len Day told the stories in sections," said Mr. Quinn...Len Day had lived in New Brunswick in the forties and had thus heard the stories in their beginnings.[9]

Like Staples's 1869 report, this is quite specific and is traced back to a person who is well documented. It is unconvincing, however, for several reasons. It is secondhand and conveyed by a source (Stevens) with known biases and questionable credibility; he was far more interested in writing creative fiction than in uncovering historical truth. In addition, some of its details are unreliable: for example, there is no trace of a Haney Landing in Minnesota on any U.S. Geological Survey topographic map, nor is there any mention of Paul Bunyan in New Brunswick folklore. And of course it is not only uncorroborated but directly contradicted by Larson's and Blegen's careful research.

1870s, Ontario: Colonel George E. Laidlaw (1860–1927), who grew up outside Toronto, sent a Bunyan tale to Charles Brown in 1925 that he called, "an old one I used to hear when I was a boy."[10] In the tale, Bunyan hides under an inverted kettle to escape mosquitoes who eventually fly off with it. This is a common motif in American folklore and is found all over the continent. It is more likely that Laidlaw in his old age grafted Bunyan onto a pre-existing motif than that he was the only Toronto resident to remember hearing a Bunyan story in the 1870s.

1880, Pennsylvania: When octogenarian logger Wesley Straw was interviewed by folklorist Rodney Loehr in Montana in 1947, he claimed to have heard Bunyan tales in Pennsylvania almost seventy years before. "[Straw] was born in Potter County, Pennsylvania in 1864 and started to work in the woods at the age of fourteen…," Loehr wrote. "Straw says that he heard the Bunyan tales in Pennsylvania in 1880. These stories were told by a Bill James, a Pennsylvanian from the hard coal region who had struck out for the woods. James was a good storyteller and Straw thinks that he invented Paul Bunyan. All of the old loggers liked to listen to the stories which James had to tell about Bunyan, his partner Paul Sockalett, and the Blue Ox, which had only one eye located in the middle of its head. In those days, Straw said, good storytellers and singers achieved a sort of local fame. Their presence at a camp was welcomed because of the entertainment they provided."[11]

This account, charming as it is, strikes one as dubious because it fails to meet the standards of proximity and plausibility, and it is uncorroborated. Straw was nearly ninety years old and recalling events that had occurred almost seventy years earlier, more than two thousand miles away. Two of the three narrative details he mentioned are found nowhere else in Bunyan tales. Like Neall in New York, if he did hear about Paul Bunyan in Pennsylvania in 1880, he is the only person on record who did: his account is not confirmed by any other logger who worked in the area at the time.

1884, Michigan: In 1963, W. H. Hutchinson wrote:

> In the summer and fall of 1901, [William] Laughead was with a timber-cruising party of Red River Lumber Company examining some of their purchases in Modoc, Shasta, and Siskiyou counties, California. The region may be pinpointed on today's maps by referring to the communities of Burney, Fall River Mills, Lookout, Hackamore and Glenburn. I asked Laughead if he had heard anything of Paul Bunyan during this early visit to what still is one of the most isolated sections of California. "I had one contact [Laughead replied]. There were three brothers named Eastman that had come out from Michigan in 1884, from the Saginaw River country. One of them was working for the party I was with as a cook and pack-train man and all that sort of stuff. He was a mountain man; he'd lived and been raised in the mountains there [Glenburn] and he had some of these Paul Bunyan gags. Never been back to Michigan, and Lord, where they lived it was a three or four day trip to the nearest railroad by the horses, and there was no lumber operation in the country. It was just virgin forest, so I don't see how he would have contacted any loggers in that time. I never went into it very deep with them because I wasn't interested in Paul Bunyan particularly at that time, but I know he'd every once in a while make a crack about Paul Bunyan, so evidently the only place he could have heard them was back in that Saginaw country."

Hutchinson glossed this with the note, "Laughead erred a little here. There was a thriving lumber industry at what are now the towns of Mt. Shasta and McCloud, California, within two or three days ride of the country where he met the Eastman brothers."[12] In fact, the Eastman brothers must have come into regular contact with other lumber industry workers between 1884 and 1901 simply to market their logs. This fact alone undermines Laughead's assumption that they must have brought the tales from Michigan in 1884.

1885, Wisconsin: Bert Taplin's clear recollection of hearing Bunyan tales north of Tomahawk, Wisconsin, in 1885 or 1886 (see chapter 4 and appendix, no. 5) is the first thoroughly reliable account so far discovered. It is specific as to place and time and was recorded directly from the observer. It even includes a complete Bunyan story that was told at the time, with unique motifs not derived from traditional folktales. Taplin had no motive for bias, his account is plausible given other known facts about Wisconsin River logging, and his evidence is independently corroborated by the separate account of Jim McKeague. Until new sources are uncovered, it remains the earliest reliable evidence of Paul Bunyan's existence as a folk hero. No convincing account can be found earlier than Taplin's description from the vicinity of Tomahawk, Wisconsin, in 1885–1886.

What, then, is the genealogy of the surviving Bunyan tales (prior to their colonization by the mass media in the 1920s)? The earliest attempts to answer this question focused on Laughead's 1914 pamphlet, *Introducing Mr. Paul Bunyan of Westwood, California*, which was long thought to be the first publication of the tales. Laughead himself said that, apart from the passing references in California already discussed, he had first heard stories about Bunyan around Bemidji between 1901 and 1908. Working backward through time, Bunyan's Minnesota history is quite simple:

1914 Red River pamphlet
1901 Laughead heard Bunyan tales at Bemidji[13]

The Michigan recension is somewhat more complex. In 1944, Professor W. W. Charters pointed out that the "Round River" sequence predated Laughead and had been printed not once but twice (in the *Detroit News* in 1910 and again, in verse, in the *American Lumberman* in 1914). Subsequent research revealed that the "Round River" stories had in fact first appeared in 1906 in the *Oscoda Press*, written by the editor's brother, James MacGillivray. In a 1951 letter to the Library of Congress folklore office, their author, MacGillivray, said that he had first heard the stories from timber cruiser Jimmy Conn (1870–1940); elsewhere he wrote that he had first heard them in 1887 on the north branch of the Au Sable River, when Conn would have been only seventeen years old. The Michigan recension therefore runs as follows:

1914 *American Lumberman*, MacGillivray/Malloch verse
1910 *Detroit News*, William MacGillivray prose
1906 *Oscoda Press*, J. MacGillivray prose
1887 Au Sable River[14]

In Wisconsin, Charles Brown always insisted that Paul Bunyan originated in the upper Wisconsin River valley, although he offered no evidence in print for that claim. Before 1922 he had heard Gene Shepard, who claimed to have invented Bunyan, say that the lumberjack hero was born forty-five miles west of Rhinelander. Then, in November 1938, Brown received Taplin's account of Bunyan tales told near Tomahawk by Bill Mulhollen in the winter of 1885–1886. The chain of Wisconsin evidence therefore goes like this, the last link being merely speculative:

1922 Charles Brown
1917 Stewart and Watt
late 1886 Jim McKeague in Tomahawk
1885–1886 Taplin/Mulhollen, north of Tomahawk
1882 Shepard[15]

The surviving evidence therefore suggests that Wisconsin has the best claim of any state to being Paul Bunyan's birthplace. Future

research, as more local newspapers are digitized and more manuscript collections cataloged online, may trace Bunyan's genealogy
to some other point of origin.

Charles Brown examined every scrap of contemporary documentation, corresponded with every important Bunyan researcher,
and talked to dozens of firsthand informants. Distinguishing between the stories and their hero, he explained Bunyan's progress
this way in 1936:

> These legends had their beginnings in the Wisconsin lum-
> ber camps in the early fifties of the past century, in the tall
> tales and other stories told by the lumberjacks in what was
> once the largest and finest stand of white pine timber in
> the world. In the succeeding thirty years, the best of these
> stories, having been told and retold in the camps, they
> had finally crystallized into their present form. At about
> this time the name of the giant lumberjack, Paul Bunyan,
> became associated with the legends and he was made the
> hero of all of them. Wisconsin is thus the true home of
> these myths. From this state lumberjacks carried them east-
> ward to Michigan, Maine and Ontario. With the westward
> spread of lumbering, in which movement some Wisconsin
> lumberman were interested, they were carried westward to
> the lumber camps of Wyoming, Oregon, Washington and
> California. Wisconsin lumberjacks also carried them into
> the yellow pine forests of the South. In all of these regions
> additional Paul Bunyan legends were created and have be-
> come a part of this rich heritage of America folklore.[16]

After looking at more evidence than Brown had available, we believe that he nevertheless understood the transmission of the tales
correctly. Traditional tales with pre-existing motifs traveled west
into Wisconsin before 1860; after the Civil War, they were aug-
mented with new stories about the early years of Great lakes lumbering; in the 1880s Paul Bunyan was inserted as their protagonist.

But Bunyan, like most of the nineteenth-century loggers on which he was based, could not be confined within the borders of any single state, and with them he traveled east, west, and south at the end of the nineteenth century. Almost from his birth, he belonged to the whole American nation.

Like the ancient forest where he was born, Bunyan's fate was to be harvested, reshaped, packaged, and sold to customers. When lumbering was still young, Henry Thoreau reflected on the destiny of a majestic white pine towering above him in the Maine woods. Though its spirit might be "as immortal as I am," its fate was to be chopped down and then sent relentlessly through mills and factories until "it comes out boards, clapboards, laths, and shingles such as the wind can take, still perchance to be slit and slit again, till men get a size that will suit…sold, perchance, to the New England Friction-Match Company!"[17]

So, too, the tough, hard-drinking, hero who inspired loggers to risk their lives in the untamed wilderness was sliced, sifted, molded, and packaged, until he became merely the sentimental stuff of picture books and fairy tales. But we all still know him and his big ox—and he still sells.

Bunyan Tales Told in Wisconsin, 1885–1915

The following stories were told aloud by Wisconsin lumberjacks between 1885 and 1915, before advertisers and publishers turned Bunyan into a national icon. They are preserved in interview notes, unpublished letters, obscure magazines, rare pamphlets, and privately printed booklets virtually unobtainable today. Most of them are published here for the first time in many decades, some for the first time ever. After introductory quotations, the stories have been arranged under the following headings: Paul Bunyan as a Character; Bunyan's Logging Operations; Bunyan's Logging Camps; Bunyan's Ox and Other Animals; Bunyan's Crew; Cooking and Eating; Wild Animals around Bunyan's Camps; Bunyan's Travels. The final item is not a tale but rather the notes on Bunyan motifs kept by Homer Watt and Bernice Stewart as they recorded stories in the field from 1914 to 1917 (see chapter 7).

The source of each tale is noted in a list at the end; a companion list gives the tales taken from each source. Apart from occasional light editing of punctuation, they are given here as they appeared in the original documents. Text enclosed in parentheses appears that way in the originals; square brackets contain editorial insertions added for clarity.

Introduction

1. Wherever there is more or less permanent isolation from the outside world of large groups of people engaged in the same occupation or at least having a community of interests, there is almost certain to spring up in time tales peculiar to that community. It is not, accordingly, surprising that such legends exist among the

lumbermen of the Great North, among a community shut off from the world for months at a time and bound together by peculiar bonds. It is among these toilers of the forests that the legends of Paul Bunyan have originated. Paul Bunyan, the greatest lumberjack who ever skidded a log, who with the aid of his wonderful blue ox and his crew of hardy lumbermen cleared one hundred million feet of pine from a single forty and performed other feats related about the roaring fires of the lumber shanties...

All lumberjacks, of course, believe, or pretend to believe, that he really lived and was the great pioneer in the lumber country; some of the older men even claim to have known him or members of his crew, and in northern Minnesota the supposed location of his grave is actually pointed out. A half-breed lumberman whom Miss Stewart interviewed asserted positively that there was a Paul Bunyan and that the place where he cut his hundred million feet from a single forty is actually on the map.

2. Paul Bunyan stories are seldom heard in these modern days, when the average lumber camp is a Babel of tongues, but they cut a big figure in the life of the old time lumberjack, and many old woodsmen will remember the first time they listened with open eyed wonder to the tales of the famous old hero of lumberjack mythology.

3. In these degenerate days, there are young fellows who would not know a peavey from a grade stick, or a round turn from a cross haul, yet they will lay claim to having worked in Paul Bunyan's camps. No credence can be placed on what such irresponsibles have to say. It is only from the veterans that one can be assured of absolute truthfulness, and it's from these truthful veterans that the following incidents were secured.

Paul Bunyan as a Character

4. Bunyan was a powerful giant, seven feet tall and with a stride of seven feet. He was famous throughout the lumbering districts for

his physical strength and for the ingenuity with which he met difficult situations. He was so powerful that no man could successfully oppose him, and his ability to get drunk was proverbial. So great was his lung capacity that he called his men to dinner by blowing through a hollow tree a blast so strong that it blew down the timber on a tract of sixty acres, and when he spoke, the limbs sometimes fell from the trees. To keep his pipe filled required the entire time of a swamper with a scoop-shovel. In the gentle art of writing Bunyan had, however, no skill. He kept his men's time by cutting notches in a stick of wood, and he ordered supplies for camp by drawing pictures of what he wanted. On one occasion only did his ingenuity fail; he ordered grindstones and got cheeses. "Oh," says Paul, "I forgot to put the holes in my grind-stones."

5. Bunyan became marooned in his upper Minnesota camp by an unusually heavy snowfall. When his food supply ran low, he fashioned a pair of snow-shoes, and went foraging through the woods. Near camp he espied a herd of moose, shot several, and captured one alive. This moose he brought to camp and broke to drive, having fashioned a harness from bark. One of Paul's men, wishing to make a trip across an 80-mile lake in that unexplored country, it was necessary to build a sledge, and hitch up the moose. Paul let his companion sleep beneath the sledge blanket while he guided the moose on their journey. As the sledge struck wide fissures in the ice, water was splashed upon the blanket, which quickly froze. On reaching the further shore, which was a precipitous hill, the moose lurched the sledge from its traces, and escaped over the brow. Being occupied with his driving across the lake, Paul was amazed to find his companion, frozen beneath a coating of ice two and a half feet thick, when he turned around. After spending a day and a half chopping his companion loose, Paul carried him on his back over forty miles away for a doctor's care.

6. One fixed rule of Paul Bunyan's was that in case of accident or mishap, tools and equipment were to be saved first. Once on the

drive a Frenchman was thrown from a log into the rushing water. Two new recruits in the crew, not knowing their employer's rule, jumped in at great risk to themselves and pulled the Frenchman out, naturally expecting commendations for their act. Instead, Paul bellowed out, "Where's the peavey?" On being told it was at the bottom of the river, as an example and warning to his crew Paul pitched the Frenchman back into the river and yelled to the crest-fallen recruits, "Get that peavey!" With much difficulty this was done, after which the Frenchman was, for the second time, pulled from the water.

7. Paul Bunyan was a good hunter. He hunted only when camp supplies were running low. He invented a shotgun that would shoot geese so high up in the air that by the time they fell to the ground they were generally spoiled. Once while hunting he spied a deer sticking its head over a log two or three miles away. Paul took careful aim and fired and the deer dropped. A few minutes later the deer again peered over the log. Paul shot again and the occurence was again repeated. With only twenty-eight cartridges Paul fired every one. With the last shot the deer stayed down. Distressed at his poor gunnery, Paul went to get his deer. Judge of his great surprise when he found twenty-eight dead deer lying behind the log, each one shot squarely between the eyes. As a trailer of game he was unsurpassed. Once he came on a moose in the woods that had died of old age. Having some spare time, Paul in a short time traced this moose back to the place where it was born.

8. Paul Bunyan was a great hunter and at times kept his camp well supplied with venison and wild fowl with his big shotgun. He could shoot ducks and geese flying so high in the air that they were often spoiled before they reached the earth. So he salted his shot to preserve them.

9. The first time the boy, Paul Bunyan, went hunting, he took his father's shotgun. After he had traveled through the New Brunswick

forest for a long way he saw a deer. It was four or five miles away. He aimed and fired at it and being anxious to see if he had killed the animal he started running toward the spot. He ran so rapidly that he outran the load and got the full charge of buckshot in the seat to his pants.

10. Now to describe the real Old Man Bunyan. He was very tall, to be exact, six axe handles from the ground, free from limbs. I might add that it took five 100-pound sacks of smoking tobacco and three rolls of tar paper to make a cigarette for the old gentleman.

11. Big Paul probably smoked the first cigarettes that were ever smoked in Wisconsin. He was very fond of his big pipe that would hold about a bushel of tobacco but he somehow got the habit. He rolled his own cigarettes of course. He would take about 200 pounds of Adams Standard, of which the jacks were all very fond, and rolled this up in a roll of tar paper. He would smoke one of these before his early morning breakfast. After a while he had to give up smoking these 'coffin nails' because his camp clerk, Johnny Inkslinger, noticing Paul's keen enjoyment of his smoking, also got the cigarette habit. Being unable to abide the smell of burning tar paper, Johnny took a section of robber hose and crammed it full of pine shavings and kinnikinick. The rich odor of Johnny's burning cigarettes was too much for Paul, so he quit and ordered his clerk to do the same. The lives and reputations of both men were probably thus saved.

12. It seems that Paul had an unusually tough beard, which he allowed to grow to an unusual length; because of the unique operation necessary for its removal. He allowed his beard to grow till its length interfered with the play of his eating tools, getting them snarled up in his whiskers on their way to his mouth. When this stage of growth was reached, Paul would call in an expert pair of wood choppers, to whom he would hand a special pair of broad axes stored in a case underneath his bunk.

Now a special grinding and honing operation took place which required a whole day to complete, and while this was under way, the bull cook made a shaving cream after Paul's personal receipt [recipe], composed of equal parts of compound lard and grease scented with Pine Oil. The application of this shaving cream required a half day to rub into Paul's Beard, and when lathering job was complete, each whisker was supported by a layer one inch thick. The two choppers were now called in to start their work. As each whisker was cut through and felled, they would call out "Timber," and when the cutting was finished and Paul's face washed clean of shaving cream, it looked like a forty acre pine slashing after the snow melted in the spring. Now, any stories you may have heard about Paul's always having been clean-shaven are just lies. I saw a man in one of those logging camps, who always shaved himself with a double-bladed axe. He claimed to be a direct descendant of one of those two whisker choppers, and he personally vouched for the veracity of this story of Paul and his whiskers.

13. One evening Julius [Naville] told Paul Bunyan that he was going to town and that if he would wait on a certain hillside, he would bring him some good snuff. Paul hadn't had any real snuff for a long time and decided to wait for Julius's return. Paul's skin was so thick and tough that the snuff he used had to be as strong as lightning and bees together in action, to be enjoyed. Julius kept his word and returned with the snuff. Paul was so eager to have some tickling his hungry nostrils once again that he took a most generous helping. The first sneeze blew the buttons off of Paul's vest and the result was a backfire that blew all the timber down between Negaunee and Marquette, Michigan. The second sneeze tore all the buttons off his trousers and as result the Iron Mountains were uncovered in Ishpeming, Michigan, three miles away. Paul also lost his teeth in sneezing.

14. My Granddaddy (poor old fellow, he's been dead many years) loved to relate the following story of how Chebomnicon Bay [Chequamegon Bay] really came into being: It seems that Paul re-

turned to camp one night (now the present site of Ashland) and strung a hammock from there to another big tree in what is now the little town of Barksdale. Paul was tired after logging three counties that day and he gave himself one gigantic push as he hopped in but his carelessness in using only 80 instead of 100 one inch log chains proved disastrous for Paul. The 80 chains snapped like a thread and down came Paul with a terrific thud with his head on the present site of Bayfield. When he arose, in rushed Lake Superior to fill up the depression now known as Chebomnicon Bay. Now my granddaddy <u>knew</u> and told me that anything he said could be RELIED upon so it must be true. Oh yes, and Mr. Brown, Grandpop said that someone ought to put down the belittling rumor that Paul logged with an axe. "Con sarn 'em," said Grandpop. "Paul was a REAL MAN. He never knew what an axe was, and never hewed down a tree with one—HE REAPED A TRACT OF TIMBER WITH HIS GIANT SCYTHE."

15. Paul Bunyan went fishing one day and caught a muskie. Instead of killing the fish, he filled his pocket with water, put the fish in it and carried it home. There he put it in the rain-water barrel. Every day he took the muskie out of the barrel and placed it on the ground. In time the fish learned to walk and before many months had passed it grew to abhor water. The muskie became very fond of Paul and Paul became as fond of his pet.

One day Paul, out for a walk, came to Rib River. When he looked around, he saw that the muskie had followed him. Paul ordered his pet to return home but the fish would not go. Paul argued with him but to no avail. Paul moved on across the river and the fish followed, moving across a log. Half-way across the log the muskie fell into the water. Paul jumped in to save his pet but before he could reach him the muskie had drowned, so he buried him there under the pine trees on the river bank.

16. I wish you would describe to me how everything looks now if you was there lately. Is there any wild potatoes growing there yet? They were black and we called them nigger spuds, which started the big fight among the Irish. I am inclosing the story the American Lumberman poet helped me get into rhyme that will tell some of the history of that camp and also a picture I made of Paul in 1911 while he was down at Woodruff on a drunk. His wife had just come to town after him with some Indians. She consented to my sketch of him when she had made him presentable by parting his hair with a hand axe and combing it with a piece of old cross-cut saw.

17. The story of Bunyan's method of paying off his crew at the end of the season shows the hero's craftiness. Discovering in the spring that he had no money on hand, Bunyan suddenly rushed into camp shouting that they had been cutting government pine and were all to be arrested. Each man thereupon seized what camp property lay nearest his hand and made off, no two men taking the same direction. Thus Bunyan cleared his camp without paying his men a cent for their labor.

Bunyan's Logging Operations

18. Either through a streak of superstition or otherwise, Paul Bunyan always selected section 37 as the seat of his lumbering operations, and it was on this particular section that all his stupendous feats were performed. It is barely possible that government plats, having no higher numbered sections than 36, may have had something to do with his choice.

19. Paul Bunyan was a pioneer lumberjack, of French-Canadian birth, with a little Scotch in him. (Sometimes quite a lot, especially when his camp would break up in the spring.) This story goes on to tell of his doings along the Big Onion River, a branch of the Wolf River, during the year 1861. He bought one single "forty" for a song. (Historians versed in Logging Lore claim it was "Casey Jones.") He was on this job six years and during the first winter put in ninety-seven million one hundred thirteen thousand feet of

logs. At times the snow was from 12 to 15 feet deep. He bought the timber on the strength of estimates made by Dave Edick and Henry Higgins, two old-time timber cruisers, who were experts in running lines through the woods, sometimes running just a few rods ahead of a timber wolf or a bear. These lines, for that reason, run a little crooked; that is why Paul got such a big over-run. Eventually the original boundary lines became entirely obliterated so that Paul's original "forty" in time took in five Upper Wisconsin counties. When he built a sawmill, promoted Dave to straw-boss and Henry to bull cook. Julius Anderson was scaler and scaled all logs with a steel tape 100 feet long, ably assisted by Fred Kalkofen as tally boy. Julius was the fastest scaler in his time and scaled so fast that Fred had to use a split lead-pencil and mark two tallies down at once.

Charley Bacon was time-keeper, keeping track of the crew of 45,000 men. Paul taught Charley not to cross the T's nor dot the I's on the time book and thus saved in one winter seven barrels of ink.

His logging roads were as straight as a crow flies and with no hills or grades. As he cut through some of these hills his men found out all about the great fertility of Langlade County soil, so most of his crew bought land from the Langlade Lumber Company in later years, and, after getting married, became permanent and prosperous farmers of Langlade County. That nearly busted up Paul's big logging operations but with his Blue Ox, "Babe," took on a logging job from this company and it is reported that he is making so much money that he will make Henry Ford blush. He was in town last week and took back a few camp supplies, comprising a carload of hams, a car of navy beans, a car of crackers, and cleaned up all the prunes in local grocery stores. Enough to last him about a week.

20. Back in the 80's Paul Bunyan set up the first of his famous camps at the forks of the Little Onion and the Big Tobacco rivers. It was the biggest lumber camp ever built, and Paul ruled with an iron hand over the 3,000 men under him. He was eight feet tall and weighed 300 pounds. He had a voice like a bull roaring, and

every man in his employ jumped when he spoke. When he yelled the noise broke the branches off the trees. It seems that Paul was a powerful heavy smoker. He had a pipe with a bowl that held about a bushel of tobacco, and he kept one cookee busy shoveling tobacco into it. He always smoked Peerless, the test of the real lumberjack.

21. There are many conflicting statements regarding the exact location of the Little Onion River and the Big Tobacco. Many place them in Northern Minnesota, but some of the old time lumberjacks claim they were located in the Dakotas, and that Paul Bunyan logged so thoroughly that he turned both these states into windswept prairies.

22. It was the winter of the blue snow that Paul Bunyan lumbered on the Gobbler Sis where it empties from the smoke stack into the Red. The lightest man in the crew weighed two hundred and all he had to do was to strap the razors for the crew to shave with on Sunday.

Big Ola, the Swead, was the only man that could drive the blue studs [oxen] on account of their being so quick the other men were too light to hold them and make them draw steady. Big Ola sprained his wrist handling a pair of five hundred pounds skidding tongs, having always used a chain in the old country, so they had to put a new man after them.

Paul always cut the timber down and drew it to the banking ground a hull tree at a time, and their it was cut in the right length. The first tree the new man hooked on, they started so quick they jerked the heart out of it.

Paul saw that the new man would spoil all of the timber, so he told him to take them to the barn and when night came he could work them on the sprinkler. Paul picked the tree up and carried it to the cook camp and used it for a dinner horn. When he blew it, you could hear it in four counties.

The lightest team in camp that winter weight 6,411 lbs, and they just kept them in the cook camp to deck fridcakes with.

That night Paul set the new man sprinkling the dry road. They were putting in a small bunch of timber that was only thirty six miles from camp. They made four trips a day. Paul thought that if they had ice roads they could make six trips. They always used the small sprinkler on the dry road and filled it at both ends of the trip. But on the return trip they walked so fast that about half of the water run out and during the night the sprinkler sprang a leak and started the Mississippi River. If you dont believe me, go west. The Mississippi River is there to prove it.

Round River camp and pyramid forty, by Eugene Shepard

FROM *PAUL BUNYAN, HIS CAMP AND WIFE,* 1929

23. Most of the exploits of Paul Bunyan center at Round River. Here Bunyan and his crew labored all one winter to clear the pine from a single forty. This was a most peculiar forty in that it was shaped like a pyramid with a heavy timber growth on all sides. The attention of skeptics who refuse to believe in the existence of the pyramid forty is certain to be called by the story-teller to a lumberman with a short leg, a member, the listener is solemnly assured, of Bunyan's crew, who got his short leg from working all winter on one side of the pyramid, and who thus earned the nickname of "Rockin' Horse." From this single forty Bunyan's crew cleared one hundred million feet of pine, and in the spring they started it down the river. Then began the difficulty, for it was not until they had passed their old camp several times that they realized that the river was round and had no outlet whatever.

24. Some time ago an old half-breed Indian told me the story of the Round river. As a young man he used to work in the logging camps and on the river drives. With true Bunyanesque spirit he said the story was true because he had been there and saw the men on the drive. Paul Bunyan was a strict disciplinarian and the men who worked for him soon learned to do just what he said implicitly and without question. One winter Paul Bunyan located a stand of huge white pines near the Round River and had only the largest cut. In the spring with the breakup he had the logs put in the Round River and selecting a crew of all young and active men he told them to keep driving the logs until they came to a saw-mill. Paul Bunyan then went about his other activities and forgot all about the log drive on the Round River. He did not return until over 40 years later. When he came to the river he saw a crew of old and stooped men with long, white whiskers who were driving a lot of what looked like fish poles on the Round River. They were the men and the logs he had started off more than 40 years before. The men did not know that the Round River ran in a complete circle and, true to Paul Bunyan's orders, they had kept driving every year hoping eventually to reach the saw-mill. Friction against each other and the rocks had worn the big logs down to the dimension of fish poles but still the men were driving on.

25. When Paul Bunyan had logged off the Onion River country, he had the Big Swede, his foreman, make a journey in search of new woods to conquer. They happened in the Leaning Pine country, where the trees stood in lines along the slope of a mountain. Each and every pine leaned in a northerly direction and the mountain range ran east and west. These were ideal conditions for Paul and his crew. He and the Big Swede returned in high good humor and announced that the camps would be moved forthwith.

The Blue Ox was harnessed, the sleep camps, cookeries and sheds were hooked together, the Ox hitched on and away they went over hill and valley until they reached the Leaning Pine country. The Big Swede explained to the crew the method of operation. They were to start on the north and cut the trees which were self-skidding, falling down row on row and rolling into the Hot Water River which skirted the mountain. Now both Paul and the Big Swede had figured out the logging scheme to a nicety, but they did not investigate the Hot Water River very closely and as a result there was a serious hitch in the season's work. When the time came for the drive the logs were started off with Paul riding on the raft directing operations. For nine days they went down the stream and suddenly Paul noticed that the front end of the drive had caught up to the rear. He sent the Big Swede to investigate and they found out that the river ran in a circle. This was a catastrophe, the worst since the winter of the Blue Snow, but Paul was not stumped.

He decided to saw the logs right there, and to do this he set up the nine-story saw mill. He sent Johnny Inkslinger, his bookkeeper, out to the outside with orders for machinery and saws. The Blue Ox hauled them in. The bandsaws and circulars ran through the whole nine stories and logs were sawed on every story. The sawdust was blown into the circular river and in time filled it solid. Paul, to amuse his men, brought in race horses, which followed the perfect circular track getting back to the starting point every Sunday. The only trouble he had all summer was with the hinges on the smokestack, which had to be lowered to let the clouds go by.

26. One winter it was about New Years when some of us visitors arrived at camp. Weather conditions had been favorable. The ice roads were well built up, and some very creditable sized loads of logs were being hauled. One of the visitors made a remark to this effect, when a woodman spoke up: "But they are no such loads as old Jake used to haul. We had to shoot his dinner up to him with a shotgun."

27. When I was at Round River in 1884 I found an old cant hook band attached to it on which was stamped 'Pat, June 8, 1862.' I didn't know Pat by name but I think he worked there all right and we called him "Rocking Horse." He had one short leg from working on the side hill. Several more of them were in the same fix—some of them live here now.

28. The site of one of Paul's camps is still plainly located, being marked in a most peculiar manner. In this case it was necessary to build the camp on a high, rounding hill, far from water. A well thirty feet in diameter and 200 feet deep was dug. For curbing, timber piles were driven in around the well. The timber in that vicinity was soon cut and the camp dismantled. As the timber piling of the well was still sound and good, it was pulled out and sawed up into logs. Within a few years, the wind had blown the sand from around the old well, leaving the bare hole sticking up many feet in the air, and which may still be seen from miles around.

29. Whirling Lake. This fabled lake, a round lake located near Paul's Sawdust River camp, was always whirling round and round. As it gained in momentum, the friction caused by its water rubbing against the shore and rocks filled the whole country with steam, smoke, and fog. This, when there was no wind to carry it away, became so dense that Paul's loggers could do no work. In attempting to reach camp, many lost their way. Some ran into trees or fell into streams, some were never seen or heard of again. Sometimes the lake changed direction in its whirling. Then the fog became just terrible. Lumberjacks and oxen who accidentally stepped into its waters were just whirled away. This lake became a terror to the camp. Many lumberjacks asked for their time and left. Paul feared that it might set other nearby lakes to whirling. The lake whirled only in the daytime, at night it was quiet. Paul sent Ole Olson to stop it, if possible. The big blacksmith went to it one evening with a crew of men and team loads of long poles. With his big sledge he drove piles across its diameter in several directions. Thus the lake was unable to start whirling. It troubled Paul no more.

30. During the winter of the blue snow, much of Paul Bunyan's work went for naught. It seems that Paul had a mortal enemy, Old Drumbeater, and after his winter's drive had been completed, Paul found that the logs he had cut were taken from Old Drumbeater's land, and his arch enemy threatened to take possession of them. This was too much for the Lumberjack King, and he assembled his river hogs once more. Collecting the logs from the pond, he drove them back upstream, and rolled them back on Old Drumbeater's land, determined that his enemy should not profit from the mistake.

Bunyan's Logging Camps

31. I have a letter from our mutual friend up the creek that states that you have rediscovered the remains of Paul Bunyun's camp and Round River that was built and used by old Paul away back in 1862, the winter of the black snow, and as I have not visited the spot for many years I am very curious to know how things look around there as I worked for Paul that winter. I was a young boy at that time and he put me wheeling prune stones away from the cook camp. I had worked about three months when he ordered me to wheel them all back. Did you see any of them anywhere? And I found when they were dry they were used by Mrs. Bunyun to make hot fires to cook her famous soft nosed pancakes. She was even more resourceful than old Paul himself.

32. At Paul Bunyan's Big Onion River Camp, in section 37 there was a forty-acre tract of land shaped like a pyramid. It had a heavy growth of pine timber on all of its four sides. It was so very high that to see its peak took a week of steady looking. It required twenty men each looking as far as he could see to do this. Several men became blind in just trying to see half-way up. Paul and his logging crew of two thousand men worked a whole winter in clearing this forty. From it he cut one hundred million feet of timber. Some of the men got one short leg from working on the steep slope. They sharpened their axe blades by holding them on boulders which they rolled downhill. The slope was so steep that the upland grouse laid square eggs to keep them from rolling out of their nests. When Paul's axemen reached the top of the pyramid in their cutting, the stumps at the bottom had sprouted and already shot up young trees seventy feet in height. Paul did not bother with these trees as they were second-growth timber and of no value to him.

33. The year of the Two Winters, when he was cutting timber in the Fool River region in northern Wisconsin, Paul Bunyan had a logging crew of a thousand men and he needed a big bunkhouse for them. That summer he hired two loggers to build it. They were small men. These men hired other undersize woodcutters and all worked night and day to construct it. When Paul's crew came to occupy it, the men had to crawl into it on their hands and knees it was so low. Paul was mortified. He tore it down and had some of his big Yankees, Canucks, and Swedes reconstruct the building. These men built it so high that telephones were needed to wake the men sleeping in the top bunks. At that some of them slept overtime. This big bunkhouse occupied twenty acres of land. It had eight entrances and sixteen exits. High as it was, Paul could kick his initials into the ceiling with calked boots. The floors of the bunks sloped so that the men could roll out easily and quickly in the morning. Whenever Paul changed the location of his camp, he put skids under the building, hitched Babe his big blue ox to it, and moved it to its new location in a jiffy.

34. One of Paul's big new bunkhouses needed a roof so he provided an immense quantity of shakes and set a big crew of lumberjacks at work, nailing them on to the structure. While they were at work a dense fog came up but the men kept right on until they finished the big job. Next day Paul went to inspect the work. He looked up and saw that, despite the hard labor of his men the day before, the bunkhouse was still without a covering. The lumberjack carpenters had nailed the shakes to the layer of fog instead of to the framework of the roof. So there was nothing else to do but to rope the fog and to spike that down to the framework. It was no easy job but with the help of the big oxen, Babe and Benny, it was finally accomplished.

35. It was the winter of the "blue snow" when Paul was first heard of. In that winter, the tale goes, there was a forty-foot fall of blue snow in Northern Minnesota. That winter they had to cut the trees from forty feet above the ground, and in the spring there was a forest of stumps forty feet high. But the pine was so big at that time that it didn't make much difference in the size of the logs.

36. As it has been so long ago since we logged on the Little Onion, I can't remember what the color of the snow was. I do remember, however, that it was so cold that winter on the Little Onion that your 400 below weather would have looked like the climate of the tropics beside it. It was so cold that words froze right in the air. All winter long the weather remained that way. If one said "Hello" he could see it hanging in the air. If a teamster swore at his team, the sound of his voice would freeze also. That spring when the thaw came you could see all of those oaths thaw out the same day. Never in all history since the beginning of man was a more terrible profane barrage thrown over than there was that spring on the Little Onion.

37. It was so cold during one winter at one of Paul's logging camps that even the fire in the big camp range froze. When a lumberjack wanted to write a letter to his home, he just stepped outdoors and shouted the words he wished to write. These froze solid. He wrapped them up in a gunnysack and sent them home. When the sack arrived, all his folks had to do was to thaw them out in or on the kitchen stove, and they had the letter just as it was spoken.

38. At Paul Bunyan's Big Onion camp on the Little Gimlet where it joins the Big Auger River, according to Paul Fournier, the snow became so deep that year [1877] that the crews had to dig down to find the tops of the tallest pines and the choppers were lowered down to the base of the trees by means of ropes. The logs were hauled to the surface with long parbuckle chains to which Babe, Paul Bunyan's Big Blue Ox, mounted on snowshoes, was attached.

The stovepipes on the shanties were lengthened so as to reach the surface by boring out logs with a long six-inch auger and linking them together. Fournier stated that on one particularly snappy day Big Joe set the boiling coffee pot on the stove and it froze up so quickly that the ice was hot. Before spring had arrived the Great lakes were frozen to the bottom and it is said would never have thawed out if Paul Bunyan had not chopped the ice out and hauled it on shore for the sun to melt.

One of the crew was kept busy picking up ears and noses that froze and dropped off the loggers and for a time threatened to tie up traffic on the tote roads. The only way the men could keep from freezing to death at night was by hanging their feet out of the bunks into buckets of oil and then setting their clothes on fire, the heavy woolen garments acting as wicks…

Hundreds of men died in the woods that year from over-exertion, it is said, as a result of carrying around the great number of overcoats they found it necessary to wear.

The following winter was the year of the blue snow, according to Fournier, and while the temperature sank to 40 and 50 below the men had become accustomed to the cold and worked throughout the winter in their shirt sleeves and straw hats…

39. One winter it was 63 degrees below zero in Paul's lumber camp and every degree 63 inches long. It was so darn cold that the flame in Paul's big lantern froze and the only way he could put it out was to break off the flame and throw it out of the bunkhouse window.

In the spring this flame thawed out and burned Paul's logging river in two. This was a calamity but Paul gave the matter careful thought. He had to mend the break so he could get his logs out. So he took his match box out of his pocket and used it to make a connection between the ends of the river. Now it is called the Soo Locks.

40. The Winter of the Big Thaw there was no snow on the ground and Paul Bunyan was hindered in hauling logs from the woods to the river landings. Fortunately for him, the Pacific Ocean was frozen over, and Brimstone Bill and Babe and Benny were kept busy hauling snow from Siberia. At this time Bill made the first ox-yokes from cranberry wood. These were very elastic and once they got started, pulled the oxen along whether they wanted to move or not. Bill never profited by his invention because other loggers stole it before he could get it patented. Bill got a lot of new and novel cusswords from the Siberians. With them he blistered all the trees for miles around Paul's camp.

Bunyan's Ox and Other Animals

41. Bunyan was assisted in his lumbering exploits by a wonderful blue ox, a creature that had the strength of nine horses and that weighed, according to some accounts, five thousand pounds, and according to others, twice that. The ox measured from tip to tip of his horns just seven feet, exactly his master's height. Other accounts declare that the ox was seven feet—or seven ax-handles—between

Bunyan and his blue ox, by William Laughead

FROM *THE MARVELOUS EXPLOITS OF PAUL BUNYAN,* 1922

his eyes, and fourteen feet between his horns. Originally he was pure white, but one winter in the woods it snowed blue snow for seven days (that was the winter of the snow-snakes) and Bunyan's ox from lying out in the snow all winter became and remained a brilliant blue. Many of the Bunyan legends are connected with the feats performed by the ox. Bunyan's method of peeling a log was as follows: He would hitch the ox to one end of the log, grasp the bark at the other end with his powerful arms, give a sharp command to the animal, and, presto, out would come the log as clean as a whistle. On one occasion Paul dragged a whole house up a hill with the help of his ox, and then, returning, he dragged the cellar up after the house. Occasionally, as might have been expected from so huge a creature, the ox got into mischief about camp. One night, for example, he broke loose and ate up two hundred feet of tow-line.

42. The blue ox measured just fourty two axe handles and a plug of tobacco between the eyes. When he ate baled hay it took three men to pull the baling wire from between his teeth. Paul had eighteen miles of crooked loging road, it was so crooked that the new teamster could not make the short turns on account of the teams not being able to hold the loads back, as the road was downhill all the way to the landing and half the way back. Paul hooked Babe, the blue ox, on one end of it and jerked it straight; and we know that Paul lumbered off the Dakotas for if you dont belive me go to the Dakotas you wont find any pine.

43. One tale of the blue ox had best be told in the words of the lumberjack who sent it to a friend of Miss Stewart's, in a letter written with very evident care and with every other word capitalized. "Paul B Driving a large Bunch of logs Down the Wisconsin River When the logs Suddenly Jamed. in the Dells. The logs were piled Two Hundred feet high at the head, And were backed up for One mile up river. Paul was at the rear of the Jam with the Blue Oxen And while he was coming to the front the Crew was trying to break the Jam but they couldent Budge it. When Paul Arrived at the Head with the ox he told them to Stand Back. He put the Ox in the old Wisc. in front of the Jam. And then Standing on the Bank Shot the Ox with a 303 Savage Rifle. The Ox thought it was flies And began to Switch his Tail. The tail commenced to go around in a circle And up Stream And do you know That Ox Switching his tail forced that Stream to flow Backwards And Eventually the Jam floated back Also. He took the ox out of the Stream. And let the Stream And logs go on their way."

44. One favorite tale connected with the blue ox is that of the buckskin harness. One day old Forty Jones of Bunyan's crew killed two hundred deer by the simple process of tripping a key-log which supported a pile of logs on a hillside above the place where the animals came to drink. The skins were made into a harness for the blue ox. Some days later while the cook was hauling a log in for fire-wood, it began to rain, the buckskin began to stretch, and by the time the ox reached camp the log was out of sight around a bend in the road with the tugs stretching back endlessly after it. The cook tied the ox and went to dinner. While he was eating, the sun came out boiling hot, dried the buckskin harness, and hauled the log into camp.

45. After Paul had logged off the Dakotas and had his logs all banked on the Mississippi, and had driven the stumps all down and made a prairie of the state, he sent Ola the big Swede, with the crew to break the roll-ways and drive them to New Orleans, but it being a foggy morning they went by Paul's logs and put in the logs of Brimstone Bill. Paul did not find out their mistake until they had driven them clear to New Orleans. He did not want to hurt the feelings of Brimstone Bill, he being the best jobber Paul had, so he fed the Blue ox eleven barrels of salt and led him down to the river to drink it, being only knee deep to him; he had to wade to the middle to drink. Babe's drinking caused the water to run up stream and it floated the logs back seven miles and twenty rods above where the rollways were.

46. A man in Bismarck, North Dakota, once wrote to Paul Bunyan that he had a good strong ox calf for sale. So Paul walked up there one evening after supper and bought him. He brought him back to his Big Onion River camp. He built a log barn for him, but Benny grew so fast that he outgrew the barn in a single night and walked off with the frame.

47. Pork was a very important article of food at Paul Bunyan's camps. In order to always have on hand an abundant supply of pork, Paul kept a large drove of hogs. These were in Brimstone Bill's keeping. This job was wished on Bill and he couldn't object. He kept the pigs in log pens, but they were always burrowing out and getting away into the woods. Bill and his helpers undertook the job of building a hog-proof fence around the pens. Before starting this work, Bill's men somehow managed to get hold of a keg of Hudnut's Budge. As a result of their inebriated condition, they built the crookedest and craziest fence that human beings ever erected. Paul Bunyan was very much disappointed in this barrier when he saw it. Just the same, the fence proved to be very effective. The hogs would burrow under it, then because of its crooked and bewildering nature, they would burrow right back again. So it held the pigs after all. They never knew, were they in or out of the enclosure?

48. Paul had a smart little dog called Elmer whom he used in his hunting. One night Paul thought that he heard a rat in a corner of the bunkhouse. Reaching beneath his bunk for his double-bit axe, he threw it in the direction of the noise. He heard a yelp. Going to the corner he found that he had cut Elmer in two. He was very fond of the dog. He put the two parts together and wrapped a gunnysack about his middle. This was done in the dark. He got the hind end of the dog placed the wrong way. The rear legs were up instead of down. Elmer got well and became the smartest hunting dog in the north woods. He could outrun any deer. He would run on one pair of legs until they were tired. Then he would turn over and use the other pair.

49. A good friend presented Paul Bunyan with a goat. This was a kind of animal Paul had no experience with. Paul kept him tied near the bunkhouse. After this rambunktious animal had butted the daylights out of everybody and everything within reach, he was turned over to the tender mercies of Brimstone Bill. Bill at first tried to control Billy with kindness, but it was just no go. After he had butted Bill right over the roof of the stable, and nearly caused his death on several other occasions, Bill learned that it was always best to have an axe or a peavy handle handy when near Billy. One day Bill tied Billy out to feed in a clearing. There was a big rock. The goat thought that it was an enemy and ran to butt it. The rock never moved. This angered Billy and he went back to butt it again. Bill watched the goat butting the stone for some time, then

he went to dinner at the cook shanty. When he returned to the battleground an hour later, the fight was still going on. Billy was gone, all but his tail, and that part of him was still running at the big rock and butting it.

50. Paul Bunyan's cow Lucy kept his camp supplied with milk. Brimstone Bill was in charge of her. She was a curious critter, part jersey and part wolf. She was always hungry. Bill soon quit trying to feed her and mostly let her forage for a living. The winter of the deep snow, when the tallest pine trees were buried to their very tops, Bill outfitted her with snowshoes, put green goggles over her eyes, and tied a big bell around her neck. He turned her out to graze among the snowdrifts. Being fooled by the goggles, she did very well.

Bunyan's Crew

51. Paul Bunyan had a great crew up in the Wisconsin pinery the year of the two winters. His men were a well-selected lot, coming from Maine, New Brunswick, Vermont, Pennsylvania, Ontario, Michigan and Wisconsin. Chris Crosshaul, the camp foreman, had such a sharp sight that he could see to the tops of the tallest pine trees in three looks.

52. This chapter of Paul's biography refers to his earlier days in Upper Wisconsin—the good old days when any man could cut and skid and log and haul as much as he wanted to, as there was pine enough for all. Then all a logger had to do was to stake out a homestead beside a stream, and timber enough to keep his crew busy during the winter.

Paul selected the famous 'round' forty, in section thirty-seven. Paul was without question the greatest logger in the land—the king-pin of them all. With a punch in either hand, he licked more men and got drunk in more new styles than any other knight of the peavie in those days.

Paul bossed that famous crew, a bunch of shouting bruisers—"Hank" Higgins, "Black" McDonald, "Tom" McCann, "Dutch"

Jake, "Red" Murphy, "Dirty" Dan, and other Dans and Nicks and Jakes from black to red, with Curley Charley Yellow- head.

It sure was just the gang that he could depend upon to break up a possible log-jam in the spring. They were generous to a fault, give a "twenty" to a bum, or clean out a bar-room and lick up all the rum.

They paid no attention to boundary lines, so east, and south and north and west they cut a swath of pines, but left the Hemlock, Spruce, Balsam and Hardwood, especially along the shores of North Wisconsin's 7,000 lakes. Paul could see far enough ahead even in those days that his old Pine slashings would some day become the playground of the people of the great middle west.

53. Some of the tales of the camp exploits concern members of Paul Bunyan's crew rather than the hero himself. One of the men, for example, had two sets of teeth, and, walking in his sleep one night, he encountered the grind-stone and chewed it to bits before he was fully aroused to what he was doing. In the adventure of another member of the crew we have the familiar tale of the man who jumped across the river in three jumps. The crew sometimes showed ingenuity on their own account as when they rolled boulders down the steep sides of the pyramid forty, and running after them ground their axes to a razor edge against the revolving stones.

Loggers sharpening their axes on the pyramid forty, by Eugene Shepard

54. Shot Gunderson was the best log-spinner in the camp. Taking a 75-foot log, he could spin it so fast with his feet that the log slid out of the bark and he walked ashore on the bubbles. Jim Liverpool was a great jumper. Planting his feet on the bank of the widest river he could jump across it in three jumps. Big Ole the Swede was the camp blacksmith. He was a very powerful man. When he struck his anvil, the ring of the metal could be heard in the next county. He alone could shoe Babe the Blue Ox. Once he carried two of Babe's shoes from his shop to the barn and sank knee deep in the solid rock at every step. Every time Babe was shod, a new iron mine had to be opened up. In his spare time Big Ole punched the holes in the camp doughnuts. Brimstone Bill was Babe's keeper. He invented swearing. His supply of cusswords was unlimited. When anything went wrong and Bill really tore loose, he could only be quieted with a tub of water.

55. Paul's cooks were far above the average in intelligence and resourcefulness, and on several occasions helped their foreman or some member of the crew out of a bad situation. One of these cooks had been given the nickname "Sourdough Sam" on account of his serving sourdough for almost every conceivable purpose. He had lost one leg by the blowing up of his sourdough barrel, but with the aid of a crutch he was still as good as the best of them. One winter a foreman had worked all winter and banked his logs in a good sized lake, taking it for granted, but without looking it up, that the lake had an outlet. It was not until the drive was started in the spring, and the foreman had drawn the logs three times around the lake, that the foreman found it was landlocked, with no outlet whatsoever. When Sourdough Sam learned of his foreman's predicament, he said, "I can fix that. Just leave it to me." Filling one of the huge water tanks with sourdough and hitching Babe the big ox to the tank, he soon dumped its contents into the lake. A mighty frothing and foaming took place, and like lava in a volcano eruption, the mixture of water and sourdough carried those logs all over a ridge several miles to a good driving stream, where they were soon on their way to the sawmills below.

56. On another occasion, one of Paul's crews was driving logs on the Niagara River when the driver, Pete Murphy, just for fun, de-

cided to run over the falls on a saw log. Of course, such a skillful driver as he had no difficulty in sticking to his log. But unfortunately he got into the whirlpool below the falls and for three weeks he circled around in the raging flood with nothing to eat except doughnuts, which were thrown to him from shore, and which he caught on the point of his peavey.

57. Brimstone Bill figures prominently in tales of Paul Bunyan's Big Onion, Little Garlic, and Gimlet River camps in Wisconsin. Bill was a tough, burly man with a florid complexion and a full white beard. His usual costume was a slouch hat, red shirt, blue jumpers, and boots. His homeland was in the Wild River country in Western Pennsylvania. There he had once been a school teacher in a backwoods school. He had both seafaring and lumberjack ancestors. From these he probably inherited his great ability to use cusswords. He is credited with having invented most of those in use today. Learning of his outstanding accomplishments in this field, Paul Bunyan hired Bill to become the boss bullwhacker in his camps...

Bill sometimes used up his entire supply of ten thousand cusswords in trying to control Benny [the young ox], and at the end of the day was speechless. The air around camp was blue for several days afterwards. On one occasion he nearly burned down the barn...

At the age of eighty years, Brimstone Bill still held the national record for profanity. No one has surpassed him since. He could still burn the bark off a big spruce tree with his flow of lurid language. During his last years in Paul's service, Brimstone compiled books of cusswords for the use of cabmen, mill hands, rivermen, railroadmen, soldiers, sailors, and other men engaged in soul-trying occupations. Paul Bunyan wept for several weeks when his faithful friend passed on. He excavated Kilauea, the largest mountain in the Hawaiian Islands, and there buried Brimstone Bill. There his body cremated itself. The mountain became a volcano, the largest and most spectacular of all craters.

58. Johnny Inkslinger, the camp clerk, was a very efficient man. He kept the time of the camp crew, paid the men, purchased supplies, sold clothing and tobacco, and performed many other duties that fall to the lot of a camp clerk. The first month that he was in Bunyan's employ he hit on the plan of leaving off the dots from the i's and the crosses from the t's. Thus he saved to Paul nineteen barrels of ink on the payroll. In his spare time, Johnny surveyed the whole United States. It was he who invented the fountain pen by attaching a hose to a barrel of ink.

59. He was accused of using a split pencil when charging the loggers for socks, tobacco and mackinaws. In this manner he charged each man double and made money for the camp. Investigation proved this accusation untrue. Johnny was as honest as the day is long. He had a big watch that he bought from a peddler. This he fixed so that it gained so much time that it paid for itself in a single week.

60. Ole the blacksmith had little or no religion. He said that he didn't need any in his line of work. To him went Shanty Boy, once the most famous entertainer in Paul Bunyan's camps and now become camp evangelist. Among his numerous other conquests, he was determined to convert Ole and set him on the right path. Ole did not attend camp revivals, so Shanty Boy took to visiting him at his forge. There the two engaged in some hot arguments. When they got to going good, sparks and flames issued from all of the shop doors and windows. The more determined the gospel shark was to make a real Christian of Ole, the more Ole decided to remain a rank heathen. One day when Shanty Boy came to the smithy to engage in a religious argument, they had a regular fight. Both were mighty men. At the end of their tussle, Ole seized the vanquished Shanty Boy and stuffed him up the forge chimney. When he emerged on the roof he was covered from head to foot with black soot. He looked more like the devil than a bush preacher. Thus ended the attempts at Ole's conversion.

Cooking and Eating

61. Having lived and worked up in this neck of the woods with Paul Bunyan during the past forty years or more, ate with him, slept with him, jailed with him, I feel better qualified to write his life history than some of these other camouflaged lumberjacks like Fred H. Shaw, Henry Higgins, Jim Werden, W. J. Knott, Lawrence Peterson, Jack Le Page, Bob Pike, and many others of the young, inexperienced class, who claim the acquaintance of Paul.

I remember his blue ox very well. In fact, I was present when he died on the "Little Gimlet," and was made into ox-tail soup by Sour Dough Sam. Of course, that is going back quite a ways. Lots of interesting things happened since then. I can recall the bigness of Paul's camp at the confluence of the "Big Auger" and the "Big Onion." There were over 300 cooks, and hundreds of flunkies, who had hams tied to their feet when they skated over the griddle on pancake days. The camp was so big that one cook got lost between the flour-bin and root-cellar and nearly starved to death before he was found.

The flunkies wore roller skates while waiting on the table. Part of the crew dinnered out, and the size of the works made the timing of meals rather difficult, so three crews were required—one going to work, one on the job, and one coming back. Big Joe, the head cook, had to start the bull cook out with the lunch sled two weeks ahead of dinner time. To call the men in for supper was another problem, so Paul had Big Ole, the blacksmith, make a dinner horn so big that no one could blow it but Big Joe or Paul himself. The first time Joe blew it he blew down ten acres of timber. The company wouldn't stand for that, so the next time he blew straight up, which caused that famous cyclone in Antigo, when so many houses were blown down in the Second ward, the H. B. Kellogg residence being the only house escaping the fury of this storm within a radius of four blocks. Later on the horn was junked and the tin used to cover the roof of the Antigo Armory and J. C. Lewis's hardware store.

"Ole," the blacksmith, had a most cranky disposition, but he was a skilled workman. One of the cooks made the doughnuts and Ole punched the holes, some of these same doughnuts being used in emergency cases for spare links on the loading chain. Every time he made a new set of shoes for the blue ox a new iron mine had to be opened up over in Minnesota. Ole was also an inventor and mechanic, and built the "down-cutter," a rig like a mowing machine, that cut down a swath of trees 500 feet wide. He also boosted Henry Ford's fortune by showing him how to get along with four less nuts on his "flivver."

The cooks used a lot of water, so Paul dug a well so deep that it took all day for the bucket to fall to the water, and a week to haul it up. They had to run so many buckets that the well was forty feet in diameter. It was cribbed with tamarack, and when the big storm of 1903 blew the sand away, the well was left sticking up 178 feet in the air.

Paul's shotgun was so big it required four dishpanfuls of powder and a keg of railroad spikes to load each barrel, and with this gun he could shoot geese so high in the air they would spoil before reaching the ground.

62. Bunyan's crew was so large that he was obliged to divide the men into three gangs; of these one was always going to work, one was always at work, and the third was always coming home from work. The cooking arrangements for so many men were naturally on an immense scale. Seven men with seven wheel-barrows were kept busy wheeling the prune-stones away from camp. The cook-stove was so extensive that three forties had to be cleared bare each week to keep up a fire, and an entire cord of wood was needed to start a blaze. One day as soon as the cook had put a loaf of bread into the oven he started to walk around the stove in order to re-move the loaf from the other side, but long before he reached his destination the bread had burned to a crisp. Such loaves were, of course, gigantic, so big, in fact, that after the crew had eaten the insides out of them, the hollow crusts were used for bunk-houses, or, according to a less imaginative account, for bunks. One legend reports that the loaves were not baked in a stove at all but in a

ravine or dried river-bed with heat provided by blazing slashings along the sides.

63. The daily discard of prune stones from Paul's Little Garlic River camp in Wisconsin was so large that Paul used them in building a bridge across the western end of Lake Superior to a camp he had in Canada. Johnny Inkslinger, the camp clerk, who was a sort of "shirttail" engineer, superintended the construction in his spare time. It took a year's supply of prune stones to accomplish this. The bridge shortened Paul's trail by 500 miles.

64. I hauled black pepper there that winter. It kept 14 four-horse teams, making four trips per day to supply the camp with pepper. I mentioned this just so the size of our ration transportation job can be imagined.

65. I am making a small sketch from an old one I made in 1862. You will find it on the face of the envelope containing this letter. It will show Mrs. Bunyun calling the men to dinner by blowing through a woodpecker's hole in a hollow stub that stood near the camp. There was a nest of owls in it then that had one short wing that flew in circles. I presume the stub was burned during the fierce forest fires of 1871.

66. I remember one day the cook was late in blowing the dinner horn. Old Paul comes dashing madly into the cook-shack, jerks the horn from its resting place, sticks the small end of it out of the window, and peals forth one long blast. Just outside of the camp stood as fine an 80 acres of white pine as ever grew. The concussion of the blast was so strong that it uprooted every single tree on the 80 and laid it flat. I am satisfied that if Paul hadn't blown into the wrong end of the horn, the whole winter cut would have been blown to the saw mills 300 miles distant.

67. All members of Paul's logging crew were very hearty eaters. Eating was a real business to them. When the men came in from their day's work in the woods, they would rush into the cook shanty in a mad scramble and seat themselves at the tables like a lot of wild men. Their bad table manners didn't please Paul Bunyan. To bring about a better order of things, he had a big dinner horn made. It was a hundred and thirty feet in diameter at the noisy end. The first time that Joe Muffraw the cook blew this horn, he held it out straight and knocked down several sections of timber. Some of the men were blown so far away that they did not get back to camp until breakfast time. Some men never returned to camp. They were later located in Nova Scotia. Paul didn't like to have his timber ruined. It was money out of his pocket. He told Joe to blow the horn up in the air the next time. Joe followed his orders the next day, and the men came running in from the woods. All seemed to work out well but the next day Paul got complaints from the U.S. Weather Bureau and from shipping companies. Blowing the big dinner horn had caused cyclones, a hurricane, and other storms. Paul then decided to junk the horn and finally sold it to an eastern railroad whose officers made it into a roof for a Union Depot.

68. At his early Big Onion River camp, Paul used a small frozen lake as a griddle. A big hole was dug under the bed of this shallow lake, filled with dry wood and this set afire. When the fire was going good, the cook and his assistants spread pancake batter on the ice. Other helpers followed with shovels, flipped the cakes, and when they were done tossed them into baskets.

69. Such a stove as Bunyan's demanded, of course, a pancake griddle of monstrous size. As a matter of fact, Bunyan's cook, Joe Mufferon, used the entire top of the stove for a griddle and greased it every morning by strapping hams to the feet of his assistant cooks and obliging them to skate about on it for an hour or so. Of this famous tale there are several versions. According to one the cook mixed his batter in a sort of concrete-mixer on the roof of the cook-shanty and spread it upon the stove by means of a connecting hose. A ver-

Bunyan's cook at work, by William Laughead FROM *THE MARVELOUS EXPLOITS OF PAUL BUNYAN*, 1922

sion from Oregon shows the influence of local conditions upon the Bunyan tales; from this version we learn that two hundred Japanese cooks with bacon-rinds or bear-steak strapped to their feet skated upon the stove before the cook spread his batter. In a Minnesota version Bunyan employs his twenty-four daughters for the same menial task. By mistake one day the nearsighted cook put into the batter several fingers of blasting-powder instead of baking-powder, and when the mixture was spread upon the griddle, the cookees made a very rapid ascent through the cook-shanty roof and never returned to camp.

70. The cooking arrangements in Paul Bunyan's famous camp were unique. Cooking for 3,000 men was no easy task. They had a cook stove so long that a man could not throw a stone from one end to the other. The cook had two little nigger boys, and he would strap slices of fat pork to their feet. They would skate up and down the stove, and the cook would follow on roller skates, pouring out the pancake batter as he went. After him came the cookee, flapping the

pancakes, and the second cookee followed throwing the cakes off into baskets carried by helpers.

71. The pancake batter was mixed with a concrete mixer and squirted on the range with a squirt gun. The cook flipped the pancakes through a hole in the roof when they were brown on one side. A man on the roof caught them and dropped them back on the range. Later an improvement in this method was made. A kernel of popcorn was placed beneath each cake. A cookee caught the pancakes in a basket when the corn popped. Later the cook added cockleburs to the batter. That made the pancakes stick to the men's slats.

72. The French Canadian lumberjacks in Paul's big camp were very fond of pea soup. His cooks tried to keep them well supplied with their favorite food. One winter day the tote teamster was driving his ox-team and sleigh across a frozen lake near Paul's camp. He was transporting a load of dried peas. Near the middle of the lake the ice suddenly broke and down into the icy water went the oxen and their load. The teamster was rescued but the oxen were drowned. The loss of the peas was a real calamity for Paul Bunyan, but he was happily probably the most resourceful man who ever lived. He set a crew of his lumberjacks to damming the lake outlet with logs. Another crew cut the brush and timber and piled it on the shores of the lake. This he set afire and boiled the lake. Paul's cook Joe Muffraw threw in a quantity of salt and pepper. When the lake cooled off, the liquid was the best of pea soup, with a fine ox-tail flavor. It was hauled to the camp in casks and the loggers had pea soup all winter. When the men were working at a distance from the camp, the cooks got the soup to them by freezing it onto pieces of rope and sticks. Some of the men drilled holes in their axe and peavy handles and filled these with soup. Their hands on the handles kept the soup always warm.

73. Some funny things occurred on his camp that winter—the winter of the black snow. Near the camp was a nice big spring—it

was a hot spring, boiling over at times. But that winter the thermometer dropped down to 66 degrees below zero, and the boys in
his crew used it for a skating rink. However, too many went onto
the ice at one time, and breaking through the ice scalded their feet,
and laid them up for a time.

One day the tote-teamster bringing supplies to Paul's camp,
drove his yoke of oxen too close to the edge of this hot-spring,
ditching his load of navy beans, ten tons or more, were lost in
the mess. Joe Sourdough, the cook, undaunted by this catastrophy,
took pepper, salt and pork, and threw them in among the beans,
and got good bean soup to last all winter. His flunkeys were kind of
mad as they had to tote the soup three miles to camp.

Paul would not allow any booze around his camp. He couldn't
help it, as every fellow that he sent to town for apple-jack would
drink it all up on the way back to camp.

But one day one of the cookees or cook-shanty rustlers, was par-
ing spuds and heard a peculiar sizzling in the suds, and found the
peelings fermenting right where they lay. "Sour-face" Murphy, the
road monkey, was standing in the doorway, and the face he wore
convinced the cook that Murphy soured the "mash" with his looks,
and when the mess was drained a gallon or more of real Irish XXX
booze resulted. Paul took Murphy off the road and made him superintendent of his private still. Later on, both Paul and Murphy
went into the Spanish American War, Paul coming back with a
major's commission but poor Murphy remained a private still.

74. That winter the camp ran out of beans, owing to the long
spell of cold weather. A huge blue ox hauled all the wood and water for the camp. This ox measured eight ax-handles between the
horns. The cook harnessed up the big blue ox and started for the
nearest town, one hundred miles up the Little Onion River and
across Little Onion Lake. They were on their way back the next
day with the beans, when the spring thaw set in. The thermometer
went from zero to eighty in the shade when the cook and the blue
ox were crossing Little Onion Lake, and the entire outfit broke

through the ice. The cook escaped drowning by climbing on the end of one of the ox's horns, and standing there with just his nose out of water, from sundown to sunup when he was rescued by Paul Bunyan and a party from the camp. Paul, it seems, was very wrathy at the loss of the beans. The breakup had come with a rush, and with no beans in camp the men would not work. The Little Onion River was a raging torrent, and quick action was necessary. Paul thought a moment, drawing at his huge pipe, and then instructed all hands to dam up the outlet of the lake. With the lake dammed, he set all hands to building fires around its shores, and within an hour the lake was a bubbling pot of bean soup, with a slight taste of beef to it. The men, with a cheer, returned to work, and at meal times the cook would open the sluice in the dam, and let out a supply of bean soup for the men working on the river one hundred miles below him.

75. Joe put some beans to soak one day,
   Out in the cook-house shanty;
   They swelled so big, the shanty filled
   And raised the cook-house off the sills!
   'Twas then Paul tired of pork and beans
   And to the cook did say:
   'Of peas, and beans, and ox-meat
   Apple sauce and stew,
   Taters in their jackets,
   Let's for a while be through!
   'Twill aid in our digestion, to have a little change;
   So now we'll have some venison; some good, wild game.

   Belle has made bushels of morphine pills,
   But they are no good for woodsmen's ills.
   We'll use them for bullets to shoot into deer;
   We'll get a supply that will last us a year!'
   Five thousand deer in just one day
   Were put to sleep and stacked like hay!

76. The inherent truthfulness of the genuine woodsman seems to have been transmitted well down to the present day. It was not over ten years ago that the writer made the acquaintance in camp of a veteran logging camp cook. He said in early days, at the close of the winter logging, some of the oxen would be found so old and worn out as not to be worth the expense of taking downriver. These were turned out into the woods to shift for themselves. In the fall following, when early operations were begun, preparatory to another winter's work, some of these oxen would be found still alive, sleek and fat, and would be butchered for camp use. The newly put-on flesh was juicy and tender, with a certain gamey appetizing flavor caused by the wild feed. To this story the faithful old cook made the following addition. Said he, "Some of those oxen were so old that there was not room enough on their horns for the animal rings denoting age, but we needed to fashion a stick with hay wire on top of the horn to record additional years."

77. Paul brought a flock of chickens to his camp on the Big Auger River. His men were fond of hen fruit and many eggs were used by the cook in preparing other food. The chickens, which were a special breed imported from China, did very well. When the supply of chicken food was low, the cook experimented with mixing sawdust with their grain. It seemed to increase their laying. Then the cook fed them only on sawdust. After a week or two of this sawdust diet, the fowls still layed but they layed knotholes instead of eggs. In the end Paul found it cheaper and easier to grow eggplants for his camp. An infirm lumberjack gathered the eggs from these plants every day.

78. An old friend once sent to Sourdough Sam a gift of a barrel of Milwaukee German sauerkraut. The teamster who brought it to the cook shanty placed it near one end of the big range without informing Sam. At about this same time another friend sent to Sam a gift of a cask of limburger cheese. This another teamster rolled into the cook shanty, depositing it among a lot of salt and sugar casks, again without informing Sam. He was blissfully ignorant of the arrival of both gifts. In the meantime the contents of both casks, aided by the heat of the nearby big range, were gaining power daily. In a few days Sam began to sniff the awful smells that were now issuing from the containers. Others who became aware of these also mentioned it to him. Thinking that there might be some dead rats somewhere about the shanty, Sam sent a number of his helpers to hunt for the carcasses. The men after a pretty thorough search found none. Every day the smells became worse. The lumberjacks, who were Canada-French, Swedes, Indian half-breeds and Maine and Vermont Yankees, now hotly objected to eating in such an odorous atmosphere. They charged Sam and his staff with the improper care of the camp garbage. So Sam was driven to an investigation of his own account. When he at last found the casks from which the terrible odors were issuing and identified their contents, he had them removed and buried in the woods a half mile away from the camp. There they attracted all of the wild animals of the forests.

79. Accidents were not uncommon in the big cook shanty. Babe the big blue ox once got in and in his efforts to sample it overturned the big kettle of pea soup which was simmering on the range. On another occasion he devoured most of a lot of Pieface Charley's pies. One day a big pot of Jimmy Beanpot's beans exploded and hot beans flew all over the shanty. The nearby jacks sought refuge under the big table and nearly overturned it. It was a week before the rain of beans ceased. Once an entire tribe of Indians got into the shanty just before supper, calmly seated themselves at the lumberjack's places, and began devouring the bread and other food already placed there. When the loggers arrived for their supper and found redmen seated at their places, they grabbed them and threw them out in a real riot. Large quantities of prunes were served at nearly every meal. Seven men with wheelbarrows labored all day from day to day in hauling prune stones away from the cook shanty. The chipmunks found and ate them and grew as big and as fierce as tigers. They sometimes attacked Paul's men and he had

to arm some of his crew with shot guns to reduce their numbers. The cook shanty was a very busy place from early morning until quite late at night. Forty helpers were kept busy opening salt, pepper, sugar, and flour barrels and as large a number in drawing and bringing water from the camp well.

Wild Animals Around Bunyan's Camps

80. Connected very frequently with the Bunyan tales are accounts of fabulous animals that haunted the camp. There is the bird who lays square eggs so that they will not roll down hill, and hatches them in the snow. Then there is the side-hill dodger, a curious animal naturally adapted to life on a hill by virtue of the circumstance that it has two short legs on the up-hill side. Of this creature it is said that by mistake the female dodger once laid her eggs (for the species seems to resemble somewhat the Australian duck-bill) wrong end around, with the terrible result that the little dodgers, hatching out with their short legs down hill, rolled into the river and drowned. The pinnacle grouse are birds with only one wing, adapted by this defect for flight in one direction about the top of a conical hill. There is little doubt that these animal stories existed outside the Bunyan cycle, and are simply appended to the central group of tales.

81. One of the strange creatures that inhabited the Little Onion Mountain at the head of the Little Onion River, during the winter of the blue snow, was the "Side Hill Gouger." There was only one Side Hill Gouger, an old female. Her two right legs were shorter than her two left ones, so she could only travel in a circle around the mountain. The animal belonged to the cat family, but was larger and more ferocious than any member of the feline tribe. It was easy to escape the Gouger, because she could only travel in one direction, and if the men got behind her she was powerless to reach them, except by backing up or running on around the mountain, which she could do with amazing celerity. The old Side Hill Gouger had a litter of little Gougers in the spring of the blue

A sidehill gouger near Bunyan's camp, by Eugene Shepard

FROM *PAUL BUNYAN, HIS CAMP AND WIFE*, 1929

snow, but she made the fatal mistake of starting them off the wrong way around the mountain, and they all rolled over and over down the hill, losing their lives in the Little Onion River, because none of them could swim. No one ever heard what became of the Old Gouger, or at least the surviving members of the old crew of lumberjacks do not remember. Perhaps she too tried to turn around one day, and was drowned in the Little Onion.

82. A strange bird, called the "Deep-Winter-Flying-Midget," made its home on the Little Onion Mountain. The bird used to frequent Paul Bunyan's camps, and the cook always kept it supplied with food. It would lay its eggs right out on the surface of the snow. Cold, instead of warmth, hatched the eggs. To prevent the eggs rolling down the mountain side, the midget always laid square eggs.

83. The Whiffenpouf Bird is one of the most curious of the Bunyan wild animals of the woods. This fowl spends most of the daylight hours on the wing. It always flies backwards, this to keep the wind out of its eyes. One naturally asks, "How does he know where he is going?" The answer to this query is that he doesn't know and doesn't care. He only wants to know where he was. The Whiffenpouf Bird has seven broods in a single year. As his kind thus multiplies very rapidly, a food famine soon overtakes any locality where a pair of these birds sets up housekeeping and all of the other wild animals must either move away or starve to death. As they sing at night only, giving imitations of popular songs, they never were popular with the lumberjacks.

84. The "Hodag" was a monster of hideous mien, a re-incarnation of the spirit of the lost ox. In Paul Bunyan's days horses were not used in the lumber camps. Oxen were the beasts of burden in the woods. Once in a while one would wander away and never be seen again. The lost oxen, according to the lumberjacks, turned into Hodags, and became as wild and terrible as they were formerly tame and peaceable. Their cry was something to make the strongest heart quake. Not many years ago "Gene" Shepherd, [*sic*] the famous Wisconsin woodsman-joker, hoaxed the whole scientific world with a photograph of a Hodag, caught in his lair. Among other things Gene had learned taxidermy, and at some expense and no end of labor, he transformed a peculiarly shaped log into as ferocious an animal in appearance as ever a Jack saw in his wildest nightmare.

85. The belief of those sturdy woodsmen was that seven years of continuous fire was necessary to exterminate the profanity which had accumulated in the body of the ox during his life...As the fire died down, there slowly issued from the great pile of ashes, a mystical animal, later to be known as the hodag.

On this particular day, just at twilight, Eugene Shepherd [*sic*], a naturalist of the north woods, taking his customary quiet stroll into the forest, strode down a favorite trail, breathing the fragrance of the tall pines and hemlocks. Suddenly, he became aware of an unusual odor in the air, which aroused his curiosity. On looking further through the depths of the foliage, he discovered a strange creature, so unlike anything he had ever seen before, that it was beyond description. Though a student of woodlore and of both prehistoric and other wild animals, Mr. Shepherd could not classify the monstrosity, which was gazing at him with glowing, green eyes and sniffing from nostrils of flaming hue.

The animal's back resembled that of a dinosaur, and his tail, which extended to an enormous length, had a spearlike end. Sharp spines, one and a half feet apart, lined the spinal column. The legs were short and massive and the claws were thick and curved, denoting great strength. The broad, furrowed forehead was covered with coarse, shaggy hair and bore two large horns. From the broad, muscular mouth, sharp, glistening white teeth protruded.

This strange animal of the woods had an alert movement and the swish of his tail made the earth tremble. When he exhaled, an obnoxious odor penetrated the atmosphere for some distance. Mr. Shepherd was trembling and speechless as he gazed on this horror of the forest. The great naturalist who had conquered all before, was at his wit's end.

86. Snow snakes. These reptiles came over from Siberia during the very cold year of the two winters when Bering trait was frozen over.

87. The statement of Edward H. Bean, director of the Chicago Zoological park, that the Indian pythons, the largest snakes ever brought into this country, were seldom over 30 feet in length may be absolutely correct as far as imported snakes are concerned but it would be an admission of ignorance to intimate that our native snakes do not occasionally grow much larger than that.

The winter of 1886–87 was known to all of the old lumberjacks in northern Wisconsin as "The Winter of the Big Snow Snakes." We had one cold spell that lasted three months with the temperature down to 30 to 60 degrees below zero most of the time. There were more snow snakes that winter than were ever seen before or since. Where they came from or where they went has always been a mystery. They never appeared until it was about 40 degrees below zero and with the first warm day they disappeared.

I was in Paul Bunyan's logging camp that winter driving a tote team hauling supplies in to our camp which was located near the head waters of the Big Auger River on section 37. On my daily trips I saw hundreds of snow snakes, most of them from 10 to 20 feet in length. One day, at the top of a long hill where I usually stopped to let my team rest, I sat on the load eating a sandwich when suddenly I heard a sniffing sound. I looked up and was nearly paralyzed to see the head of a large snow snake not over three feet from my face...

88. During the winter of the big blue snow, the famous snow snakes made their appearance. They froze up in the winter, and the Jacks used them for skids. In the spring they would thaw out. The first thing a snow snake did when he thawed out was to make for the river for a drink, and carrying the logs on their backs. It saved the men a lot of unnecessary work.

89. The hangdown. This ferocious animal lives in the Big Woods near the logging camps, where it hangs from the limbs of trees, either head down or head up, either way making no difference to its digestion. It climbs up a tree after the manner of a sloth, its long claws enabling it to clasp the branches and pull its body up. It is hunted by the lumberjacks, as its skin brings a high price. Greenhorns in the logging camps are sent out to hunt it with a tub and an axe. It is hunted at night. The greenhorn must meet it when it is on the ground, deftly cover it with the tub and then kill it with the axe. If he fails to cover it—well—goodbye, greenhorn. The animal gets its share of greenhorns every year.

90. Only recently a retired woodsman acquaintance related the following. A friend of his said he was one day rowing across a lake, but despite all his efforts he realized he was making no headway, in fact was going backward. Looking around to ascertain the cause, he saw that a huge school of fish like a great wave was pushing the boat back, when he was soon landed high and dry many feet inland, with the entire beach covered two feet deep with the struggling fish. Then, said he, "a large herd of deer came down to the lake, and ate those fish up, slick and clean." In the face of such indisputable testimony, still there are persons who in their wisdom declare that deer do not eat fish.

91. Some of the fish in the Big Onion country had peculiar habits. For instance there were the upland perch. These fish were hardly ever near the water. They were generally on the wing and nested in the tall trees, like birds. The only way to get them was with a gun.

One had to shoot fast and straight to knock down enough of them for a mess.

Then there were the whirligig fish. They were very fond of cheese. They were taken in the winter time through holes cut in the ice. They always swam in circles, so the men smeared the edges of the holes with limburger cheese to attract them. The fish would smell the cheese and coming to the holes would swim round in circles faster and faster until being unable to stop themselves. In their mad circling they would fairly whirl clear out of the water, then falling on the ice they were easily gathered up.

Another kind of fish were the giddy fish. These fish also arose to the surface at the ice holes in large schools. They were small fish and very elastic, like pieces of India rubber. The easiest way to get them was not with a hook and line or spear. When they rose to the surface one of the men would lean over and hit one of the fish a smart rap with a paddle. That would send the fish to the bottom, and then striking the bottom he would immediately, being elastic, bounce right up to the surface again. Then the other fish in the school, following this leader, would also begin to bounce. So they would continue bouncing up higher and higher at every bounce until all bounced themselves right out of the water. Here on the ice the men killed them with axes handles or clubs.

Some of the fish were really dangerous. The big gar fish had snouts so armed with saw teeth that they would sometimes saw right thru a big log to get at a juicy lumberjack. Many lost their lives in this way. Once in the water they quickly made mincemeat of a man.

There are other yarns which Wisconsin lumberjacks tell of the curious fish which inhabited the waters and woods in the vicinity of some of Paul's logging camps. One of these tells of the muskie in one of the lakes which was of such gigantic proportions that when finally hooked it took all of Paul's crew and his ox teams to draw him out of the water. The hole which his removal left in the bottom was so large that for months afterward the lumberjacks could walk right in the without getting their feet wet.

92. Paul Bunyan, giant Wisconsin lumber-king giant, long ago had a logging camp up in the Pelican Lake country. In the lake near the camp there was a big muskelunge. It was a tremendous fish. The loggers knew of its great size by the way in which it churned up the lake in great waves.

They made up their minds to catch this great fish. One day they baited a thick rope with a side of pork and cast it into the water. Ole the camp blacksmith had forged a hook as big as an anchor for the line.

Soon they saw the line drawn under the water and then they knew that they had hooked the big fish. All of the men in the camp took hold of the line and tried to pull the fish out of the water. It was a big task, as he was very strong. By their united strength they pulled him toward the shore, then, all of a sudden, he turned and dragged half the crew into the water. They struggled with him all day and made little progress. Only by harnessing Babe, the Big Blue Ox, and all of the other ox teams in the camp to the line did they finally succeed in pulling the big fish out of the lake.

His leaving the lake left so big a hole in the water that for a long time afterwards Paul's men could walk into the lake with rubber boots on without getting their feet wet. The crew had fish, fish chowder and fishballs for dinner for a month after the big fish was caught.

93. In his old time logging camps on the Big Onion River in Wisconsin, Paul Bunyan always made it a practice to serve fish to his crews on Friday, if possible. Not that the river pigs, bull nurses, and jam busters in Paul's crews liked fish, all of the jacks, except the Swedes, would have preferred sow belly or salt horse. As it was, the boys were always sorry to see Friday come around. Some said that serving fish or fish balls on that day was just another of Johnny Inkslinger, the camp clerk's, damned camp economies. Not content with saving money by cutting down the ink supply in his bookkeeping, Johnny had Paul introduce fish among the camp grub. Sometimes, however, the supply of codfish and mackerel ran low or was exhausted and Paul's camp cooks had to resort to the native fish of the streams and lakes about the Big Onion camp. These were generally very abundant, so abundant in fact sometimes in the spring of the year that they clogged the streams and held up the log drives. At such times Paul had to muster his whole crew to break up these fish jams with axes and pike-poles or even resort to charges of dynamite before he could clear the way for his big logs.

94. Paul Bunyan, when logging off the present state of North Dakota, had similar troubles with big mosquitos. These actually carried away many of his men. At about this time he learned of the existence of a particularly large and ferocious race of bumble-bees in Texas and he sent one Joe Muffraw, his camp cook, South to secure a lot of them and to drive them North to his camp. These domesticated bumble-bees were as large and formidable as he expected them to be. When released they immediately attacked and sadly worsted the mosquito tribe. All went well in the camp for a while until some of his bees entered into friendly relations with and intermarried with the mosquitos. The result was a cross which was more powerful and bloodthirsty than the mosquitos, because of having a stinger at each end of its body.

95. When Paul Bunyan's men were logging in the Chippewa River region, they were greatly troubled by the mosquitoes. These insects didn't mind the cold weather, they were as active and bloodthirsty then as at any other time of the year. The chief difficulty in fighting them lay in the very large size of some of the larger species. These were so big that they could straddle the river banks and pick the lumberjacks right out of the passing

Mosquito-bees at Bunyan's camp, by William Laughead
FROM *THE MARVELOUS EXPLOITS OF PAUL BUNYAN*, 1922

batteaux. Sometimes a crew would catch one of them in this position, quickly tie some of their legs to convenient trees, and then use them as a bridge across the river.

Bunyan's Travels

96. Not all of the Bunyan stories are concerned with Bunyan's life in the Round River or the Big Onion camps. There are several accounts of his exploits far from the forests of the north-central states. It is said that when he was once dredging out the Columbia River, he broke the dredge, and, sticking it into his pocket, walked to the nearest blacksmith shop in South Dakota, had it repaired, and returned to the Oregon camp before dark. Besides his blue ox Bunyan had, according to some versions, so many oxen that their yokes, piled up, made twenty cords of wood. One day he drove all of these animals through a hollow tree which had fallen across a great ravine. When he reached the other side, he found that several of the oxen had disappeared, and, returning, he discovered that they had strayed into a hollow limb.

97. In logging in the big forests of the Northwest, in Washington and Oregon, Paul Bunyan's men encounter some big difficulties. Out there the rivers often run in narrow and deep gorges. Some of these are only five or six feet wide and five hundred feet deep. Once a logging crew was running logs down one of these streams. They were making but small progress. The logs kept piling up in the stream bed. Paul's foreman, Chris Crosshaul, stationed a lumberjack at each end of the gorge, and had these men turn the river on its side with their peavies. There was no further trouble after that. Chris was a mighty resourceful camp boss.

98. When Paul had lumbered off the Dakotas and made a prairie of the state, some one told him of the great cypress swamps of Louisiana where the timber grew so fast it was dangerous to walk through it at night or when the dew was on for fear of being caught between the trunks and crushed.

The natives thought the timber could never be logged. Paul sent word by the wild geese that he was coming down in the spring. The natives were able to talk with the geese, their language being similar. But they thought their timber would look small to Paul so they picked out a nice thrifty cypress tree on the banks of the river, seven feet two inches through. They drew all the manure in the state of Louisiana around it, and set up four derricks, one on each side, and stretched the trunk. In a short time they got the tree growing fourteen feet ever night.

When Paul came down he was surprised to find such timber and sent back after the long saw that would reach across forty acres of land. He thought that by sending Jim Liverstone he could beat the train. Jim being the fastest man in camp. Being able to jump any river in three jumps.

While Jim was after the saw, Paul thought that to pass away the time he would go hunting, some one having sent him a saw tooth hound from the old country. They being supposed to be the fastest things on four legs. Paul was sure that the hound could catch anything running. He only took his ax with him. They had not been in the woods long before they started a luferlang. Now a luferlang is an animal with a dark blue strip running the length of its back, the tail being in the middle center of its back. It could run either way without turning around. Paul was so mad to see the luferlang run a short distance and sit down and waite for the hound, that he threw his axe and cut the hound exactly through the middle, lacking a half inch. Paul felt so bad over losing his temper that he sewed the hound together, but being in a hurry he got him twisted but it proved to be a great blessing for the hound, for when he got tired running with his front feet he would flop over and run on his hind legs, so that he never got tired, which enabled him to catch any animal in the woods.

When Liverstone Bill [*sic*] returned with the long saw, Paul felled the big cypress tree. There was a flying squirrel in the top that hit the saw tooth hound with such force square between the eyes that it killed him. Paul buried the hound and now they find great bones all over the state of Louisiana and they think that they are the bones of some pre-historic animal, but they are nothing but the bones of Paul's old saw-tooth hound.

Paul had trouble a plenty in lumbering the great cypress swamps. He found that the handles of the seven great choppers axes were too short to even notch the trees, they being only eleven feet and one half inch, but he overcame the trouble by putting a rope on the handle of his own ax, then he could cut forty acres at one swing.

99. In his spare time, when not engaged in lumbering, Paul Bunyan, the lumberjack hero, sometimes turned his attention to agriculture. One year he planted the entire state of Iowa to corn. That was the year of the hot-hot summer.

His corn crop was growing very nicely, the stalks were already 15 feet tall and earing-out well, when a spell of very hot weather came along. It grew steadily hotter and hotter. The corn matured very rapidly. Still hotter became the weather. The corn ears were ripened and the kernels fell on the ground. In many places they covered the ground to the dept of a foot or more. Still the terrible heat increased. Now the kernels began to pop. The popping was incessant and soon the ground was hidden beneath three or four feet of white popped corn. Now a big wind from Kansas swept the fields, piling the white corn up in drifts and great heaps. Some of Paul's cattle had strayed into the fields for food and many of these oxen and cows, believing that there had been a great snowstorm, actually froze to death before they could be rescued. Some of Paul's farm-hands were also badly frost-bitten or suffered from frozen noses, ears, fingers and toes. All of this happened during the hot-hot-hot summer of which many lumber-jacks can tell. There never was such a torrid year. Over in Illinois where Paul was trying to grow grapes, the fruit swelled to such great size that in the great heat the grapes burst and the rivers of grape juice flooded out completely a number of Mississippi River towns.

Appendix

100. Research Notes of Bernice Stewart and Homer Watt, 1914–1916

Cook Camp Tales

It took seven men working constantly with wheelbarrows to haul the prune stones away from camp.

The cook stove was so large that it was necessary to clean three forties bare each week to keep a fire in it.

It took a cord of wood to start a fire.

One day the cook put a batch of dough in one side of the oven and before he could run around the stove to the other side, the dough had not only baked but burned. It was all the cook could do to throw a stone across the top of his stove.

The cook baked loaves so large that after the soft part was eaten out the crusts were large enough for bunks for the men. Another version is that they were large enough for sleeping shanties.

Some say he baked these large loaves in a ravine and set the slashings on fire around the ravine.

He had to make so many pancakes it was necessary to use the entire top of the stove as a griddle. Cookees with sides of bacon strapped to their feet skated around to grease the griddle. The batter was mixed in a huge container on the roof and dropped through on the griddle. The cakes were served with a cart and pitchfork. One cook undertook to make twelve acres of pancakes.

One time the cook made a mistake and put several fingers of blasting powder in the pancake batter in place of soda. The first pancake put on the griddle blew the two boys who greased griddles so high they never returned.

One time Paul's tote-teamster tipped a load of peas over in a lake. Paul added salt and pepper, set the slashing on fire and made enough pea soup to last the crew all winter. Some versions say he dammed up the outlet, and sluiced the pea soup down the river to his crew as they needed it. Other versions say he spilled the peas in a hot spring. Still others have it that the team hitched to the wagon went down to flavor the soup.

Paul froze pea soup to sticks and sent it out in the woods to his crew in this way.

The potato parings were left in a pail by the cookee. One day Sour-faced Murphy looked at them and his look was so sour the parings fermented and made some Irish booze. Murphy was kept as the camp distillery.

One day the camp cook got lost between the root cellar and the flour bin and came near starving to death before he was rescued.

The cook one day made such hard doughnuts that the blacksmith had to put the holes in them. Paul said they were all right but would taste better if the holes were larger.

Paul always hired 100 men with wooden legs to mash potatoes.

Sour dough is used in camps to make a great many things. The cook once made so much of it that Paul used it to dam up a river and turn its course the other way so that he could get his logs out of a lake which had no outlet and into which he had driven them by mistake.

When the cook was sick Paul made biscuits for the crew. The biscuits were so hard no one could eat them—not even Paul, so he and the crew threw them at various bothersome beasts around the shanties. Paul shot the last biscuit at an old black cat with such strength that the cat landed behind the moon where she is still barked at by dogs.

Paul Bunyan, Personal appearance, pets, friends etc.

Paul Bunyan was seven feet tall and had a stride of seven feet. Some say he was seven axe handles tall.

Paul had great lung capacity. One day the cook could not blow the new dinner horn. Paul took it and with one blast he laid several acres of trees flat. Sometimes when he spoke the limbs fell from trees.

He smoked a huge pipe most of the time. The barrel was so large he always hired two men to fill it.

Paul's constant companion was the big blue ox. Its weight was either five or ten thousand pounds. It was either seven feet or seven axe handles between the tips of the horns. The French Canadians say he was "seven feet between de two hie."

Paul could not write. He kept his men's time by cutting notches in a log. When he ordered grindstones from town he received cheeses and remarked that he forgot to put the holes in the grind stones.

The blue ox had the strength of nine horses. He was pure white until he slept out all winter the time of the blue snow.

Logging Adventures

Paul Bunyan logged all one winter on the pyramid forty from which he took ten million feet of pine. The pyramid was so high it took three weeks to see the top, and three men looking at once could hardly see the peak. This place was near the Little Onion or the Big Onion, Round River, or where the Little Gimlet empties into the Big Auger. It was also on section 37, and was three weeks this side of Quebec.

When Paul wanted to peel a log he hitched the ox to the log while he grasped the bark. The ox jerked the log right out of its bark.

One day the logs jammed in the river and no one could break the jam. Paul backed the blue ox into the river and shot at it with a big rifle. The ox thought the shots were flies and switched his tail with such vigor that the water started flowing the other way and loosened the jam.

Paul worked all winter on the one forty—the pyramid—and all his crew developed short legs on one side from working on the side of a hill.

In the spring he put his logs in the river and passed his own canoes with them three times before he realized that the river was round.

The crew on the pyramid forty was so large that Paul kept one group going to work, one coming from work, and one working all the time.

The winter Paul logged on the pyramid forty there was blue snow and a great deal of it.

There were also snow snakes that winter. Paul made use of them. Some were so large that he used them for skids on which to pile his big rollaways. In the spring they crawled to the river carrying the logs with them. The little snow snakes he saved, to cool his summer camps with.

Once Paul got in a hurry to get his logs to the river. Instead of cutting the timber in the woods he hauled the whole sections down to the river—6 sections a day for 6 days a week. Late Saturday nite he hauled down a section, but he never carried it back because he didn't work on Sunday. Hence there is no longer a section 37.

The snow was forty feet deep on one place where Paul logged. He came back the next winter and logged the stumps.

One time Paul had no money with which to pay his crew. So he rushed into camp exclaiming that they had cut government pine and would be arrested. He told the crew to each grab a piece of camp equipment and run, and for no two men to go the same way. This they did and Paul was rid of his crew.

Paul logged off North Dakota one winter, and any one who does not believe he was a good logger, may take a look at N. D.

While logging in the west among the large timber Paul used a tremendous number of small oxen as well as the big blue ox. One day he drove them into a hollow tree and never recovered them all for they ran up the hollow limbs and were lost.

Other Tales of Paul

Paul and the blue ox were a strong pair. One day they hauled a house up hill and returned and hauled the cellar up after it.

Paul and a friend of his killed over 200 deer one time by tripping the key log of a big rollaway and letting the logs roll down hill to the place where the deer came to drink. It took all of these deer to make a harness for the blue ox.

One day the cook's flunkey hitched up the blue ox in the new harness and went for a big pine log for fire wood. It rained as he was bringing the big log up hill toward the camp. He beat the ox and hurried to camp but when he arrived there was no log. The harness had stretched and left the log at the bottom of the hill. The harness was thrown over a stump and the sun came out, dried the harness and dragged the log up hill.

A member of Paul's crew was noted for his two sets of teeth. One night he walked in his sleep and ground several grindstones to bits before he realized what he was doing.

One of the crew bet that he could cross a wide river by jumping. To the crew's surprise he stopped in mid air, humped up and jumped again and made the river in three jumps.

Paul's crew ground their axes by rolling stones down the pyramid forty and holding their axes to the rolling stones. In this way they put on razor edges.

When Paul was logging in Oregon, he had to dredge out the Columbia River. One day the dredge broke, so he put it in his pocket and walked back to Dakota to have it mended. It was late the same night when he returned to camp.

Paul snowshoed from Oregon to Minnesota one day and on his return trip it grew warm and the sun warped one snow shoe. Without his realizing it, he did not cover as much ground with his left as with his right snow shoe and before he knew it he landed in San Francisco.

Paul sometimes worked on his father's farm in the summer time. One time they raised a large water melon and when they were harvesting it they forgot to prop it up on the hillside before cutting the vine. It rolled down hill and washed out several yards of railroad track at the bottom.

One day Paul hitched the blue ox to a stump in one corner of a forty. The stump was a big pine one and in so deep that the ox couldn't budge, but when Paul urged, the old ox turned the forty acres right around before he could be stopped.

The blue ox's shoes were so heavy that when the blacksmith carried them he sunk almost knee deep in solid rock at each step.

Paul always watered the ox in the Mississippi, but he could water him but once a day because the ox lowered the water from ten to fifteen feet and stranded a large number of boats.

One winter Paul found a pine log so large he had to log all winter on it with his entire crew. When it came to skidding it down to the river he hitched the blue ox to it, also the large number of small oxen he owned. He had to haul it across a ravine, and the little oxen made no impression on the log, but the blue ox pulled and pulled and soon the log was on one side of the ravine, the blue ox on the other with all the little oxen strung like beads across the top of the ravine.

Paul owned a trained army of chicadees which he used as "warners." In the morning when he turned his crew in on a piece of timber the trees fell so fast that the birds and beasts did not have time to leave. He always sent the chickadees out the night before to let all living things know that he was coming.

When the blue ox finally dies some of Paul's old crew skinned him. The hide was tremendous, and a terrible wind came along just as they had finished skinning him and blew the hide up into the sky. Once in a while what we think is a dark cloud is actually the hide of the ox, as we can readily see by the shape.

No account of Paul's death is ever given except that the blue ox died from weeping when his master cashed in.

A mound near a swamp in northern Minnesota is sometimes known as Paul's grave.

One winter Paul iced a logging road so deep that it did not thaw out in the spring. The next year a crew went in near the road logging and thought it was a river. In the spring they put their logs in it and drove them down to a mill. The logging road has been a creek ever since—Main Creek.

Paul greased a hole in the ice to catch fish. The fish loved the smell of grease and as they came up to get a better whiff the shape of the fish made it so they popped out on top of the ice and were ready to be hauled away by the sleigh box full.

Paul had a dog—a wonderful deer hound that rounded up several hundred deer every time he went to the woods. One day as he was going very fast he ran into a cross cut saw and was cut right in two. Paul was worried but he picked up the two pieces and slapped them together. To his surprise he had put them together the wrong way. But he had doubled the dog's efficiency— he ran on two legs till he was tired, then flopped over and ran on the other two.

Paul told his crew they could cut as far from the edge of his forty as a lumberjack could throw an ax.

One time at a summer log-peeling camp the mosquitos were so thick a man had to crawl under an old iron kettle to save himself. He hammered on the inside of the kettle to scare the pests away, and soon the whole kettle was lifted and carried away. He had hammered the bills into the kettle.

An Irish lumberjack had had hard luck trying to kill a deer for his family to eat, so he clubbed a porcupine to death and carried it home. "I'll take it for the children to eat with the petaties—a little of something is better than a great deal of nothing."

One of the old-timers filled his old muzzle loader extra full one day before he shot at a deer. When the gun was fired the barrel exploded and the pieces killed a deer. A limb on a nearby tree on which several partridges were sitting, split and caught them all by their feet. The concussion stunned two rabbits. The man dressed his game and started across the river for his bear. On the way over his boots filled with fish.

Once when Paul was caught in a big snow storm he crawled in a leaning hollow tree to spend the night. He went down so far he had no idea how he would get out, but in the morning he saw a bear climbing down. He seized the bear by the tail and was hauled out. He did not shoot the bear even though he was out bear-hunting.

Paul must have had a wife for she made him some linen trousers. They were a very strong pair as was proved one day when the ox hurrying back to camp ran right through a big stump. Paul went through after him, but the stump snapped shut just as Paul emerged. His trousers were caught in the stump, but instead of tearing they pulled the stump up by the roots.

One day Paul met a bear on a side hill. He had no gun with him so he had to use his brain to fight the bear. He threw a big stone at him, but to no avail. Then he picked up a big club and hit the animal over the head, but on came the bear. Soon Paul knew that he must fight the bear bare handed So he took a deep breath in order that he might haul off and give the bear a big blow. As he breathed deeply a button flew off his vest and hit the bear between the eyes, killing it instantly.

Other stories

When Joe Mufferon died, the sad news was carried back to camp. Pete Legout said, "Hum? Joe dead? Dat's funny. He never done dat before."

One winter in the woods was very cold. The barn boss could not blow his lantern out no matter how hard he tried. Finally he discovered that the flame was frozen, so he picked it off and threw it away.

The dinner horn also froze that winter, and one night the cook blew and blew and could not get a sound out of it. When he brought it in the house he hung it up behind the stove. At last it thawed out, and kept the crew awake by blowing all nite—all the wind the cook had put into it at supper time.

One old lumberman invented a gun and frying pan combination. If he wanted to hunt all he needed to do was turn the affair into a gun. When he cooked his food he turned it into a frying pan. One day when he was cooking bacon, he saw some Indians about to attack him. He didn't want to waste his bacon, so quick as a cat he threw the bacon into the air to turn it o'er, converted the pan into a gun, killed the Indians, turned it back into a pan and caught the bacon as it was coming down.

An old lumberman one time paddled to an Island to camp for the night. He had no ammunition left, so he felt badly when he saw a beautiful buck on the island just as he arrived. Near him was a wild cherry tree from which the fruit had dried leaving only the stones hanging to the trees. He filled his old muzzle loader with these stones, crept up close to the buck and shot, but the animal dashed away. He hunted and hunted but couldn't find the beast although he knew he had injured it. The next spring as he was paddling across the river he saw a small tree growing right up out of the lake. He came closer and saw that it was a cherry tree, and he recognized the buck that he had killed with cherry stones.

One old lumberman fell through a hole in the ice one winter and did not come up for some time. He declares he was under that icy water exactly forty minutes because he had looked at his watch just before he went down, and he was thoughtful enough to glance at it as soon as he came up.

One day the old ox got hungry and ate up over two hundred feet of tow line.

Source of Each Tale (by Number)

Although many of the items listed here were created after 1920, the tales in them were generally collected from informants who recalled hearing them in the woods long before that date. Most of these sources are discussed at length in previous chapters.

1. Stewart, K. Bernice, and Homer A. Watt. "Legends of Paul Bunyan, Lumberjack." *Transactions of the Wisconsin Academy of Arts, Sciences, and Letters* (1916), 640.
2. Rockwell, J. E. "Some Lumberjack Myths." *Outer's Book* (Milwaukee, WI), February 1910, 160.
3. Bartlett, William. "Paul Bunyan and Other Logging Camp Yarns" (ca. 1927) in his *Papers, 1821–1934, 1944–1962.* Eau Claire Mss BY, at the Area Research Center, McIntyre Library, University of Wisconsin, Eau Claire, WI, box 10 folder 9.
4. Stewart and Watt, 1916, 642–643.
5. Taplin, Bert, told by Bill Mulhollen to Bert Taplin, winter of 1885–1886 (see chapter 4); quoted in a letter from H. J. Kent to Charles Brown, November 9, 1938, in the W. W. Charters Papers, Children's Literature Research Collection, University of Minnesota.
6. Bartlett, 1927.
7. Brown, Charles E. *Paul Bunyan and Tony Beaver Tales. Tall Yarns of the Prince of American Lumberjacks and of His Southern Cousin Tony Beaver as Told in the Logging camps in the North and South.* Madison, WI: C. E. Brown, 1930, 11.
8. Brown, Charles E. *Sourdough Sam, Paul Bunyan's Illustrious Chief Cook and Other Famous Culinary Artists of his Great Pinery Logging Camps, Old Time Tales of Kitchen Wizards, the Big Cook Shanty, the Camp Fare, the Dinner Horn, and Sam's Cook Book. Dedicated to the Memory of Eugene S. Shepard, Matt R. Stapleton, and Otis W. Terpening, Wisconsin Woodsmen.* Madison, WI: Charles E. Brown, Wisconsin Folklore Society, 1945.
9. Wadsworth, B., sent to Charles Brown, Children's Literature Research Collection, University of Minnesota, box 16 folder 1.
10. Jenderny, Fred. "That Lumber Camp." *Stars and Stripes* (Paris, France), June 13, 1919, 4.
11. Kearney, Luke, told to Charles E. Brown, Milwaukee, December 15, 1930, Children's Literature Research Collection, University of Minnesota, box 17 folder 1.
12. Kaufman, Elmer, told to Charles Brown in Antigo, WI, no date, Children's Literature Research Collection, University of Minnesota, document TM26 in box 16.
13. Deadman, Charles A. Interview notes, U.S. Works Progress Administration. Federal Writers' Project. *Records, 1936–1939: Folklore Wisconsin,* reel 6, frame 674.

14. Schmidt, E. E., to Charles Brown, May 17, 1929, in the W. W. Charters Papers, University of Minnesota Libraries.

15 Unattributed interview notes, U.S. Works Progress Administration. Federal Writers' Project. *Records, 1936–1939: Folklore Wisconsin*, reel 5, frame 305.

16. Shepard, Eugene. "Mrs. Paul Bunyan Even More Resourceful than Her Husband." *New North* (Rhinelander, WI), May 11, 1922, 1.

17. Stewart and Watt, 1916, 647.

18. Bartlett, 1927.

19. Shaw, Fred A. "Paul Bunyan, Inventor of Logging. His Autobiography [sic]." *Langlade Clippings* (Antigo, WI), February 12, 1923, 5. Tearsheets in box 8 folder 14, Children's Literature Research Collection, University of Minnesota.

20. Rockwell, 1910, 157.

21. Rockwell, 1910, 160.

22. Terpening, Otis. "The Myths of Paul Bunyan…" Four-page manuscript, undated but ca. January 1932, in box 5 of the Charles Brown Papers, Wis Mss HB, at Wisconsin Historical Society.

23. Stewart and Watt, 1916, 644–645.

24. Jones, A. P., sent to Charles Brown, March 1, 1935, in the W. W. Charters Papers, Children's Literature Research Collection, University of Minnesota.

25. Wisconsin Folklore Society. "Additional Paul Bunyan Legends, Copied from Wisconsin Folklore Society Manuscripts." Children's Literature Research Collection, University of Minnesota, box 16.

26. Bartlett, 1927.

27. Shepard, 1922, 1.

28. Bartlett, 1927.

29. Brown, Charles E. *Ole Olson. Tales of the Mighty Swede Blacksmith of Paul Bunyan's Wisconsin and Other Great Logging Camps , His Smithy, Shoeing Babe the Blue Ox, the Camp Dinner-horn, Paul's Watch, Whirling Lake, Sky Pilot, the Vacation, and Other Stirring Yarns of the Pineries. Dedicated to Harry G. Dyer, Lakeshore Kearney, Jos. Lucius, Otis W. Terpening.* Madison, WI: Charles E. Brown, Wisconsin Folklore Society, 1945, 2.

30. Rockwell, 1910, 160.

31. Shepard, 1922, 1.

32. Brown, Charles E. *Paul Bunyan Classics. Authentic Original Stories Told in the Old Time Logging Camps of the Wisconsin Pineries. Paul Bunyan Super-Lumberjack, His Camp and Logging Crew, Babe the Blue Ox, the Pyramid Forty, Pea Soup Lake, the Round River Drive, the Buckskin Harness, the Reversible Dog, the Big Mosquitos, and Other Tall Tales. Dedicated to Gladys J. Haney, W. W. Charters, "Ranger Mac" Mcneel.* Madison, WI: Charles E. Brown, Wisconsin Folklore Society, 1945, 4.

33. Brown, Charles E. *Flapjacks from Paul Bunyan's Cook Shanty. Miscellaneous Yarns Dedicated to James J. McDonald, Dr. C. A. Deadman, Lake Shore Kearney, August Derleth, H. J. Kent.* Madison, WI: Charles E. Brown, Wisconsin Folklore Society, 1941, 1.

34. Terpening, Otis, sent to Charles Brown, no date, Children's Literature Research Collection, University of Minnesota, Mss. TM34 in box 16.

35. Rockwell, 1910, 157.

36. Jenderny, 1919, 4.

37. Brown, *Flapjacks...*, 1941, 4.

38. "Some Cold Days in Bunyan's Camp. 68 Below Zero in Onion Camp on Big Auger River in 1877." *Rice Lake Chronotype*, January 14, 1925, 1.

39. Brown, Charles. "Paul Bunyan and the Great Lakes. Bunyan Yarns Collected by Charles E. Brown, Madison, Wisconsin, from Lake Michigan Lumberjack-sailors at Milwaukee and elsewhere, 1906–1915." Children's Literature Research Collection, University of Minnesota, mss. TM 40, box 16 folder 2.

40. Brown, Charles E. *Brimstone Bill, Famous Boss Bullwhacker of Paul Bunyan's Camps. Tall Tales of His Exploits. Babe and Benny, the Great Lakes, Hauling Snow, Cow Lucy, Goat Billy, Paul's Pigs, His Courting, Saw Mills, Babe Sick and Finis for Bill. Dedicated to H. J. Kent and Alonzo W. Pond.* Madison, WI: Charles E. Brown, Wisconsin Folklore Society, 1942, 3.

41. Stewart and Watt, 1916, 643.

42. Terpening, "The Myths of Paul Bunyan...," 1932.

43. Stewart and Watt, 1916, 644.

44. Stewart and Watt, 1916, 643–644.

45. Terpening, "The Myths of Paul Bunyan...," 1932.

46. McDonald, James, told to Charles E. Brown, no date, Children's Literature Research Collection, University of Minnesota, mss. TM 27, box 16.

47. Brown, *Brimstone Bill*, 1942, 4.

48. Brown, *Paul Bunyan Classics*, 1945, 5.

49. Brown, *Brimstone Bill*, 1942, 4.

50. Brown, *Brimstone Bill*, 1942, 3.

51. Brown, *Paul Bunyan Classics*, 1945, 2.

52. "Paul Bunyan—Inventor of Logging." *Langlade Clippings* (Antigo, WI), March 1924 (page numbers missing). Tearsheets in box 8 folder 14, Children's Literature Research Collection, University of Minnesota.

53. Stewart and Watt, 1916, 647.

54. Brown, *Paul Bunyan Classics*, 1945, 2.

55. Bartlett, 1927.

56. Bartlett, 1927.

57. Brown, *Brimstone Bill*, 1942, 1.

58. Brown, *Paul Bunyan Classics*, 1945, 3.

59. Brown, Charles E. *Johnny Inkslinger. Deacon Seat Tales of Paul Bunyan's Industrious Camp Clerk at His Sawdust River Camp in Wisconsin. Dedicated to*

Louis A. Maier, President of the Mystic Knights of the Blue Ox. Madison, WI: Charles E. Brown, Wisconsin Folklore Society, 1944, 2.

60. Brown, Charles E. *Ole Olson,* 3.
61. Edick, Dave. "Paul Bunyan—Inventor of Logging." *Langlade Clippings* (Antigo, WI), May 22, 1923, 9–10. Tearsheets in box 8 folder 14, Children's Literature Research Collection, University of Minnesota.
62. Stewart and Watt, 1916, 645.
63. Brown, Charles E. "Paul Bunyan and the Great Lakes…" Children's Literature Research Collection, University of Minnesota, mss. TM 40, box 16 folder 2.
64. Jenderny, 1919, 4.
65. Shepard, 1922, 1.
66. Jenderny, 1919, 4.
67. Brown, *Flapjacks…,* 1941, 2.
68. Brown, *Flapjacks…,* 1941, 1.
69. Stewart and Watt, 1916, 645–646.
70. Rockwell, 1910, 157.
71. Brown, *Flapjacks…,* 1941, 2.
72. Brown, *Paul Bunyan Classics,* 1945, 4.
73. "Paul Bunyan—Inventor of Logging."
74. Rockwell, 1910, 158.
75. Shepard, Eugene S., and Karretta Gunderson Shepard. *Paul Bunyan; His Camp and Wife.* Tomahawk, WI: The Osborne Press, 1929, 19.
76. Bartlett, 1927.
77. Brown, *Flapjacks…,* 1941, 3.
78. Brown, *Sourdough Sam,* 1945, 3.
79. Brown, *Sourdough Sam,* 1945, 3.
80. Stewart and Watt, 1916, 647.
81. Rockwell, 1910, 158–159.
82. Rockwell, 1910, 159.
83. Terpening, Otis, sent to Charles E. Brown, 1931, Children's Literature Research Collection, University of Minnesota, mss. TM 83, box 17 folder 4.
84. Rockwell, 1910, 159–160.
85. Kearney, Luke Sylvester. *The Hodag, and Other Tales of the Logging Camps.* Wausau, WI, 1928, 11–13.
86. McDonald, James, told to Charles E. Brown, no date, Children's Literature Research Collection, University of Minnesota, mss. TM 27, box 16.
87. Gleason, Edward. "Those Paul Bunyan Snow Snakes." *Capital Times* (Madison, WI), April 27, 1936.
88. Rockwell, 1910, 158.
89. Twenhofel, W. H., told to Charles E. Brown, 1940. Children's Literature Research Collection, University of Minnesota, box 16.
90. Bartlett, 1927.

91. Carney, John. "The Fish of Paul Bunyan's Day. Told to C. E. Brown by John Carney, ex-lumberjack of Wausau, Wisconsin." Undated. Charles Brown Papers, Wis Mss HB, at the Wisconsin Historical Society, box 5.
92. Hobbs, George. "The Big Fish. Paul Bunyan Tale told to C. E. Brown by George Hobbs, ex-lumberjack, at Pelican Lake, Wisconsin, August, 1930." Children's Literature Research Collection, University of Minnesota, mss. TM 82, Box 17 folder 4.
93. Carney, "The Fish of Paul Bunyan's Day…"
94. Balch, James. "Told by James Balch, a South Carolinian, Nov. 22, 1931." Charles Brown Papers, Wis Mss HB, at the Wisconsin Historical Society, box 5.
95. McCann, Robert, told to Charles E. Brown, 1934, Children's Literature Research Collection, University of Minnesota, mss. TM 13, box 16.
96. Stewart and Watt, 1916, 648.
97. Barrett, W. W., sent to Charles E. Brown, 1932, Children's Literature Research Collection, University of Minnesota, mss. TM28, box 16.
98. Terpening, "The Myths of Paul Bunyan…," 1932.
99. "The Hot-Hot Summer, as told to Charles E. Brown, Feb. 20, 1930." Charles Brown Papers, Wis Mss HB, at the Wisconsin Historical Society, box 5.
100. Watt, Homer, and Bernice Stewart. Notes, ca. 1914–1916, on Bunyan tales collected in the field. Contained in an April 22, 1941, letter from Watt to Professor W. W. Charters in the Paul Bunyan Collection, Children's Literature Research Collection, Univ. of Minnesota, box 16, folder 6.

Tales from Each Source (by Creator)

Balch, James. "Told by James Balch, a South Carolinian, Nov. 22, 1931." Charles Brown Papers, Wis Mss HB, at the Wisconsin Historical Society, box 5. 94

Barrett, W. W., sent to Charles E. Brown, 1932, Children's Literature Research Collection, University of Minnesota, mss. TM28, box 16. 97

Bartlett, William. "Paul Bunyan and Other Logging Camp Yarns" (ca. 1927) in his *Papers, 1821–1934, 1944–1962*. Eau Claire Mss BY, at the Area Research Center, McIntyre Library, University of Wisconsin, Eau Claire, WI, box 10 folder 9. 3, 6, 18, 26, 28, 55, 56, 76, 90

Brown, Charles E. *Brimstone Bill, Famous Boss Bullwhacker of Paul Bunyan's Camps. Tall Tales of His Exploits. Babe and Benny, the Great Lakes, Hauling Snow, Cow Lucy, Goat Billy, Paul's Pigs, His Courting, Saw Mills, Babe Sick and Finis for Bill. Dedicated to H. J. Kent and Alonzo W. Pond*. Madison, WI: Charles E. Brown, Wisconsin Folklore Society, 1942. 40, 47, 49, 50, 57

Brown, Charles E. *Flapjacks from Paul Bunyan's Cook Shanty. Miscellaneous Yarns Dedicated to James J. McDonald, Dr. C. A. Deadman, Lake Shore Kearney, August Derleth, H.J. Kent*. Madison, WI: Charles E. Brown, Wisconsin Folklore Society, 1941. 33, 37, 67, 68, 71, 77

Brown, Charles E. *Johnny Inkslinger. Deacon Seat Tales of Paul Bunyan's Industrious Camp Clerk at His Sawdust River Camp in Wisconsin. Dedicated to Louis A. Maier, President of the Mystic Knights of the Blue Ox.* Madison, WI: Charles E. Brown, Wisconsin Folklore Society, 1944. **59**

Brown, Charles E. *Ole Olson. Tales of the Mighty Swede Blacksmith of Paul Bunyan's Wisconsin and Other Great Logging Camps , His Smithy, Shoeing Babe the Blue Ox, the Camp Dinner-horn, Paul's Watch, Whirling Lake, Sky Pilot, the Vacation, and Other Stirring Yarns of the Pineries. Dedicated to Harry G. Dyer, Lakeshore Kearney, Jos. Lucius, Otis W. Terpening.* Madison, WI: Charles E. Brown, Wisconsin Folklore Society, 1945. **29, 60**

Brown, Charles E. "Paul Bunyan and the Great Lakes. Bunyan Yarns Collected by Charles E. Brown, Madison, Wisconsin, from Lake Michigan Lumberjacksailors at Milwaukee and elsewhere, 1906–1915. Children's Literature Research Collection, University of Minnesota, mss. TM 40, box 16 folder 2. **39, 63**

Brown, Charles E. *Paul Bunyan and Tony Beaver Tales. Tall Yarns of the Prince of American Lumberjacks and of His Southern Cousin Tony Beaver as Told in the Logging camps in the North and South.* Madison, WI: C. E. Brown, 1930. **7**

Brown, Charles E. *Paul Bunyan Classics. Authentic Original Stories Told in the Old Time Logging Camps of the Wisconsin Pineries. Paul Bunyan Super-Lumberjack, His Camp and Logging Crew, Babe the Blue Ox, the Pyramid Forty, Pea Soup Lake, the Round River Drive, the Buckskin Harness, the Reversible Dog, the Big Mosquitos, and Other Tall Tales. Dedicated to Gladys J. Haney, W. W. Charters, "Ranger Mac" Mcneel.* Madison, WI: Charles E. Brown, Wisconsin Folklore Society, 1945. **32, 48, 51, 54, 58, 72**

Brown, Charles E. *Sourdough Sam, Paul Bunyan's Illustrious Chief Cook and Other Famous Culinary Artists of his Great Pinery Logging Camps, Old Time Tales of Kitchen Wizards, the Big Cook Shanty, the Camp Fare, the Dinner Horn, and Sam's Cook Book. Dedicated to the Memory of Eugene S. Shepard, Matt R. Stapleton, and Otis W. Terpening, Wisconsin Woodsmen.* Madison, WI: Charles E. Brown, Wisconsin Folklore Society, 1945. **8, 78, 79**

Carney, John. "The Fish of Paul Bunyan's Day. Told to C. E. Brown by John Carney, ex-lumberjack of Wausau, Wisconsin." Undated. Charles Brown Papers, Wis Mss HB, at the Wisconsin Historical Society, box 5. **91, 93**

Deadman, Charles A. Interview notes, U.S. Works Progress Administration. Federal Writers' Project. *Records, 1936–1939: Folklore Wisconsin,* reel 6, frames 670–675. **13**

Edick, Dave. "Paul Bunyan—Inventor of Logging." *Langlade Clippings* (Antigo, WI), May 22, 1923, 9–10. Tearsheets in box 8 folder 14, Children's Literature Research Collection, University of Minnesota. **61**

Gleason, Edward. "Those Paul Bunyan Snow Snakes." *Capital Times* (Madison, WI), April 27, 1936. **87**

Hobbs, George. "The Big Fish. Paul Bunyan Tale told to C. E. Brown by George Hobbs, ex-lumberjack, at Pelican Lake, Wisconsin, August, 1930." Children's

Appendix

Literature Research Collection, University of Minnesota, mss. TM 82, Box 17 folder 4. **92**

"The Hot-Hot Summer, as told to Charles E. Brown, Feb. 20, 1930." Charles Brown Papers, Wis Mss HB, at the Wisconsin Historical Society, box 5. **99**

Jenderny, Fred. "That Lumber Camp." *Stars and Stripes* (Paris, France), June 13, 1919, 4. **10, 36, 64, 66**

Jones, A.P., sent to Charles Brown, March 1, 1935, in the W. W. Charters Papers, Children's Literature Research Collection, University of Minnesota. **24**

Kaufman, Elmer, told to Charles Brown in Antigo, WI, no date, Children's Literature Research Collection, University of Minnesota, document TM26 in box 16. **12**

Kearney, Luke Sylvester. *The Hodag, and Other Tales of the Logging Camps.* Wausau, WI, 1928, 11–13. **85**

Kearney, Luke, told to Charles E. Brown, Milwaukee, December 15, 1930, Children's Literature Research Collection, University of Minnesota, box 17 folder 1. **11**

McCann, Robert, told to Charles E. Brown, 1934, Children's Literature Research Collection, University of Minnesota, mss. TM 13, box 16. **95**

McDonald, James, told to Charles E. Brown, no date, Children's Literature Research Collection, University of Minnesota, mss. TM 27, box 16. **46, 86**

"Paul Bunyan—Inventor of Logging." *Langlade Clippings* (Antigo, WI), March 1924 (page numbers missing). Tearsheets in box 8 folder 14, Children's Literature Research Collection, University of Minnesota. **52, 73**

Rockwell, J. E. "Some Lumberjack Myths." *Outer's Book* (Milwaukee, WI), February 1910. **2, 20, 21, 30, 35, 70, 74, 81, 82, 84, 88**

Schmidt, E. E., to Charles Brown, May 17, 1929, in the W. W. Charters Papers, University of Minnesota Libraries. **14**

Shaw, Fred A. "Paul Bunyan, Inventor of Logging. His Autobiography [sic]." *Langlade Clippings* (Antigo, WI), February 12, 1923, 5. Tearsheets in box 8 folder 14, Children's Literature Research Collection, University of Minnesota. **19**

Shepard, Eugene. "Mrs. Paul Bunyan Even More Resourceful than Her Husband." *New North* (Rhinelander, WI), May 11, 1922. **16, 27, 31, 65**

Shepard, Eugene S., and Karretta Gunderson Shepard. *Paul Bunyan; His Camp and Wife.* Tomahawk, WI: The Osborne Press, 1929. **75**

"Some Cold Days in Bunyan's Camp. 68 Below Zero in Onion Camp on Big Auger River in 1877." *Rice Lake Chronotype*, January 14, 1925, 1. **38**

Stewart, K. Bernice, and Homer A. Watt. "Legends of Paul Bunyan, Lumberjack." *Transactions of the Wisconsin Academy of Arts, Sciences, and Letters* (1916). **1, 4, 17, 23, 41, 43, 44, 53, 62, 69, 80, 96, 100**

Taplin, Bert, told by Bill Mulhollen to Bert Taplin, winter of 1885–1886 (see chapter 4); quoted in a letter from H. J. Kent to Charles Brown, November 9, 1938, in the W. W. Charters Papers, Children's Literature Research Collection, University of Minnesota. **5**

Appendix

Terpening, Otis. "The Myths of Paul Bunyan…" Four-page manuscript, undated but ca. January 1932, in box 5 of the Charles Brown Papers, Wis Mss
HB, at Wisconsin Historical Society. **22, 42, 45, 98**

Terpening, Otis, sent to Charles Brown, no date, Children's Literature Research
Collection, University of Minnesota, Mss. TM34 in box 16. **34**

Terpening, Otis, sent to Charles E. Brown, 1931, Children's Literature Research
Collection, University of Minnesota, mss. TM 83, box 17 folder 4. **83**

Twenhofel, W. H., told to Charles E. Brown, 1940, Children's Literature Research Collection, University of Minnesota, box 16. **89**

U.S. Works Progress Administration. Federal Writers' Project. *Records, 1936–1939:
Folklore Wisconsin.* Unattributed interview notes, reel 5, frame 305. **15**

Wadsworth, B., sent to Charles Brown, Children's Literature Research Collection, University of Minnesota, box 16 folder 1. **9**

Wisconsin Folklore Society. "Additional Paul Bunyan Legends, Copied from
Wisconsin Folklore Society Manuscripts." Children's Literature Research
Collection, University of Minnesota, box 16. **25**

Bibliography

The literature on Great Lakes logging is immense, as is that on American folklore. Listed here are only those sources actually cited in the text or otherwise essential to my research. They are divided as follows (parts II and III are arranged chronologically to reveal the evolution of the Bunyan literature):

    I. Manuscripts and Unpublished Sources
    II. Printed Texts of the Tales from Wisconsin
    III. Printed Texts of the Tales from Other States
    IV. Other Primary Sources
    V. Secondary Sources
    VI. Bibliographical Ghosts

Citations to local newspaper articles that omit page numbers are taken from *Wisconsin Local History & Biography Articles,* a set of scrapbooks in the Wisconsin Historical Society Library that can be viewed online at www.wisconsinhistory. org/wlhba.

I. MANUSCRIPTS AND UNPUBLISHED SOURCES

Before the Bunyan stories became famous in 1925, at least seven people actively tried to collect the oral tradition directly from lumberjacks:

1. Parrish S. Lovejoy (1884–1942), Michigan forester; his Bunyan correspondence and manuscripts are now in the Archives of Michigan in Lansing.
2. Richard R. Fenska (1884–1966), a forester raised in Rhinelander, Wisconsin, who went on to teach at the University of Montana (1912), Syracuse University (1921), and Columbia University (1943). He started collecting the tales in his youth in the 1890s; he told correspondents that he intended to publish a Bunyan collection as early as 1921 and as late as 1941, but none ever appeared. No Bunyan materials have survived among his professional papers, and his personal papers have not been found.
3. William Laughead (1882–1958), advertising executive for the Red River Lumber Company of Minneapolis; printed ephemera from his Bunyan ad campaigns and other company records are in the Children's

Literature Research Collection at the University of Minnesota. His incoming Bunyan correspondence at the Forest History Society in Durham, NC, came to light only after this book went to press.

4. Homer A. Watt (1884–1948), professor of English at the University of Wisconsin until 1917 and then New York University; his papers are in the possession of his family, who report that they contain no field notes or other evidence of his 1914–1920 Bunyan research; the papers of his research partner, Bernice Stewart (if any survived) could not be located.

5. Esther Shephard (1891–1975), graduate student at Reed College in 1921 and later professor at San Jose State College; her papers at the University of Washington contain few Bunyan research notes and almost nothing on her sources.

6. William W. Bartlett (1861–1933), local historian of Eau Claire, Wisconsin; his papers in the McIntyre Library at the University of Wisconsin–Eau Claire, contain letters, notes, clippings, and an unpublished manuscript written ca. 1927 about the tales.

7. Charles Brown (1872–1946), museum director at the Wisconsin Historical Society; his papers are divided between two repositories. The Wisconsin Historical Society in Madison owns his official files as museum director, microfilm of his WPA Wisconsin Folklore Project records, and a large collection of his other manuscripts. Only a small amount of Bunyan material survives in the Madison papers; instead, most of his Bunyan material was given by his widow in the 1960s to the Children's Literature Research Collection at the University of Minnesota, where they are interspersed among the W. W. Charters papers.

In addition, W. W. Charters (1875–1952), professor of education at Ohio State University, collected Bunyan material as a hobby. During the 1940s, Charters carried on a voluminous correspondence with the collectors named previously, as well as editors of Bunyan anthologies. His correspondence in the Children's Literature Research Collection at the University of Minnesota contains a wealth of documentation on how Bunyan editors obtained their stories.

These are the people who formed the major collections of unpublished records documenting the oral tradition about Paul Bunyan. Details on each collection are given here.

Badger State Folklore Society. *Records, 1946–1956.* Wisconsin Historical Society Archives Collection Mss 174 (three archives boxes).

Bartlett, William. *Papers, 1821–1934, 1944–1962.* Eau Claire Mss BY, at the Area Research Center, McIntyre Library, University of Wisconsin, Eau Claire, WI. Box 1, folder 5 contains letters about Bartlett's winter 1913–1914 travels in lumber camps. Box 1, folder 6 contains several letters between Bartlett and Stewart, Watt, Malloch, WHS director M. M. Quaife, and Eugene Shepard. Box 1, folder 7 includes his letters home from a January 1919 visit to camps. Box 10, folder 9 contains a seventeen-page manuscript in Bartlett's hand on the Bunyan tales, including their collection, publication, and authenticity, and a handful of the tales themselves; only a few paragraphs of this was published in his book. Box 10, folder 9 also contains photos by Shepard and a photocopy of his "Round River" plagiarism, marked to highlight its differences from the MacGillivray-Malloch text.

Beatty, Arthur. *Papers*. University of Wisconsin Archives, series 7/10/8/2-5 at Steenbock Library, Madison, WI.

Brown, Charles E. *Papers*. Wis Mss HB, at the Wisconsin Historical Society, 816 State St., Madison, WI 53706. Boxes 5 and 6 contain several letters from informants and summaries of interviews, all dated during the 1930s. The great bulk of Brown's Bunyan materials is not here but rather in the Children's Literature Research Collection at the University of Minnesota.

Fenska, Richard Robert. *R. R. Fenska Papers, 1910–1915*. Series 9/24/9 in the University of Wisconsin–Madison Archives, Steenbock Library, Madison, WI.

Lovejoy, Parrish Storrs. *Papers*. Archives of Michigan, Michigan Library and Historical Center, 702 W. Kalamazoo St., Lansing, MI. The most relevant segment is Series 7–11 of record group 63-12, *"Manuscripts of Articles Written by P. S. Lovejoy, 1902–1940, 1916–1926."* His Bunyan-related correspondence and manuscripts are in Box 30, "Paul Bunyan Series, 1916–1923" and Box 31, "Paul Bunyan Tales."

Milner, Harold E. *Essay and Letters, 1941–1942*. SC1243 in WHS Archives.

Northland Historical Society (WI) *Meetings on Lumber Camps, the Jesuits, and Eugene Shepard* [sound recording], 1960. Wisconsin Historical Society Archives, Tape 458A, Madison, WI. The October 9, 1960, session includes more than an hour of reminiscences and group discussion about Shepard led by local historian Isabel Ebert; very little concerns Bunyan.

Paul Bunyan Collection, Children's Literature Research Collection, Room 113, Andersen Library, 222 21st Avenue South, Minneapolis, MN 55455. Manuscripts, artwork, printed publications, and ephemera arranged into ten series in twenty-seven boxes, including papers of W. W. Charters, William Laughead and the Red River Lumber Company, James Stevens, and Charles and Dorothy Brown. The most useful portions for this study were:
Series 3: W. W. Charters Papers:
Correspondence, alphabetical, boxes 4 and 5;
Correspondence with Charles and Dorothy Brown, box 6 folders 7–9
Series 5: Red River Lumber Company: Boxes 10–12 contain printed ephemera from his Bunyan ad campaigns and other company records but very little correspondence.
Series 6: Paul Bunyan Story Manuscripts, Poetry, Plays, and Recordings: Boxes 16 and 17 contain Charles Brown's Bunyan materials missing from

his papers in Madison, both original and later typescript copies. The clean typescripts were made for Charters in the 1940s by the Browns, at his request; the original materials, which include early interview summaries and notes apparently from the WPA Wisconsin Folklore Project, were presented by Dorothy Brown later. Box 16 folder 6 contains the only surviving records from Homer Watt's and Bernice Stewart's 1914–1916 collecting activities.

Series 10: Paul Bunyan Collection Correspondence:

Other Charles E. Brown materials are in box 3, folder 12, and box 4, folder 3.

Shepard, Eugene S. *Ephemera sent by Shepard to W. H. Killen, 1896–1916*, Wisconsin Historical Society Archives collection PH7-345.

Shepard, Eugene S. *Papers, 1915–1975*. Wisconsin Historical Society Archives SC1152. A single folder of miscellaneous manuscripts that includes a handful of Shepard's letters and a broadside reprint of "The Round River Drive." Shepard's personal papers became the property of his first wife in a 1911 divorce settlement and have not been located.

Shepard, Layton, 1892– . *Interview, 1963*. SC 1004, at the Wisconsin Historical Society, Madison, WI. Much detail on his father, Eugene Shepard, including his Bunyan stories and writings.

Shephard, Esther. *Papers, 1921–1955*, Accession No. 0994-001 in the Special Collections Division, at Allen Library, University of Washington, Seattle, WA, contain a series called "Paul Bunyan correspondence, notes, research material, etc." with virtually nothing about the sources from whom she collected her stories.

State Historical Society of Wisconsin. State Historical Museum. *Curators' general correspondence files, 1908–1982, 2000–2001*. Series 972, at the Wisconsin Historical Society, Madison, WI. Contains Charles Brown's official correspondence as museum director, including scattered letters relating to Bunyan.

Stevens, James. "Interview, 1957" in *Forest History Association Lumberjack Interviews*, Minnesota Historical Society, collection P2385. Thirty-three pages.

Stevens, James. *James Stevens Papers, 1883–1966*. University of Washington Manuscript Collection No.: 2008. Allen Library, University of Washington, Seattle, WA 98195-2900. Contains a box of Bunyan short stories and various clippings, but the bulk of his Bunyan manuscripts had already been given to the Children's Literature Research Center at the University of Minnesota when this collection was acquired in 1965–1966.

Timlin, William Henry. *Autobiography, 1915*. Wisconsin Historical Society Archives, call. no. SC 245.

U.S. Office of Indian Affairs. *Letters received by the Office of Indian Affairs, 1824–81*; National Archives microfilm publications microcopy no. 234 (Washington, DC: National Archives, 1956–1959), reel 152, Chippewa Agency.

Bibliography

U.S. Works Progress Administration. Federal Writers' Project. *American Life Histories: Manuscripts from the Federal Writers' Project, 1936–1940.* Online at http://lcweb2.loc.gov/ammem/wpaintro/wpahome.html.

U.S. Works Progress Administration. Federal Writers' Project. Writers' Program. Wisconsin. *Folklore Project records, 1935–1937.* (1 archives box). Wisconsin Historical Society Archives Collection Wis Mss IZ. Incomplete correspondence and administrative records of the Wisconsin Folklore Project, 1935–1937; does not include field notes or Bunyan material (see next entry).

U.S. Works Progress Administration. Federal Writers' Project. *Records, 1936–1939: Folklore Wisconsin* (Washington, DC: Library of Congress Photoduplication Service, 1984). Microfilm 19045; 7 reels. Records of the Wisconsin Folklore Project consisting of prose summaries of field interviews and some unedited manuscript notes. Contains very few Bunyan materials (see chapter 8); some of the missing material appears to be among papers Dorothy Brown gave to the Children's Literature Research Collection, University of Minnesota, in the 1960s.

Watt, Homer A. *Paul Bunyan, The Lumberjack.* Fifty-page manuscript version of the tales, with poems by his son William W. Watt, written in 1943 for his grandchildren; in the possession of his granddaughter, Barbara Friend, Northampton, MA.

Watt, William Whyte. *The Olden Days: A Random Remembering.* Manuscript memoir by the son of Homer Watt, written ca. 1978 for his children; in the possession of his daughter, Barbara Friend, Northampton, MA.

Wisconsin Academy of Sciences, Arts and Letters. *Records, 1869–1989.* Wisconsin Historical Society Archives collection Mss 429. Unfortunately, records from the years when Bernice Stewart and Homer Watt presented their Bunyan research to WASAL conferences and published it in their *Transactions* do not survive.

II. PRINTED TEXTS OF THE TALES FROM WISCONSIN

1910a Rockwell, J. E. "Some Lumberjack Myths." *Outer's Book* (Milwaukee, WI), February 1910, 157–160.

1910b "Frozen Snakes Used as Skids: Nature Fakers Put to Shame by These Classy Stories from the Lumber Camp." *Washington Post*, February 6, 1910, "Miscellany" section, 1; a straightforward reprint of 1910a.

1910c "North Woods Myths Passing: Tales of Bunyan and Other Lumberjacks Bring Back Old Days. Gene Shepherd's [*sic*] Hodag. Famous Fake of Rhinelander Man a Product of Backwoods Cleverness—Bunyan a Character." *Wisconsin State Journal*, May 23, 1910. Reprints the tales that had appeared in the *Washington Post* and *Outer's Book*.

1916 Stewart, K. Bernice, and Homer A. Watt. "Legends of Paul Bunyan, Lumberjack." *Transactions of the Wisconsin Academy of Sciences, Arts, and Letters* (1916): 639–651. Actually published in March 1917.

Bibliography

1917a "Logging Camp Yarns." *Eau Claire Telegram*, [month missing] 31, 1917. A reprint of MacGillivray and Malloch's "Round River" poem.

1917b Shepard, Eugene S. *The Round River Drive*. Rhinelander, WI: C. C. Collins Lumber Co., no date. Dating uncertain. This is a trifold booklet plagiarizing Malloch and MacGillivray's 1914 poem, with only a few place names changed to locate it in Wisconsin. Shepard also printed this text as an undated broadside (copies in WHS Archives collection PH7-345 and William Bartlett Papers), which he was still mailing out in 1922.

1917c "Extracts from Paul Bunyan Yarns." *Eau Claire Telegram*, April 20, 1917. A reprint of Stewart and Watt's *WAASL Transactions* texts.

1919 Jenderny, Fred. "That Lumber Camp." *Stars and Stripes* (Paris, France), June 13, 1919, 4.

1921 "Paul Bunyan, Noted Pioneer in Land Clearing." *Vilas County News*, December 21, 1921. Close reprint of Stewart and Watt's *WAASL Transactions* texts.

1922a Brown, Charles E. *American Folk Lore. Paul Bunyan Tales, prepared for the use of students of the University of Wisconsin Summer Session*. Madison, WI: 1922. Reprinted 1927. Brown's first collection of the tales, eight pages.

1922b Shepard, Eugene. "Mrs. Paul Bunyan Even More Resourceful Than Her Husband." *New North*, May 11, 1922. Purports to be a letter to judge A. H. Reid of Wausau, reminiscing about Shepard's days working for Paul Bunyan at the Round River camp in 1862; the only printing of any Bunyan tales by Shepard during his lifetime, in his own words.

1923a Shaw, Fred A. "Paul Bunyan, Inventor of Logging. His Autobiography [sic]." *Langlade Clippings* (Antigo, WI), February 12, 1923, 5. Tearsheets in box 8 folder 14, Children's Literature Research Collection, University of Minnesota. Local tales that overlap only slightly with other published versions.

1923b Edick, Dave. "Paul Bunyan—Inventor of Logging." *Langlade Clippings* (Antigo, WI), May 22, 1923, 9–10. Tearsheets in box 8 folder 14, Children's Literature Research Collection, University of Minnesota. Local anecdotes that overlap only slightly with other published versions.

1923c Hopkins, Bert E. "Paul Bunyan Only True American Myth." *The Wisconsin Magazine*, 1, no. 3 (June 1923): 32–33, 57–59; reprinted in *Wisconsin State Journal*, June 10, 1923, 15. Reprints tales from Laughead, Smits, and Brown.

1924 "Paul Bunyan—Inventor of Logging." *Langlade Clippings* (Antigo, WI), March 1924 (page numbers missing). Tearsheets in box 8 folder 14, Children's Literature Research Collection, University of Minnesota. Local stories that overlap only slightly with other published versions.

1925 "Some Cold Days in Bunyan's Camp. 68 Below Zero in Onion Camp on Big Auger River in 1877." *Rice Lake Chronotype*, January 14, 1925, 1.

1927a [Brown, Charles E.] "Yarns of Paul Bunyan's Boyhood," *The Wisconsin Magazine*, March 1927: 19, 26. About twenty paragraphs of anecdotes with no attributions, very similar to 1927b. Brown's authorship established in 1948 by Dorothy Brown.

Bibliography

1927b Brown, Charles E. *American Folk Lore. Paul Bunyan Tales. Prepared for the Use of Students of the University of Wisconsin Summer Session. Second Issue.* Madison, WI: 1927. Although this 1927 printing acknowledges Shephard's 1924 and Stevens's 1925 books, it includes no tales from either one and is in fact almost identical to the 1922 printing, eight pages.

1928 Kearney, Luke Sylvester. *The Hodag, and Other Tales of the Logging Camps.* Wausau, WI: 1928. Contains Eugene Shepard's version of the Round River Drive; doesn't explicitly tell any other Bunyan tales but uses six of the motifs.

1929a Bartlett, William W. *History, Tradition and Adventure in the Chippewa Valley.* Eau Claire, WI: the author, 1929. Contains only a few of the stories he collected.

1929b Brown, Charles E. *Paul Bunyan Tales: Paul Bunyan Mythical Hero of the American Lumber Camps.* Madison, WI: 1929. A revised and expanded collection, quite different from that of 1922/1927, twelve pages.

1929c Jones, Edward Richard. *Bunyan's Progress, a Volume of Verse on Paul Bunyan Up to Date.* Madison, WI: E. R. Jones, 1929. A pamphlet of Bunyan poems; the author was a university instructor in agricultural engineering.

1929d Shepard, Eugene S., and Karretta Gunderson Shepard. *Paul Bunyan; His Camp and Wife.* Tomahawk, WI: The Osborne Press, 1929. Includes a thoughtful preface by Shepard and dozens of the stories put into verse by his widow.

1930a Brown, Charles E. *Paul Bunyan and Tony Beaver Tales. Tall Yarns of the Prince of American Lumberjacks and of His Southern Cousin Tony Beaver as Told in the Logging camps in the North and South.* 1st ed. Madison, WI: C. E. Brown, 1930.

1930b Brown, Charles E. "River Pigs and Bull Punchers." *Wisconsin Alumni Magazine*, December 1930. Reprints stories already found in Brown's pamphlets.

1930c. Jones, Edward Richard. *Paul Bunyan, Preface and Progress.* Madison, WI: the author, 1930. More fictional stories by the university instructor.

1931 McDonald, James J. "Paul Bunyan and the Blue Ox." *Wisconsin Blue Book* Madison, WI: Democrat Printing Company, 1931, 113–128. Retells several dozen of the key stories that the author considers most relevant to Wisconsin.

1933a Brown, Charles E. "Paul Bunyan's Blue Ox." *The Wisconsin Octopus*, November 1933. Reprints stories already found in Brown's pamphlets.

1933b Watt, Homer A. "Paul Bunyan Provides for his Crew." In *The Rise of Realism*, Lewis Wann, 270–273. New York: The Macmillan Co., 1933.

1934 Alvord, Thomas G. *Paul Bunyan and Resinous Rhymes of the North Woods.* New York: The Derrydale Press, 1934. Although the author claims the manuscript was more than twenty years old before it was printed, it employs some of Laughead's names.

1935 Brown, Charles E. *Paul Bunyan Natural History, Describing the Wild Animals, Birds, Reptiles, and Fish of the Big Woods about Paul Bunyan's Old Time Logging Camps. Habitat and Habits of the Flitterick, Gumberoo, Hangdown, Hidebehind, Hodag, Luferlang, Rumptifusel, Sliver Cat, Shagamaw, Goofus Bird, Hoop Snake, Whirligig Fish and Others*. Madison, WI: C. E. Brown, 1935.

1936a Watt, Homer A. "When Gran'pa Logged for Paul." In *Literature and Life*, edited by Edwin Almiron Greenlaw, William H. Elson, Christine M. Keck, Clarence Stratton, Robert C. Pooley, and Dudley H Miles, vol. 3: 422–427. Chicago: Scott, Foresman and Co., 1936. A four-volume high school literature textbook.

1936b Gleason, Edward. "Those Paul Bunyan Snow Snakes." *Capital Times* (Madison, WI), April 27, 1936. Fictional reminiscence sent in from Osseo, Wisconsin.

1937 Brown, Charles E. *Paul Bunyan, American Hercules. Wisconsin Tall Tales of the Prince of American Lumberjacks and His Logging Crews for Story Telling at the Campfire and Fireside*. Madison, WI: C. E. Brown, 1937.

1940 Raihle, Paul H. *The Valley Called Chippewa*. Cornell, WI: Chippewa Valley Courier, 1940. Contains three pages of tales mostly derived from printed sources but with some that are new; unnamed "old timers" are acknowledged as sources.

1941 Brown, Charles E. *Flapjacks from Paul Bunyan's Cook Shanty. Miscellaneous Yarns Dedicated to James J. McDonald, Dr. C. A. Deadman, Lake Shore Kearney, August Derleth, H. J. Kent*. Madison, WI: Charles E. Brown, Wisconsin Folklore Society, State Historical Museum, 1941. Published ca. July 10, 1941.

1942 Brown, Charles E. *Brimstone Bill, Famous Boss Bullwhacker of Paul Bunyan's Camps. Tall Tales of His Exploits. Babe and Benny, the Great Lakes, Hauling Snow, Cow Lucy, Goat Billy, Paul's Pigs, His Courting, Saw Mills, Babe Sick and Finis for Bill. Dedicated to H. J. Kent and Alonzo W. Pond*. Madison, WI: Charles E. Brown, Wisconsin Folklore Society, 1942. Advertised as in preparation and available soon in the *Capital Times* on August 18, 1942.

1944 Brown, Charles E. *Johnny Inkslinger. Deacon Seat Tales of Paul Bunyan's Industrious Camp Clerk at His Sawdust River Camp in Wisconsin. Dedicated to Louis A. Maier, President of the Mystic Knights of the Blue Ox*. Madison, WI: Charles E. Brown, Wisconsin Folklore Society, 1944.

1945a Brown, Charles E. *Ole Olson. Tales of the Mighty Swede Blacksmith of Paul Bunyan's Wisconsin and Other Great Logging Camps , His Smithy, Shoeing Babe the Blue Ox, the Camp Dinner-horn, Paul's Watch, Whirling Lake, Sky Pilot, the Vacation, and Other Stirring Yarns of the Pineries. Dedicated to Harry G. Dyer, Lakeshore Kearney, Jos. Lucius, Otis W. Terpening*. Madison, WI: Charles E. Brown, Wisconsin Folklore Society, 1945. Published ca. August 1945.

1945b Brown, Charles E. *Paul Bunyan Classics. Authentic Original Stories Told in the Old Time Logging Camps of the Wisconsin Pineries. Paul Bunyan Super-Lumberjack, His Camp and Logging Crew, Babe the Blue Ox, the Pyramid Forty, Pea Soup Lake, the Round River Drive, the Buckskin Harness, the Reversible Dog, the Big Mosquitos, and Other Tall Tales. Dedicated to Gladys J. Haney, W. W. Charters, "Ranger Mac" Mcneel.* Madison, WI: Charles E. Brown, Wisconsin Folklore Society, 1945. Published ca. August 1945.

1945c Brown, Charles E. *Shanty Boy, Bard of Paul Bunyan's Wisconsin and Michigan Logging Camps. Tales of the Great Singer, Storyteller, and Dancer, the Blue Hills, Paul's Farm Camp Evangelist, and Old Abe's Visit. Dedicated to Dorothy Moulding Brown, Lorraine Charlotte Alfred, Helene Stratman-Thomas.* Madison, WI: Charles E. Brown, Wisconsin Folklore Society, 1945. Published ca. August 1945.

1945d Brown, Charles E. *Bunyan Bunkhouse Yarns. Original Tall Tales told in Paul Bunyan's Logging Camps on the Big Onion, the Little Garlic, the Gimlet, the Sawdust, the Round, and Other Famous and Fabulous Streams in the Old Northwest. Paul Bunyan, Super-Lumberjack, His Logging Crew and Camps, Babe the Great Blue Ox, the Pyramid Forty, Pea Soup Lake, the Round River, the Buckskin Harness and other Tall Tales. Dedicated to the Memory of the Thousands of Old Northwest Lumberjacks Who Worked for Paul in Those Camps or Who Knew Men Who Did.* Madison, WI: Charles E. Brown, Wisconsin Folklore Society, 1945. Issued ca. November 7, 1945.

1945e Brown, Charles E. *Sourdough Sam, Paul Bunyan's Illustrious Chief Cook and Other Famous Culinary Artists of his Great Pinery Logging Camps, Old Time Tales of Kitchen Wizards, the Big Cook Shanty, the Camp Fare, the Dinner Horn, and Sam's Cook Book. Dedicated to the Memory of Eugene S. Shepard, Matt R. Stapleton, and Otis W. Terpening, Wisconsin Woodsmen.* Madison, WI: Charles E. Brown, Wisconsin Folklore Society, 1945. Published December 5, 1945.

1948 Brown, Dorothy. *What Say You of Paul?* Madison, WI: privately printed, 1948. A one hundred–page paper-covered booklet assembling anecdotes collected 1905–1946; includes stories originally printed in her husband's various booklets and found among his papers; contributors are sloppily acknowledged, and sources of individual tales are not identified.

III. EARLY PRINTED TEXTS OF THE TALES FROM OTHER STATES

1904 "Caught on the Run." *Duluth News Tribune*, August 4, 1904, 4.

1906 "Round River." *Oscoda Press*, August 10, 1906. The first printing of any complete tales, written by James MacGillivray from tales he heard in 1887 on the Au Sable River in Michigan.

1910 MacGillivray, William. "The Round River Drive." *Detroit News*, July 24, 1910. Prose, slightly edited and printed by the original author's brother.

1914a "The Round River Drive." [poem] *American Lumberman*, April 25, 1914, 33. No authorship stated. Reprinted in Will MacGillivray's *Oscoda Press*, June 5, 1914, where it was attributed to James McGillivray and Douglas Malloch; plagiarized by E. S. Shepard in Rhinelander, Wisconsin, about 1916.

1914b Harrigan, W. D. "Paul Bunyan." *American Lumberman*, June 13, 1914. A letter to the editor that contains several tales.

1914c Davis, G. M. "Paul Bunyan's Mosquitoes." *American Lumberman*, June 13, 1914. The classic story, in a letter to the editor.

1914d Davis, G. M. "In Paul Bunyan's Cook Shanty." *American Lumberman*, July 18, 1914, 44. Headed "Saginaw, Mich.," this story tells of a traveler visiting Paul's camp who is startled at the sight of his enormous oxen (not named) and flees from the camp in terror.

1914e Goodman, B. J. "Another Story of Bunyan's Oxen." *American Lumberman*, July 18, 1914, 44. Headed "Little Lake, Mich.," this story recounts the exploits of the giant cook Swede Charlie and includes the motif of beans falling through ice and swelling in the lake, among others.

1914f Laughead, William B. *Introducing Mr. Paul Bunyan of Westwood, Cal.* Minneapolis: Red River Lumber Co., 1914. The first separate publication of any of the stories, this booklet was mailed to the company's business contacts.

1916a Albright, Charles Albert [pseudonym of P. S. Lovejoy]. "Chronicle of Life and Works of Mr. Paul Bunyan." *American Lumberman*, June 17, July 8, August 12 and 26, September 30, November 11, 1916; August 11, 1917; and June 29, 1918. A fictional account of a scholar's attempt to research Bunyan's life by interviewing loggers; he is strung along in typical fashion. The series is long, funny, and includes illustrations of the stories, which are given in credible dialect. Laughead's character names are not used, and many motifs are unrecorded elsewhere.

1916b Johnston, A. M. "Lumberjack Songs While You Wait." *American Lumberman*, June 24, 1916, 27. Headed "Ludington, Mich.," this is a poem in bad French-Canadian dialect that does not repeat any widely known motifs.

1916c Laughead, William B. *Tales about Paul Bunyan. Vol. II.* Minneapolis: Red River Lumber Co., 1916. Slightly expanded from the 1914 edition.

1919a "Paul Bunion and Swede Charlie Have Awful Experience with Midsummer Thaw." *Four L Bulletin* (Portland, OR), 1, no. 7 (September 1919): 30. Paul climbs falling snowflakes in a freak Fourth of July storm.

1919b Backus, R. L. "Working on the Drive." *American Lumberman*, July 19, 1919, 63. A poem in Swedish dialect whose geographic origin is not given.

1919c Cummings, Harry L. "All Together, Boys." *The Stars and Stripes* (Paris, France), May 23, 1919, 4. A Minnesota native compares the AEF dining halls to Paul's camp and tells other tales. Mentions the blue ox but not by name, and uses familiar motifs about him.

Bibliography

1919d Turney, Ida Virginia. *Paul Bunyan Comes West.* Eugene, OR: University of Oregon Press, 1919. Date verified by University of Oregon library staff from payroll records; tales collected from Western newspapers and live informants, then strung together into a fictional narrative. A very fragile booklet reprinted in expanded form on equally fragile paper in 1928.

1920a Anderson, Al W. "Paul Runyon Bunyun Is With Us Again." *Camp and Mill News* (Seattle, WA), 2, no. 8 (July 1920): 14. A tale from Tacoma, Washington, about the digging of Puget Sound.

1920b Rourke, Constance. "Paul Bunyon." *New Republic* 23 (July 7, 1920): 176–179. Discusses logging, the body of tales; describes the collection of P. S. Lovejoy and gives some tales from it.

1920c Smits, Lee J. "The Epic Lumberjack. He Did Wonders. Let's Collect Yarns. Do You Know Any?" *Seattle Star*, November 17, 18, 19, 20, 22, 23, 24, 25, 26, 27, and 29, 1920. Tales submitted by readers. Most are from the Pacific Northwest, though a few are set in the Great Lakes.

1920d Utke, G.A. "As We Drove the Michagamme." *American Lumberman,* January 3, 1920, 64. A shanty song.

1921a Frost, Robert. "Paul's Wife." *The Century Magazine,* 103, no. 1 (November 1921): 83–89.

1921b Olsen, Charles O. "Paul Bunion Gets a Bear Hide." *Four-L Bulletin* (Portland, OR), 3, no. 5 (May 1921): 38. A shanty song.

1921c Shephard, Esther. "The Tall Tale in American Literature." *Pacific Review* 2 (1921): 402–414. After reviewing the comic tradition in American folklore and placing the Bunyan tales in this context, relates several stories collected in the Pacific Northwest without providing details about the source of each.

1922a Calland, Annice. "Excerpts from the Book of Paul Bunyan." *American Lumberman,* September 2, 1922, 79. A poem with unique motifs and none of Laughead's names.

1922b DeWitt, Harry. "The Listening Post." *Morning Oregonian* (Portland, OR), February 7–April 2, 1922. Tales contributed by readers. Most are tales from the Northwest, with no mention of Wisconsin.

1922c *Four L Bulletin* (Portland, OR). Very brief tales contributed by readers appear in the following issues: 4, no. 3 (March 1922): 27; 4, no. 4 (April 1922): 36; and 4, no. 5 (May 1922): 34–35. Three of the stories mention Wisconsin, but there is no other connection. ·

1922d Laughead, William B. *The Marvelous Exploits of Paul Bunyan : as told in the camps of the white pine lumbermen for generations, during which time the loggers have pioneered the way through the north woods from Maine to California : collected from various sources and embellished for publication.* Minneapolis: Red River Lumber Co., 1922. This is the publication that brought the tales to public notice. Thirty-six pages, including card covers.

1922e "Paul Bunyan and His Big Blue Ox." *Kansas City Star* (Kansas City, MO) August 21, 1922, 16. Laughead credited this five-column article with causing a wave of interest in the 1922 booklet and forcing them to reprint another five thousand copies; contains many of the tales from his book.

1922f Morbeck, G.C. "Paul Bunyan—An Authentic Account of His Pre-Historic Activities." *The Ames Forester* (Ames, IA), 10 (1922): 101–103. Reprints stories first published elsewhere.

1922g Shawe, Victor. "When Finn Meets Finnegan." *Saturday Evening Post,* June 3, 1922, 8–9. Opens with two paragraphs about Bunyan that convinced James Stevens there might be a market for the Bunyan tales he had heard in camps.

1922h Utke, G. A. "A New Paul Bunyan Story." *American Lumberman*, August 5, 1922, 45. Opens, "La Madera, N.M., July 31. Have just finished reading a pamphlet about Paul Bunyan, which was issued by the Red River Lumber Co., Westwood, Calif." and supplements it.

1923a Langerock, Hubert. "The Wonderful Life and Deeds of Paul Bunyon." *The Century Magazine*, 106, no. 1 (May 1923): 23–33. Nearly verbatim plagiarism of Laughcad's 1922 booklet.

1923b Malloch, Douglas. "In Which Paul Bunyan Again Demonstrates His Superiority Over the Rest of Mankind." *American Lumberman*, January 20, 1923, 79. A brief note by Malloch after receiving a letter from "W. B. L., of Minneapolis, Minn."

1923c Morbeck, G. C. "Paul Bunyan, an Authentic Account of His Pre-Historic Activities." *Ames Forester* (Ames, IA), 10 (1923). Fictional stories with no attribution.

1924a Clark, Gregory. "Paul Bunyan: Superman Hero of the Lumberjacks." *Toronto Star Weekly*, January 19, 1924. Comments on Bunyan's rising popularity in the United States and tells some tales.

1924b "Origin of Paul Bunyan Stories." *American Lumberman*, June 7, 1924, 38. A correspondent in the Pacific Northwest asks for information from readers.

1924c Shephard, Esther. *Paul Bunyan*. Seattle: The McNeil Press, 1924. The first book-length anthology, combining tales from earlier printed sources with others collected in the Pacific Northwest to form a consecutive narrative supposedly told by one Angus Campbell; reprinted, illustrated by Rockwell Kent, 1941 and 1952. First (1924) edition, 235 pages.

1925 Stevens, James. *Paul Bunyan*. New York: Alfred Knopf, 1925. Stevens's expanded and rewritten versions of the tales he had heard in western camps; no sources cited. The most popular and frequently cited anthology of the tales; reprinted with a new introduction, 1948.

1926 Wadsworth, Wallace. *Paul Bunyan and His Great Blue Ox*. New York: Doran, 1926. The first children's version; there was a separate trade issue by Doubleday and a special Doubleday issue "for Parents' Institute" the same year. The Doran issue was advertised in the *New York Times* on October 24, 1926.

1927a Bowman, James Cloyd. *The Adventures of Paul Bunyan*. New York: The Century Co., 1927. The second children's versions of the tales.

1927b "America's Only Folk-Lore Character: Paul Bunyan, Mythical Hero of the Logging Camps, and the Exploits of His Husky Axemen at Last Find a Permanent Place in Literature and College Classics." *American Weekly*, October 30, 1927, 8. Reprints many stories; quotes Fenska, Shephard, Turney, and Laughead; and describes Charles Brown's pamphlets. A Hearst newspapers Sunday supplement that reached 4,758,000 readers in 1927.

1932 Stevens, James. *The Saginaw Paul Bunyan*. New York: A. A. Knopf, 1932. More fictional stories written after a research trip to Michigan. Woodcuts by Richard Bennett.

1946 Newton, Stan. *Paul Bunyan of the Great Lakes*. Chicago: Packard & Co, 1946. Highly embellished and fanciful tales from Michigan's Upper Peninsula.

1947 Felton, Harold W. *Legends of Paul Bunyan*. New York: A. A. Knopf, 1947. The largest and, despite its substantial flaws, still the standard anthology of the tales, collected from many different publications.

IV. OTHER PRIMARY SOURCES

Local newspaper articles lacking page numbers can be found online at www .wisconsinhistory.org/wlbha.

Aldridge, Frank. "Old-timer Recounts Changes in Wisconsin's Logging Industry." *Antigo Journal*, December 21, 1923.

Alft, William. "History of Logging Era on Wolf River." *Antigo Journal*, June 8, 1932.

"An Interesting Letter on Lumberjacks and River Hogs." *Banner-Journal* (Black River Falls, WI), January 23, 1935.

Beck, Earl Clifton. *Lore of the Lumber Camps*. Ann Arbor, MI: University of Michigan Press, 1948.

Beck, Earl Clifton. *They Knew Paul Bunyan*. Ann Arbor, MI: University of Michigan Press, 1956.

Blanchard, Louie. *The Lumberjack Frontier: The Life of a Logger in the Early Days on the Chippeway* ("Told from the Recollections of Louis Blanchard by Walker D. Wyman, with the assistance of Lee Prentice"). River Falls, WI: University of Wisconsin–River Falls Press, 1976.

Brennan, James. "Life in Lumber Camps, with Circuses Recalled by Early Eden Resident." *Fond du Lac Reporter*, March 19, 1929.

Brown, Charles E. "Paul Bunyan a Wisconsin Product, Without Doubt." *Wisconsin State Journal*, October 26, 1935. Makes no attempt to prove the claim in its title, and includes many facetious comments.

Bruncken, Ernest. *North American Forest and Forestry*. New York: G. P. Putnam's, 1900.

Bullen, C. A. "C. A. Bullen Gives Interesting Sketch of his Busy Life in the Valley." *Eau Claire Telegram*, April 8, 1916.

Clarke, John C. "Timber Product, Wisconsin Valley. What Its Product in Lumber Has Been since 1833, Shown by the Output of the Mills." *Wausau Daily Record*, July 24, 1905.

Crosshaul, Cal [George Slecht]. "Paul Bunyan's Log. The Great American Epic." *The Forester* (Mercer, WI), July 31, 1931.

Cummings, Frank E. "Confessions of a Camp Cook. Frank E. Cummings Tells of Life in Woods Over Forty years Ago." *Eau Claire Leader*, March 15, 1916.

Cummings, Frank E. "The Camp Cook, Cranky at Times." *Eau Claire Telegram*, April 24, 1916.

Dana, Bob. *Role of the Lumberjack During the Pioneer Days*. 2d ed. Antigo, WI: Dana, 1975.

Defebaugh, James. *History of the Lumber Industry of North America*. Chicago: The American Lumberman, 1906–1907.

Drake, Horace. "Indians and Logging Camps on Site of Rice Lake in 1877." *Rice Lake Chronotype*, January 18, 1928.

Dyer, Harry G. "Upper Mississippi River Life." *La Crosse Tribune*, April 29, 1929.

Eke, Paul. "Early Days in Rusk County." *Ladysmith Journal*, May 3, 1923.

Fitzmaurice, John W. *The Shanty-Boy, or, Life in a Lumber Camp. Being Pictures of the Pine Woods in Descriptions, Tales, Songs and Adventures in the Lumbering Shanties of Michigan and Wisconsin*. Cheboygan, MI: Democrat Steam Print, 1889.

Frohlicher, John C. *Timber!: the Bygone Life of the Northwoods Lumberjacks*. Stockton, IL: Hill House, 1984.

Griffith, E. M. *Report of the State Forester of Wisconsin for 1909 and 1910*. Madison, WI: 1911, 30.

Hader, Elmer S. "A Gallery of American Myths." *The Century Magazine* 107, no. 6 (April 1924): 894.

Hallock, Charles. "Life Among the Loggers." *Harper's New Monthly Magazine* 20, no. 118 (March 1860): 437–455.

"Harry G. Dyer, Madison Resident, Recounts Old Raftsmen's Tales about Upper Mississippi River." *La Crosse Tribune and Leader-Press*, January 24, 1932

"He Talks of Old History." *Wausau Record*, July 24, 1906.

Henry, Charles H. "Cruising, Surveying, Logging and Log Driving and Dam Building in Pioneer Days of North Wis." *Eau Claire Leader*, March 9, 1916.

Holden, W. H. "Early Camp Life Reminiscences Told by Holden." *Eau Claire Telegram*, November 10, 1916.

Holden, W. H. "Tells of Logging Camp in the Pioneer Days." *Eau Claire Leader*, December 8, 1916.

Holley, John M. "History of the Lumber Industry; Comprehensive Paper on Western Wisconsin." *La Crosse Chronicle*, October 21, 1906.

Holley, John M. "Waterways and Lumber Interests of Western Wisconsin." *Proceedings of the State Historical Society of Wisconsin for 1906*. Madison, WI: State Historical Society of Wisconsin, 1907, 208–215.

Holt, William Arthur. *A Wisconsin Lumberman Looks Backward*. Oconto, WI: 1948.

"Life Closes for Gene Shepard." *New North*, March 29, 1923. Obituary.

"The Log Jam on the Chippewa." *Harper's Weekly* 13 (June 5, 1869): 360 (full-page illustration) and 365 (one-paragraph notice).

Longyear, John Munro. *Landlooker in the Upper Peninsula of Michigan: from the Reminiscences of John Munro Longyear*. Marquette, MI: Marquette County Historical Society of Michigan, 1960.

"'Looking Pine' in Wisconsin." *The Wisconsin Lumberman*, 2, no. 4 (July1874): 352–354.

Lovejoy, Parrish Storrs. "Legend Unending, Beginnings Unknown: P. S. Lovejoy on Paul Bunyan." *Forest History* 11 (January 1968): 37–38.

Lueth, Henry. "Radio Entertains Woodsmen Now: Used to Be Wolves." *La Crosse Tribune and Leader-Press*, February 3, 1924.

"Lumbering in Chippewa Valley." *Eau Claire Telegram*, February 2, 1916.

Maunder, Elwood. "An Interview with James Stevens. The Making of a Folklorist." *Forest History* 7 no. 4 (Winter 1964): 2–19.

McDonald, Marian Jenne. "The Legend of Paul Bunyan." B.A. thesis, University of Wisconsin, 1928.

Milwaukee Public Museum. *Annual Report of the Board of Trustees of the Public Museum of the City of Milwaukee*. 1896–1906.

Nelligan, John E. "The Life of a Lumberman by John E. Nelligan, as told to Charles M. Sheridan." *The Wisconsin Magazine of History* 13, no. 1 (September 1929): 3–65; Part 2, 13, no. 2 (December 1929): 131–185; Part 3, 13, no. 3 (March 1930): 241–304. Nelligan's editor included this note: "Apparently Nelligan, despite his diversified experience in the woods of New Brunswick, Maine, Pennsylvania, Michigan, and Wisconsin, had hardly so much as heard of the redoubtable Paul or of his blue ox, Babe. Why this was so we can only surmise. Perhaps it was because he employed so largely foreign-born—especially Irish—lumberjacks instead of natives. At all events he could not remember anything worth while and at the good last [his ghostwriter] Sheridan was forced to take a few items out of a book; for Bunyan stories belonged in the chapter on camp recreation." The Bunyan tales that Sheridan put into Nelligan's mouth came from Laughead and Stevens; they are located in volume 13, no. 2, (December 1929): 179–180.

Page, Martin. "The Days in the 50s—Martin Page." *Eau Claire Leader*, February 23, 1917.

Pederson, Thomas. "Some Recollections of Thomas Pederson." *Wisconsin Magazine of History* 21, no. 2 (December 1937): 175–190.

Bibliography

"Radio Entertains Woodsmen Now: Used to Be Wolves." *La Crosse Tribune and Leader-Press*, February 3, 1924.

Robins, J. D. "Paul Bunyan." *The Canadian Forum* 6, no. 61 (October 1925): 146–150.

Roos, C. A. "The Trail of the Lonesome Pine: Reminiscences of the Days of the Lumberman on the St. Croix." *Balsam Lake Ledger* (WI), November 23, 1916.

Rosholt, Malcolm Leviatt. "Paul Bunyan and the Round River Drive: A Communication." *Wisconsin Magazine of History* 65 no. 1 (Autumn 1981): 36–38. On Eugene Shepard's plagiarism of the "Round River Drive."

Roth, Filibert. *On the Forestry Conditions of Northern Wisconsin.* Wisconsin Geological and Natural History Survey. Bulletin no. 1, Economic Series no. 1. Madison, WI: The State of Wisconsin, 1898

Sargent, Charles S. *Report on the Forests of North America Exclusive of Mexico.* 47th Cong., 2d sess., Misc. Doc. 42, part 9.

Shepard, Eugene. "Reminiscences of..." *New North*, December 12, 1912.

[Slecht, George]. *Cal Crosshaul Interpreting the Oral Literature of the Lake States Lumberjack.* Hudson, WI: Northern Forest Baking Bureau, [1939?].

Smith, Harlan. "Recent Work of the Wisconsin Archeological Society." *Science, A Weekly Journal Devoted to the Advancement of Science* (July–December 1905): 152–155.

Snilloc, Tap [Matt Stapleton]. "The Tale of the Lumberjack." *Stevens Point Daily Journal*, June 7 and 14, 1930.

Springer, John S. *Forest Life and Forest Trees: Comprising Winter Camp-Life among the Loggers, and Wild-wood Adventure. Descriptions of Lumbering Operations on the Various Rivers of Maine and New Brunswick.* (New York: Harper Brothers, 1851).

Stephenson, Isaac. *Recollections of a Long Life, 1829–1915.* (Chicago: privately printed, 1915).

Stevens, James. "Iron Man of the Saginaw." *American Mercury* 21 (December 1930): 484–492.

Stevens, James. "Mythical Hero of Loggers. Logger Deserts Ax for Pen." *Los Angeles Times,* June 28, 1925, 26.

Tabor, Edward O., and Stith Thompson. "Paul Bunyan in 1910." *The Journal of American Folklore* 59, no. 232 (April–June 1946): 134–135.

U.S. Bureau of the Census. *Report on Manufacturing Industries in the United States at the Eleventh Census: 1890. Part III: Selected Industries.* Washington, DC: GPO, 1895.

U.S. Congress. Senate. Committee on Indian Affairs. *Condition of Indian Affairs in Wisconsin: Hearings before the Committee on Indian Affairs.* 61st Cong., 2d sess., 1910.

Van Doren, Carl. "Paul Bunyan Goes West," *A Roving Critic.* New York: Alfred A. Knopf, 1923, 105–107. A note on Bunyan's growing popularity.

Vinette, Bruno. "Early Lumbering on the Chippewa." *Wisconsin Magazine of History* 9 no. 4 (July 1926): 442–447.

Warren, George Henry. *The Pioneer Woodsman as He Is Related to Lumbering in the Northwest.* Minneapolis: Press of Hahn & Harmon Company, 1914.

"Where Wisconsin Lumber Goes." *The Wisconsin Lumberman,* 3, no. 3 (December 1874): 217–223.

"The Wisconsin Loggers." *Harper's Weekly* 29 (March 28, 1885): 196 (suite of illustrations) and 203 (three short paragraphs).

Wisconsin Bureau of Labor and Industrial Statistics. *Biennial Report.* Madison, WI: 1885.

Wisconsin Legislature, Committee on White Slave Traffic and Kindred Subjects. *Report and Recommendations of the Wisconsin Legislative Committee to Investigate the White Slave Traffic and Kindred Subjects.* Madison, WI: 1914.

Yohn, Madge. "All Around the Town." *Capital Times* (Madison, WI), December 30, 1942.

V. SECONDARY SOURCES

Ames, Carleton C. "Paul Bunyan—Myth or Hoax." *Minnesota History* 21, no.1 (1940): 55–58.

Barton Albert O. "Wisconsin's Charles Brown." *Wisconsin Archeologist* 25, no. 2 (June 1944): 45–54.

Baughman, Ernest Warren. *Type and Motif-index of the Folktales of England and North America.* The Hague: Mouton & Co., 1966. Indiana University. Folklore series, no. 20.

Beck, Horace P. *The Folklore of Maine.* Philadelphia: J.P. Lippincott, 1957.

Charters, W. W. "Paul Bunyan in 1910." *Journal of American Folklore* 57, no. 225 (July 1944): 188–189.

Cornell, Richard A. "Knights of the Spike-soled Shoe: Lumbering on the Chippewa." *Wisconsin Magazine of History* 89, no. 4 (Summer 2006): 38–47.

Cronon, Edmund David, and John W. Jenkins. *The University of Wisconsin: A History, Volume 3.* Madison, WI: University of Wisconsin Press, 1994.

Dorson, Richard M. *American Folklore & the Historian.* Chicago: University of Chicago Press, 1971.

Dorson, Richard M. *Bloodstoppers and Bearwalkers.* Cambridge, MA: Harvard University Press, 1952.

Dorson, Richard M. *Jonathan Draws the Long Bow.* Cambridge, MA: Harvard University Press, 1946.

Dorson, Richard M. "Paul Bunyan in the News, 1939–1941." *Western Folklore* 15, no. 1 (January 1956): 26–39; 15, no. 3 (July 1956): 179–193; 15, no. 4 (October 1956): 247–261.

Dorson, Richard M. "Review of *Legends of Paul Bunyan* by Harold W. Felton." *Journal of American Folklore* 64, no. 252 (April–June 1951): 233–235.

Dorson, Richard M. "Review of, *Wisconsin Is My Doorstep* by Robert E. Gard (New York: Longmans, Green and Co., 1948. Pp. xvi+ 194. $3.50.)." *Journal of American Folklore* 62, no. 244 (April–June 1949): 201.

Fishwick, Marshall W. "Sons of Paul: Folklore or Fakelore?" *Western Folklore* 18, no. 4 (October 1959): 277–286.

Fowke, Edith. "In Defense of Paul Bunyan." *New York Folklore* 5 (Summer 1979): 43–51.

Fries, Robert F. *Empire in Pine: The Story of Lumbering in Wisconsin, 1830–1900*. Madison: State Historical Society of Wisconsin, 1951.

Gartenberg, Max. "Paul Bunyan and Little John." *Journal of American Folklore* LXII (October–December 1949): 416–422.

Gartenberg, Max. "W. B. Laughead's Great Advertisement." *Journal of American Folklore* 63 (October–December 1950): 444–449.

Godfrey, Anthony. *A Forestry History of Ten Wisconsin Indian Reservations under the Great Lakes Agency, Precontact to the Present*. Salt Lake City, UT: U.S. West Research Inc., 1996. "Prepared for the U.S. Department of the Interior, Bureau of Indian Affairs, Branch of Forestry, Minneapolis Area Office."

Halpert, Herbert. "A Note on Haney's Bibliography of Paul Bunyan." *The Journal of American Folklore* 56, no. 219, Elsie Clews Parsons Memorial Number (January–March, 1943): 57–59.

Haney, Gladys J. "Paul Bunyan Twenty-Five Years After." *The Journal of American Folklore* 55, no. 217 (July–September, 1942): 155–168.

Hanft, Robert M. *Red River: Paul Bunyan's Own Lumber Company and Its Railroads*. Chico, CA: Center for Business and Economic Research, California State University, 1980.

Harty, John Patrick. "Legendary Landscapes: A Cultural Geography of the Paul Bunyan and Blue Ox Phenomena of the Northwoods." PhD diss., Department of Geography, Kansas State University, 2007. Online at http://krex .ksu.edu/dspace/bitstream/2097/413/1/JohnPatrickHarty2007.pdf.

Hennigar, Mary Jane, Daniel Hoffman, and Ellen J. Stekert. "The First Paul Bunyan Story in Print." *Journal of Forest History* 30, no. 4 (1986): 175–181.

Hoffman, Daniel G. *Paul Bunyan, Last of the Frontier Demigods*. Philadelphia: University of Pennsylvania Press for Temple University Publications, 1952. The best and most thorough historical analysis of the later publications and their place in American culture.

Holmes, Fred L. *Badger Saints and Sinners*. Milwaukee, WI: E. M. Hale and Company, 1939.

Hutchinson, W. H. "The Caesarean Delivery of Paul Bunyan." *Western Folklore* 22, no. 1 (January, 1963): 1–15.

Kates, James. *Planning a Wilderness: The Great Lakes Cutover Region*. Minneapolis: University of Minnesota Press, 2001.

Kortenhof, Kurt D. *Long Live the Hodag: The Life and Legacy of Eugene Simeon Shepard, 1854–1923*. 2d ed. Savage, MN: Hodag Press, 2006.

Bibliography

Larson, Agnes. *The White Pine Industry in Minnesota: A History.* Minneapolis: University of Minnesota Press, 2007.

Laughead, William B., and W. H. Hutchinson. "The Birth of Paul Bunyan." *Forest History* 16, no. 3 (1972): 44–49.

Leary, James P., ed. *Wisconsin Folklore.* Madison: University of Wisconsin Press, 1998. Reprints Stewart and Watt, with a brief headnote on the Bunyan tales in Wisconsin.

Leopold, Aldo. "Obituary: P. S. Lovejoy." *The Journal of Wildlife Management* 7, no. 1 (January 1943): 125–128.

Loduha, Bonnie C. *A Bibliography of Wisconsin Forest History.* Wausau: Forest History Association of Wisconsin, [1980?].

Loehr, Rodney C. "Some More Light on Paul Bunyan." *Journal of American Folklore* 64 (October–December 1951): 405–407.

Loomis, C. Grant. "A Tall Tale Miscellany, 1830–1866." *Western Folklore* 6, no. 1 (January 1947): 28–41.

Myer, Linda. "Lumberjills." *Wisconsin Trails* 20, no. 4 (Winter 1979): 31–33. Includes quotes from and photographs of women working as camp cooks, after 1900.

O'Rourke, Michael. "Paul Bunyan Lives!" *Capitalism, Nature, Socialism* 14, no. 2 (June 2003).

Peterson, Dale Arthur. "Lumbering on the Chippewa: The Eau Claire Area, 1845–1885." PhD thesis, University of Minnesota, 1970.

Ripp-Shucha, Bonnie. "'This Naughty, Naughty City': Prostitution in Eau Claire from the Frontier to the Progressive Era." *Wisconsin Magazine of History* 81, no. 1 (Autumn 1997): 30–54.

Rogers, D. Laurence. *Paul Bunyan: How a Terrible Timber Feller Became a Legend.* Bay City, MI: Historical Press, 1993.

Rohe, Randall. "The Evolution of the Great Lakes Logging Camp 1830–1930." *Journal of Forest History* 30 (January 1986): 17–28.

Rohe, Randall. "The Material Culture of an 1870s' Logging Camp." *Material Culture* 28, no. 1 (1996): 1–68.

Rosholt, Malcolm Leviatt. *Lumbermen on the Chippewa.* Rosholt, WI: Rosholt House, 1982.

Rosholt, Malcolm Leviatt. *The Wisconsin Logging Book, 1839–1939.* Rosholt, WI: Rosholt House, 1980.

Schmaltz, Norman J. "P. S. Lovejoy: Michigan's Cantankerous Conservationist." *Journal of Forest History* 19, no. 2 (1975): 72–81.

Schmaltz, Norman John. "Cutover Land Crusade: The Michigan Forest Conservation Movement, 1899–1931." PhD thesis, University of Michigan, 1972.

Schmidt, Diane. "When Women Came to the Woods." In *Proceedings of the Twelfth Annual Meeting of the Forest History Association of Wisconsin.* Eau Claire, WI: Chippewa Valley Museum, September 11–12, 1987, 20–21.

Starr, Mary Agnes. *Pea Soup and Johnny Cake*. Madison, WI: Red Mountain Publishing House, 1981.

Stitt, J. Michael, and Robert K. Dodge. *A Tale Type and Motif Index of Early U.S. Almanacs*. New York: Greenwood Press, 1991.

Taradash, Daniel. *The Real Paul Bunyan*. Fifty-six-minute video produced in 2006 (?); available through http://therealpaulbunyan.com/. Interviews with tour guides and resort owners in seven states, especially Minnesota, who reveal how Bunyan became an icon of northwoods tourism.

Walls, Robert Eric. "The Making of the American Logger: Traditional Culture and Public Imagery in the Realm of the Bunyanesque." PhD diss., Indiana University, 1997.

Wisconsin Archeologist 25, no. 2 (June 1944). Entire issue consists of a tribute to Charles E. Brown on his retirement from state service.

Wood, Richard G. *A History of Lumbering in Maine, 1820–1861*. (Orono, ME: University of Maine Press, 1935.

Wrone, David. "The Economic Impact of 1837 and 1842 Chippewa Treaties." *American Indian Quarterly* 17, no. 3 (Summer 1993): 329–340.

VI. BIBLIOGRAPHICAL GHOSTS

Although cited in various sources, the following articles could not in fact be located:

1893 "Munchausen in the Pineries." *Eau Claire Free Press*, March 6, 1893. This article is mentioned twice in Brown's and Charters's correspondence. Brown believed that he had originally received the citation from Ida Turney but could never locate the article in the newspaper's files. I could not find it in the *Eau Claire Daily Leader*, the *Evening Free Press*, the *Sunday Morning Forum*, or the *Weekly Free Press*. There was also a *Daily Free Press*, but no copies survive in the Wisconsin Historical Society or the Eau Claire Public Library.

1923 "Paul Bunyan, New Light." *Park Falls Herald*, October 6, 1923. No issue was published on this date; nothing was found in the entire month of October.

1929 "The Indian Paul Bunyan." *Antigo* _____, June 26, 1929. This was mentioned in letters by Charles Brown and W. W. Charters but not found in the Antigo *Daily Journal* or the *Weekly News Item*.

NOTES

CHAPTER 1

1. Richard Dorson, "Paul Bunyan in the News, 1939–1941. Part III," *Western Folklore* 15, no. 4 (October 1956): 260; "Review of, *Paul Bunyan of the Great Lakes* by Stan Newton," *Western Folklore* 6, no. 4 (October 1947): 398.

2. Daniel G. Hoffman, *Paul Bunyan, Last of the Frontier Demigods* (Philadelphia: University of Pennsylvania Press, 1952 and 1983); Robert Eric Walls, "The Making of the American Logger: Traditional Culture and Public Imagery in the Realm of the Bunyanesque" (PhD diss., Indiana University, 1997); John Patrick Harty, "Legendary Landscapes: A Cultural Geography of the Paul Bunyan and Blue Ox Phenomena of the Northwoods" (PhD diss., Kansas State University, 2007).

3. Richard Dorson, "Review of *Legends of Paul Bunyan* by Harold W. Felton," *Journal of American Folklore* 64, no. 252 (April–June 1951): 235.

4. A third large group of early Bunyan tales, written 1916–1918 by Michigan forester P. S. Lovejoy, has completely escaped scholars: Charles Albert Albright [pseudo.], "Chronicle of Life and Works of Mr. Paul Bunyan," *American Lumberman*, June 17, July 8, August 12 and 26, September 30, and November 11, 1916; August 11, 1917; and June 29, 1918. I am grateful to James Milostan of the Kohler Art Center for leading me to this source.

CHAPTER 2

1. David Wrone, "The Economic Impact of 1837 and 1842 Chippewa Treaties," *American Indian Quarterly* 17, no. 3 (Summer 1993): 332; see also Charles S. Sargent, *Report on the Forests of North America Exclusive of Mexico*, 47th Cong., 2d sess.; Misc. doc. 42, part 9 (Washington, DC: U.S. Census Office, 1884), 554.

2. Horace Drake, "Indians and Logging Camps on Site of Rice Lake in 1877," *Rice Lake Chronotype*, January 18, 1928 [newspaper citations that omit page numbers are taken from scrapbooks at the Wisconsin Historical Society called *Wisconsin Local History & Biography Articles*, online at www.wisconsinhistory.org/wlhba].

3. Excellent accounts of a timber cruiser's work are found in "'Looking Pine' in Wisconsin," *Wisconsin Lumberman* 2, no. 4 (July1874): 352–354; Charles H. Henry, "Cruising, surveying, logging and log driving and dam building in pioneer days of north Wis," *Eau Claire Leader*, March 9, 1916; and George

Henry Warren, *The Pioneer Woodsman as He is Related to Lumbering in the Northwest* (Minneapolis: Press of Hahn & Harmon Co., 1914).

4. Horace Drake, "Indians and Logging Camps on Site of Rice Lake in 1877," *Rice Lake Chronotype*, January 18, 1928.

5. "Where Wisconsin Lumber Goes," *The Wisconsin Lumberman* 3, no. 3 (December 1874): 217–223. For a contemporary summary of logging, see Ernest Bruncken, *North American Forest and Forestry* (New York: G. P. Putnam's, 1900), 81–88. A lively account of the process, told by a practitioner, is the second installment of John Nelligan's "The Life of a Lumberman…," *Wisconsin Magazine of History* 13, no. 2 (December 1929): 131–185.

6. Otis Terpening to Charles Brown, March 1, 1931, in the Charles Brown Papers, Wisconsin Historical Society Mss. HB, box 5.

7. Randall Rohe, "The Evolution of the Great Lakes Logging Camp, 1830–1930," *Journal of Forest History* 30 (January 1986): 20.

8. Robert F. Fries, *Empire in Pine: the Story of Lumbering in Wisconsin*, 1830–1900 (Madison: State Historical Society of Wisconsin, 1951), 28–34, 88–91.

9. U.S. Census. *Report on Manufacturing Industries in the United States at the Eleventh Census: 1890. Part III: Selected Industries* (Washington, DC: GPO, 1895), 615–617.

10. James Defebaugh, *History of the Lumber Industry of North American* (Chicago: The American Lumberman, 1906–1907), 507–510; Fries, *Empire in Pine*, 204, 206.

11. Fries, *Empire in Pine*, 18–22; Wisconsin Bureau of Labor and Industrial Statistics, *Biennial Report* (Madison, WI: 1885), 216; J. M. Holley, "History of the Lumber Industry; Comprehensive Paper on Western Wisconsin," *La Crosse Chronicle*, October 21, 1906.

12. Richard R. Fenska, "Lumbering Notes [1910–1911]," University of Wisconsin Archives, Series 9/24/9, unpaginated, but pages [97–98].

13. Ibid., [99]; Charles Henry, "Cruising, surveying, logging and log driving and dam building in pioneer days of north Wis," Eau Claire Leader, March 9, 1916; E. M. Griffith, *Report of the State Forester of Wisconsin for 1909 and 1910* (Madison, WI: 1911), 5.

14. Griffith, *Report of the State Forester*, 39; Anthony Godfrey, *A Forestry History of Ten Wisconsin Indian Reservations under the Great Lakes Agency, Precontact to the Present* (Salt Lake City, UT: U.S. West Research Inc., 1996), 131–132; Paul Eke, "Early Days in Rusk County," *Ladysmith Journal*, May 3, 1923.

15. C. Grant Loomis, "A Tall Tale Miscellany, 1830–1866," *Western Folklore* 6, no. 1 (January 1947): 28–41.

16. Esther Shephard to Mellis Hartshorn, March 7, 1934, Shephard Papers, University of Washington, box 2, folder 20.

17. Richard M. Dorson, *Jonathan Draws the Long Bow* (Cambridge, MA: Harvard University Press, 1946); Horace P. Beck, *The Folklore of Maine* (Philadelphia: J. P. Lippincott, 1957), 241.

18. James Stevens, *Paul Bunyan* (New York: Alfred Knopf, 1925), 1; Edith Fowke, "In Defense of Paul Bunyan," *New York Folklore* 5 (Summer 1979): 43–51.

19. Max Gartenberg, "Paul Bunyan and Little John," *Journal of American Folklore*, LXII (October–December, 1949): 416–422; Marius Barbeau to W. W. Charters, December 5, 1941, box 4 folder 2, W. W. Charters Papers, Children's Literature Research Collection, University of Minnesota.

20. D. Laurence Rogers, *Paul Bunyan: How a Terrible Timber Feller Became a Legend* (Bay City, MI: Historical Press, 1993).

21. Shephard to Mellis Hartshorn, March 7, 1935, Shephard Papers, University of Washington, box 2, folder 20.

22. Laidlaw to Brown, March 4, 1924, in the W. W. Charters Papers, Children's Literature Research Collection, University of Minnesota.

23. Rogers, *Paul Bunyan: How a Terrible Timber Feller*, 89–119; "When Paul Bunyan Crashed the Headlines," *Milwaukee Journal*, February 10, 1948, 14; James Stevens, "Iron Man of the Saginaw," *American Mercury* 21 (December 1930): 484–492.

24. Charles E. Brown to Albert H. Griffith, February 5, 1943, in Wisconsin Historical Society. State Historical Museum. *Curators' General Correspondence Files, 1908–1982, 2000–2001*, Series 972, at the Wisconsin Historical Society Archives, box 2.

25. Elwood R. Maunder, "The Making of a Folklorist: An Interview with James Stevens," *Forest History*, 4, no. 4 (Winter 1964): 16; Stars and Stripes, April–May 1919.

CHAPTER 3

1. Isaac Stephenson, *Recollections of a Long Life, 1829–1915* (Chicago: privately printed, 1915), 77–78; Richard G. Wood, *A History of Lumbering in Maine*, 1820–1861 (Orono: University of Maine Press, 1935), 231–232.

2. Martin Page, "The Days in the 50s—Martin Page," *Eau Claire Leader*, February 23, 1917; William Alft, "History of Logging Era on Wolf River," *Antigo Journal*, June 8, 1932; James Johnston, *Papers, ca. 1920, 1929*, University of Wisconsin–River Falls Area Research Center, Mss. River Falls SC 307: 60–61, 72–73.

3. William Timlin, *Autobiography, 1915*, Wisconsin Historical Society Archives SC 245: 35.

4. U.S. Census, 1880, Wisconsin, exported from Ancestry.com; 1880 census totals available through the University of Virginia Geospatial and Statistical Data Center; Wisconsin. Bureau of Labor and Industrial Statistics, *Biennial Report* (Madison, WI: 1885), 38.

5. Matthias Martin, special agent, to James W. Denver, Commissioner of Indian Affairs, February 12, 1859, United States Office of Indian Affairs,

Letters received by the Office of Indian Affairs, 1824–81; National Archives microfilm publications microcopy no. 234 (Washington, DC: National Archives, 1956–59), reel 152, frames 126–129; "Ira Isham Tells of Indian Feast," *Rice Lake Chronotype*, December 24 1924; Horace Drake, "Indians and Logging Camps on Site of Rice Lake in 1877," *Rice Lake Chronotype*, January 18, 1928; Edward Dupuis, *Oral History Interview* (1953), Wisconsin Historical Society Archives, SC2916; Paul Kirkendall, *Reminiscences, undated*, University of Wisconsin–River Falls Area Research Center, Mss. River Falls SC 119: 12; Letter, January 8, 2008, from Timm Severud, Lac Court Oreilles Tribal Preservation Office; U.S. Census, 1880, Wisconsin, exported from Ancestry.com.

6. Stephen J. Herzberg, "The Menominee Indians: From Treaty to Termination," *Wisconsin Magazine of History* 60, no. 4 (summer, 1977): 277–289; *Condition of Indian Affairs in Wisconsin: Hearings before the Committee on Indian Affairs, United States Senate, on Senate resolution no. 263*, 61st Cong., 2d sess. (Washington, DC: 1910), 997–998.

7. Godfrey, *A Forestry History*, 33–35, 44.

8. U.S. census data tabulated in University of Virginia Geospatial and Statistics Data Center; during some census years, only "Negro males" were counted for this analysis; Harry G. Dyer, "Upper Mississippi River Life," *La Crosse Tribune*, April 29, 1929.

9. "Harry G. Dyer, Madison Resident, Recounts Old Raftsmen's Tales about Upper Mississippi River," *La Crosse Tribune and Leader-Press*, January 24, 1932.

10. William Alft, "History of Logging Era on Wolf River," *Antigo Journal*, June 18, 1932.

11. Frank E. Cummings, "Confessions of a Camp Cook. Frank E. Cummings Tells of Life in Woods Over Forty years Ago," *Eau Claire Leader*, March 15, 1916; Linda Myer, "Lumberjills," *Wisconsin Trails* 20, no. 4 (Winter 1979): 31–33.

12. John E. Nelligan, "The Life of a Lumberman by John E. Nelligan, as told to Charles M. Sheridan," Part II, *Wisconsin Magazine of History* 13, no. 2 (December 1929): 182–183; Diane Schmidt, "When Women Came to the Woods," in *Proceedings of the Twelfth Annual Meeting of the Forest History Association of Wisconsin* (Eau Claire, WI: Chippewa Valley Museum, September 11–12, 1987), 20–21.

13. John Fitzmaurice, *The Shanty Boy, or Life in a Lumber Camp…*(Cheboygan, MI: Democrat Steam Print, 1889), 113; Charles E. Brown, *Ole Olson. Tales of the Mighty Swede Blacksmith of Paul Bunyan's Wisconsin and Other Great Logging Camps…*(Madison: Charles E. Brown, Wisconsin Folklore Society, 1945), 3.

14. Lucius to Charles Brown, March 30, 1941, in the Charles E. Brown Papers, Wisconsin Historical Society, box 5, folder 4; Lucius gave his age

in a September 23, 1958, interview, SC 703 at the Wisconsin Historical Society.

15. "Radio Entertains Woodsmen Now: Used to Be Wolves," *La Crosse Tribune and Leader-Press*, February 3, 1924.

16. Thomas Pederson, "Some Recollections of Thomas Pederson," *Wisconsin Magazine of History* 21, no. 2 (December 1937): 186; Fitzmaurice, *The Shanty Boy*, 104.

17. Fitzmaurice, *The Shanty Boy*, 39, 116.

18. Richard A. Cornell, "Knights of the Spike-soled Shoe: Lumbering on the Chippewa," *Wisconsin Magazine of History* 89, no. 4 (summer 2006): 38–47; Fries, *Empire in Pine*, 219–220; "The Tale of the Lumberjack," *Stevens Point Daily Journal*, June 14, 1930.

19. F. E. Cummings, "The Camp Cook, Cranky at Times," *Eau Claire Telegram*, April 24, 1916.

20. Terpening to Charles Brown, June 21, 1931, in the Charles Brown Papers, Wisconsin Mss HB at the Wisconsin Historical Society, box 5.

21. Quoted in Walls, "The Making of the American Logger," 137, 387; Otis Terpening to Charles Brown, October 23, 1931, in the Charles E. Brown Papers, box 5; Malcolm Leviatt Rosholt, *Lumbermen on the Chippewa* (Rosholt, WI: Rosholt House, 1982), 195.

22. U.S. Works Progress Administration, Federal Writers' Project, "W. G. Leonard," *American Life Histories: Manuscripts from the Federal Writers' Project, 1936–1940*, online in the Library of Congress American Memory collection at http://lcweb2.loc.gov/ammem/wpaintro/wpahome.html.

23. Fries, *Empire in Pine*, 207.

24. William Arthur Holt, *A Wisconsin Lumberman Looks Backward* (Oconto, WI: 1948), 36, 44.

25. U.S. Works Progress Administration, "W. G. Leonard."

26. Charles Brown Papers, box 5.

27. Terpening to Brown, February 11, 1931, in the Charles Brown Papers at the Wisconsin Historical Society, Box 5.

28. Edith Dodd Culver, "610 Ellis and the Hospital Children," *Wisconsin Magazine of History* 60, no. 2 (Winter, 1976–1977): 117.

29. Undated recollection in the Charles Brown Papers at the Wisconsin Historical Society, box 5.

30. James Brennan, "Life in lumber camps, with circuses recalled by early Eden resident," *Fond du Lac Reporter*, March 19, 1929.

31. "Marinette's Foul Dens," *Chicago Tribune*, November 1, 1887, 1.

32. "The Truth about Our Northern Dives," *Wisconsin State Journal*, February 10, 1888, 4.

33. Louie Blanchard, *The Lumberjack Frontier: The Life of a Logger in the Early Days on the Chippeway* (River Falls: University of Wisconsin–River Falls Press, 1976), 77–78; see also Bonnie Ripp-Shucha, "'This Naughty, Naughty

City': Prostitution in Eau Claire from the Frontier to the Progressive Era," *Wisconsin Magazine of History* 81, no. 1 (Autumn, 1997): 30–54.

34. Wisconsin Legislature, Committee on White Slave Traffic and Kindred Subjects, *Report and Recommendations of the Wisconsin Legislative Committee to Investigate the White Slave Traffic and Kindred Subjects* (Madison, WI: 1914), 38; U.S. Works Progress Administration, "W. G. Leonard."
35. Richard Dorson, *Bloodstoppers and Bearwalkers* (Cambridge: Harvard University Press, 1952), 186–187.
36. Cummings, "The Camp Cook."
37. Fitzmaurice, *The Shanty Boy*, 233.
38. Cummings, "The Camp Cook."
39. See Walls, "The Making of the American Logger," chapter 5, for a discussion of this aspect of logging culture.
40. Charles H. Henry, "Cruising, surveying, logging and log driving and dam building in pioneer days of north Wis.," *Eau Claire Leader*, March 9, 1916. His image of three crews—one coming, one working, and one going—was also found in a popular Bunyan story at the time.
41. Fries, *Empire in Pine*, 215–220; Walls, "The Making of the American Logger," chapter 5.

CHAPTER 4

1. Dorson, *Bloodstoppers and Bearwalkers*, 7.
2. Dorson, *Jonathan Draws the Long Bow*; Ernest Warren Baughman, *Type and Motif-index of the Folktales of England and North America* (The Hague: Mouton & Co., 1966), Indiana University Folklore series, no. 20; J. Michael Stitt and Robert K. Dodge, *A Tale Type and Motif Index of Early U.S. Almanacs* (New York: Greenwood Press, 1991).
3. John S. Springer, *Forest Life and Forest Trees: Comprising Winter Camp-Life among the Loggers, and Wild-wood Adventure* (New York: Harper Brothers, 1851).
4. William W. Bartlett, *History, Tradition and Adventure in the Chippewa Valley* (Eau Claire, WI: the author, 1929), 233.
5. John E. Nelligan, "The Life of a Lumberman by John E. Nelligan, as told to Charles M. Sheridan," *Wisconsin Magazine of History* 13, no. 1 (September 1929): 8; Warren, George Henry, *The Pioneer Woodsman as He Is Related to Lumbering in the Northwest* (Minneapolis: Press of Hahn & Harmon Company, 1914).
6. Sterling North to Charles Brown, August 22, 1940, in the W. W. Charters Papers, Children's Literature Research Collection, the University of Minnesota.
7. Blanchard, *The Lumberjack Frontier*; U.S. Works Progress Administration. Federal Writers' Project. *Records, 1936–1939: Folklore Wisconsin*, reel 6,

frames 670–675; Mary Agnes Starr, *Pea Soup and Johnny Cake* (Madison, WI: Red Mountain Publishing House, 1981), 35.

8. Richard M. Dorson, "The Shaping of Folklore Traditions in the United States," *Folklore* 78, no. 3. (Autumn, 1967): 179; Richard M. Dorson, "Review of Legends of Paul Bunyan by Harold W. Felton," *Journal of American Folklore* 64, no. 252 (April–June 1951): 234.

9. Maunder, "Making of a Folklorist," 22; Marshall W. Fishwick, "Sons of Paul: Folklore or Fakelore?" *Western Folklore* 18, no. 4 (October 1959): 278–279.

10. Constance Mayfield Rourke, "Paul Bunyon [*sic*]," *New Republic*, July 7, 1920, 177; Charles Albright [P. S. Lovejoy], "Chronicle of Life and Works of Mr. Paul Bunyan," *American Lumberman*, June 17, July 8, August 12 and 26, September 30, November 11, 1916; August 11, 1917; and June 29, 1918.

11. P. S. Lovejoy to W. W. Charters, April 5, 1941, in the W. W. Charters Paper's, Children's Literature Research Collection, University of Minnesota.

12. W. H. Hutchinson, "The Birth of Paul Bunyan," *Forest History* 16, no. 3 (1972): 48–49.

13. Rourke, "Paul Bunyon [*sic*]," 177.

14. H. J. Kent to Charles Brown, November 9, 1938, in the W. W. Charters Papers, Children's Literature Research Collection, University of Minnesota.

15. William Bartlett, *Papers, 1821–1934, 1944–1962*, Eau Claire Mss BY, at the Area Research Center, McIntyre Library, University of Wisconsin, Eau Claire, WI. Box 10, folder 9; Rodney Loehr, "Some More Light on Paul Bunyan," *Journal of American Folklore* 64, no. 254 (October–December 1951): 407.

16. Bartlett, Box 10 folder 9.

17. Terpening to Brown, undated four-page letter marked "Wild Animals of the Pine Woods," in Charles E. Brown Papers, Wis Mss HB, box 5.

18. K. Bernice Stewart and Homer A. Watt, "Legends of Paul Bunyan, Lumberjack," *Transactions of the Wisconsin Academy of Arts, Sciences, and Letters* (1916): 641–642.

19. Marian Jenne McDonald, "The Legend of Paul Bunyan" (BA thesis, University of Wisconsin, 1928), 59–60.

20. Rourke, "Paul Bunyon [*sic*]," 177.

21. Dorson, "Review of *Legends of Paul Bunyan* by Harold Felton," 234.

22. Stewart and Watt, "Legends of Paul Bunyan," 639.

CHAPTER 5

1. Laughead to E. Shepard May 5, 1923. Esther Shepard Papers, University of Washington, Box 3, folder 5; George Laidlaw to Brown, May 26, 1924, in W. W. Charters Papers, Children's Literature Research Collection, University of Minnesota.

Notes to pages 66–76

2. John E. Nelligan, "The Life of a Lumberman by John E. Nelligan, as told to Charles M. Sheridan," *Wisconsin Magazine of History* 13, no. 1 (September 1929): 8.
3. See chapter 11 for a discussion of earlier claims.
4. H. J. Kent to Brown, November 9, 1938, in W. W. Charters Papers, Children's Literature Research Collection, University of Minnesota; Dorothy Brown described Taplin's account to the Douglas County Historical Society in 1940, *Superior Telegram*, November 13, 1940.
5. 1910 U.S. Census; Wisconsin marriage certificate; Wisconsin Adj. General Muster Rolls; *Stevens Point Gazette*, November 28, 1885, 4; Kent to Brown, November 11, 1938, in the W. W. Charters Papers, Children's Literature Research Collection, University of Minnesota.
6. *Wautoma Argus*, October 21, 1943.
7. Kent to Brown, November 11, 1938, in the W. W. Charters Papers, Children's Literature Research Collection, University of Minnesota.
8. Brown to Mellor Hartshorn, March 15, 1934, in the Brown Papers, Wis Mss HB, Wisconsin Historical Society, box 5; Brown to W. W. Charters, September 24, 1943, in the W. W. Charters Papers, Children's Literature Research Collection, University of Minnesota.
9. Brown to Hartshorn, March 15, 1934.
10. *Eau Claire Daily Telegram*, March 31, 1933.
11. Bartlett, *Papers, 1821–1934, 1944–1962.*
12. "Logging Camp Yarns," *Eau Claire Telegram*, [March?] 31, 1917; "Extracts from Paul Bunyan Yarns," *Eau Claire Telegram*, April 20, 1917; Bartlett, *Papers, 1821–1934, 1944–1962.*
13. Appendix, no. 4.
14. Appendix, nos. 19, 22, and 51.
15. Appendix, nos. 22 and 52.
16. Loomis, "A Tall Tale Miscellany," 40; appendix nos. 7, 15, 28, 36, 37, 44, 47, and 48.
17. Appendix, nos. 4, 5, 9, 23, 32, 39, 41, 51, 61, 68, 72, and 73.

CHAPTER 6
1. "Life Closes for Eugene Shepard," *New North*, March 29, 1923.
2. Layton Shepard, *Interview, 1963*, SC 1004, at the Wisconsin Historical Society.
3. Shepard, Interview; Luke Sylvester Kearney, *The Hodag, and Other Tales of the Logging Camps* (Wausau, WI: 1928), 9–17; Kurt D. Kortenhof, *Long Live the Hodag: The Life and Legacy of Eugene Simeon Shepard, 1854–1923*, 2nd ed. (Savage, MN: Hodag Press, 2006), 90–99.
4. Lucius, September 23, 1958, oral history interview, SC 703 at the Wisconsin Historical Society; "Some of Gene Shepard's Jokes and Pranks. Stories Told to Charles E. Brown by Joe Lucius at Solon Springs, October 26, 1934,"

Charles E. Brown papers, WI Mss. HB at the Wisconsin Historical Society, box 6. Seven-page manuscript.

5. Shepard, *Interview*, 3.

6. Quoted in Fred Holmes, *Badger Saints and Sinners* (Milwaukee, WI: 1938), 472–473.

7. *Wisconsin State Journal*, October 26, 1935; Charles E. Brown, *Paul Bunyan and Tony Beaver Tales* (Madison, WI: C. E. Brown, 1930), 1; *Paul Bunyan, American Hercules* (Madison, WI: C. E. Brown, 1937), 1; Pinchot to Lovejoy, October 28, 1920, in Lovejoy Papers, Archives of Michigan, Lansing, MI, box 31, folder 1.

8. Kortenhof, *Long Live the Hodag*, 43–44; 1880 U.S. Census for Knowlton, Wisconsin.

9. Kortenhof, *Long Live the Hodag*, 76.

10. Shepard to W. H. Killen, December 19, 1916, in *Ephemera sent by Shepard to W. H. Killen, 1896–1916*, Wisconsin Historical Society Archives collection PH7-345; Hutchinson, "The Birth of Paul Bunyan," 47. The first of Shepard's tales so far found in print date from 1922, though three of his pictures were included in "Paul Bunyan, Noted Pioneer in Land Clearing" in the *Vilas County News*, December 21, 1921.

11. *Ephemera sent by Shepard to W. H. Killen, 1896–1916*, Wisconsin Historical Society Archives collection PH7-345; a marked copy, collating Shepard's text with Malloch's, is in the William Bartlett Papers, Eau Claire Mss BY, McIntyre Library, University of Wisconsin, Eau Claire, WI, box 10 folder 9.

12. Shepard to Bartlett, March 30, 1917; Malloch to Bartlett, April 28, 1917, in the Bartlett Papers, box 10 folder 9; Brown note, Children's Literature Research Collection, University of Minnesota, box 16 folder 5; the history of its subsequent attribution to Shepard is summarized in Malcolm Leviatt Rosholt, "Paul Bunyan and the Round River Drive: a Communication," *Wisconsin Magazine of History* 65, no. 1 (Autumn 1981): 36–38.

13. Eugene Shepard, "Mrs. Paul Bunyan Even More Resourceful than Her Husband," *New North*, May 11, 1922; Charles Brown to W. W. Charters, September 24, 1943, in the Charters Papers, Children's Literature Research Collection, University of Minnesota.

14. See the appendix for the texts of his other tales; Shepard, "Mrs. Paul Bunyan"; William B. Laughead, *The Marvelous Exploits of Paul Bunyan: as told in the camps of the white pine lumbermen for generations, during which time the loggers have pioneered the way through the north woods from Maine to California: collected from various sources and embellished for publication* (Minneapolis: Red River Lumber Co., 1922), 23.

15. This drawing was printed in "Paul Bunyan, Noted Pioneer in Land Clearing," *Vilas County News*, December 21, 1921; Pinchot to Lovejoy, October 28, 1920, Lovejoy Papers, box 31 folder 1. There is some reason to suspect that Shepard lied about being its creator.

16. Bartlett Papers, box 10 folder 9; Kortenhof, *Long Live the Hodag*, 104; phone interview with Kurt Kortenhof, August 16, 2007.

17. Eugene S. Shepard and Karretta Gunderson Shepard, *Paul Bunyan: His Camp and Wife* (Tomahawk, WI: The Osborne Press, 1929). Karretta Shepard to W. W. Charters, December 7, 1940, in Charters Papers, Children's Literature Research Collection, University of Minnesota.

18. Shepard and Shepard, *Paul Bunyan: His Camp and Wife*, 19.

CHAPTER 7

1. "Caught on the Run," *Duluth News Tribune*, August 4, 1904, 4.

2. Kay Houston, "The Man Who Could Out-Lumber Paul Bunyan," *Detroit News*, June 14, 1996.

3. "When Paul Bunyan Crashed the Headlines," *Milwaukee Journal*, February 10, 1948, 14, clipping in Children's Literature Research Collection, University of Minnesota, box 8 folder 6; MacGillivray had given the same account to the *Plymouth Mail* (MI) a year earlier.

4. MacGillivray's 1951 letter is quoted in D. Laurence Rogers, *Paul Bunyan: How a Terrible Timber Feller Became a Legend* (Bay City, MI: Historical Press, 1993), 89–94; the textual history of the Michigan Round River tales is described in Mary Jane Hennigar, Daniel Hoffman, and Ellen J. Stekert, "The First Paul Bunyan Story in Print," *Journal of Forest History* 30, no. 4 (1986): 175–181.

5. J. E. Rockwell, "Some Lumberjack Myths," *Outer's Book* (Milwaukee, WI), February 1910, 157–160. Only one copy of this article appears to survive in American libraries.

6. Obituary, *Chicago Tribune*, December 10, 1953, C18.

7. Rockwell, "Some Lumberjack Myths," 157.

8. "To the Rainy River," *New North*, August 13, 1891 (reprinted in Kortenhof); *Duluth Evening News*, June 30, 1901, 8.

9. Rockwell, "Some Lumberjack Myths," 157.

10. "Frozen Snakes Used as Skids: Nature Fakers Put to Shame by These Classy Stories from the Lumber Camp," *Washington Post*, February 6, 1910 (in the "Miscellany" section, page 1); "North Woods Myths Passing: Tales of Bunyan and Other Lumberjacks Bring Back Old Days. Gene Shepherd's [*sic*] Hodag. Famous Fake of Rhinelander Man a Product of Backwoods Cleverness—Bunyan a Character," *Wisconsin State Journal*, May 23, 1910.

11. W. D. Harrigan, "Paul Bunyan," *American Lumberman*, June 13, 1914; one version from the Pacific Northwest casts the ham skaters as Japanese; see Stewart and Watt, "Legends of Paul Bunyan," 647.

12. "The Round River Drive," *American Lumberman*, April 25, 1914, 33; *Oscoda Press*, June 5, 1914, 9; W. W. Charters, "Paul Bunyan in 1910," *Journal of American Folklore* 57, no. 225 (July 1944): 189, quotes a letter from MacGillivray explaining the authorship of the 1914 verse version.

13. Snow: Baughman, *Type and Motif-index*, 574; harness: Loomis, "A Tall Tale Miscellany," 38; voice and tree: Dorson, *Jonathan Draws the Long Bow*, 128, 164; hodag: *History and Directory of Kent County, Michigan*, (Grand Rapids, MI: Daily Eagle Steam Printing House, 1870), 28.

14. "Caught on the Run," *Duluth News Tribune*, August 4, 1904, 4; James MacGillivray, "Round River," *Oscoda Press*, August 10, 1906; Rockwell, "Some Lumberjack Myths," 157–160; William B. Laughead, *Introducing Mr. Paul Bunyan of Westwood, Cal.* (Minneapolis: Red River Lumber Co., 1914).

15. *Duluth News Tribune*, May 3, 1917, 6; *Who's Who in the Central States* (Chicago: Larkin, Roosevelt and Larkin, 1947), 775.

16. Houston, "The Man Who Could Out-Lumber Paul Bunyan."

17. P. S. Lovejoy to W. W. Charters, April 5, 1941, in the W. W. Charters Papers, Children's Literature Research Collection, University of Minnesota.

18. Laughead to E. Shephard, May 5, 1923, Esther Shephard Papers, University of Washington, Box 3, folder 5; James MacGillivray, "The Round River Drive," *Detroit News*, July 24, 1910.

19. Bartlett, *Papers, 1821–1934, 1944–1962*; Brown to Martha Merrill, February 8, 1936, in State Historical Society of Wisconsin, State Historical Museum, Curators' general correspondence files, 1908–1982, 2000–2001.

20. Esther Shephard, *Paul Bunyan* (Seattle: McNeil Press, 1925), 11.

CHAPTER 8

1. Watt's obituary, *New York Times*, October 5, 1948.

2. Charles Brown to W. W. Charters, October 29, 1943, in the W. W. Charters Papers, Children's Literature Research Collection, University of Minnesota; Bernice Stewart to William Bartlett, March 29, 1917, in William Bartlett Papers, Eau Claire Mss BY, McIntyre Library, University of Wisconsin, Eau Claire, WI, box 1, folder 6; "Two Antigo Young Ladies Win Prizes," *Daily Journal* (Antigo, WI), January 6, 1910, 5; *The Badger* (student yearbooks) 1913–1916; *Wisconsin State Journal*, April 9, 1916.

3. *La Crosse Tribune*, April 24, 1907; *New York Times*, October 5, 1948; *Cornell Alumni News*, XX, no. 27 (March 28, 1919).

4. Wisconsin Academy, *Transactions*, 1915–1918.

5. Homer Watt to Milo M. Quaife, June 10, 1916, in William Bartlett Papers, Box 1, folder 6. No recordings have been found.

6. Watt to Charters, April 22, 1941, in Children's Literature Research Collection, University of Minnesota, box 16 folder 6.

7. Bartlett Papers, box 10 folder 9; *Eau Claire Telegram*, April 20, 1917.

8. *New York Times*, October 5, 1948, 36.

9. Stewart and Watt, "Legends of Paul Bunyan," 639–640.

10. Brown to Charters, October 29, 1943, and Watt to Charters, August 12, 1942, both in the W. W. Charters Papers, Children's Literature Research Collection, University of Minnesota.

11. Watt to Quaife, June 10, 1916, and Quaife to Bartlett, December 11, 1916, both in the William Bartlett Papers, box 1 folder 6; Watt to P. S. Lovejoy, August 2, 1920, in the Lovejoy papers, Archives of Michigan, Lansing, MI, box 31, folder 1.

12. Watt to Charters, April 22, 1941, Children's Literature Research Collection, University of Minnesota, box 16 folder 6.

13. Stewart to Bartlett, March 29, 1917, in the William Bartlett Papers, box 1 folder 6; Watt to P. S. Lovejoy, August 2, 1920, in the Lovejoy papers, Archives of Michigan, Lansing, MI, box 31, folder 1.

14. Watt to Quaife, June 10, 1916, and Quaife to Bartlett, March 13, 1917, both in William Bartlett Papers, box 1 folder 6; Wisconsin Academy, *Transactions* (1916): 639–651. The academy's records for those years have not survived.

15. Stewart and Watt, "Legends of Paul Bunyan," 641.

16. Ibid., 643.

17. Bruno Vinette, "Early Lumbering on the Chippewa," *Wisconsin Magazine of History* 9, no. 4 (July 1926): 443–444; Watt to Charters, April 22, 1941, in Children's Literature Research Collection, University of Minnesota, box 16, folder 6 (see appendix).

18. Hoffman, *Paul Bunyan*, 45.

19. "Ledger of Income and Expenditures, 1899–1930," Wisconsin Academy *Records, 1869–1989*, Wis Mss 429 in the Wisconsin Historical Society Archives, box 5, folder 7; Watt to P. S. Lovejoy, August 2, 1920, in the Lovejoy papers, Archives of Michigan, Lansing, MI, box 31, folder 1.

20. Stewart and Watt, "Legends of Paul Bunyan," 641–642.

21. Ibid., 641.

22. Ibid., 648–649.

23. For the state of the discipline at the time, see Jerrold Hirsch, "Folklore in the Making: B. A. Botkin," *Journal of American Folklore* 100, no. 395 (January–March, 1987): 3–38.

24. Stewart and Watt, "Legends of Paul Bunyan," 649–650.

25. Ibid., 649–652; L. G. Sorden and Isabel J. Ebert, *Logger's Words of Yesteryear* (Madison, WI: 1956).

26. *Wisconsin Alumni Magazine*, November 1918, February 1920, and June 1920; 1930 U.S. Census, Population Schedule: Bronxville, Westchester Co., New York, NARA microfilm T626, roll 1659, p. 5, image 644; Social Security Death Index ("Campbell, Catherin B" links to her husband).

27. *New York Times*, October 5, 1948, 36.

28. Lewis Wann, *The Rise of Realism* (New York: Macmillan Co., 1933), 270–273.

29. Ibid., 779.

30. Homer A. Watt, "When Gran'pa Worked for Paul" in Greenlaw, Elson, Keck, et al., *Literature and Life* (Chicago: Scott, Foresman and Co., 1922–1947) (Watt's stories first appeared in the 1936 edition); *New York Times*, October 5, 1948.

CHAPTER 9

1. *Milwaukee Journal*, January 29, 1880, 8; *Capital Times* (Madison, WI), December 22, 1940, 2; John Gregory, "Charles Edward Brown, Early Milwaukee Background," *Wisconsin Archeologist* 25, no. 2:43–44; Brown to Roy W. Carlson, July 17, 1931, in *Museum Curators' Correspondence*, Series 972 at the Wisconsin Historical Society Archives, box 3; Milwaukee city directories 1889–1899.

2. Milwaukee Public Museum, *Annual Report*, 1898–1906.

3. *Wisconsin Magazine of History* 2, no. 2 (December 1944): 133–134.

4. Brown to Otis Terpening, February 5, 1931, in *Museum Curators' Correspondence*, Series 972, Wisconsin Historical Society; Brown to Charters, September 24, 1943, in the W. W. Charters Papers, Children's Literature Research Collection, University of Minnesota.

5. *Wisconsin Archeologist* 25, no. 2 (June 1944): 46–48; Brown to Scott H. Goodnight, in *Museum Curators' Correspondence*, Series 972, Wisconsin Historical Society; Edmund David Cronon and John W. Jenkins, *The University of Wisconsin: A History*, Volume 3 (Madison: University of Wisconsin Press, 1994), 759–760; "America's Only Folk-Lore Character: Paul Bunyan, Mythical Hero of the Logging Camps, and the Exploits of His Husky Axemen at Last Find a Permanent Place in Literature and College Classics," *The American Weekly*, October 30, 1927, 8.

6. Brown to E. H. Burnham, November 26, 1930, in *Museum Curators' Correspondence*, Series 972, Wisconsin Historical Society; Watt to W. W. Charters, August 12, 1942, and Brown to Charters, September 15, 1942, both in W. W. Charters Papers, Children's Literature Research Collection, University of Minnesota Libraries.

7. Register of the Laidlaw Papers at Trent University (www.trentu.ca/admin/library/archives/74-011.htm); Charles Pelham Mulvany, *History of the Northwest Rebellion* (Toronto: 1886), 242; some of their letters are in Museum Curators' Correspondence, Series 972, at the Wisconsin Historical Society, and others in the W. W. Charters Papers, Children's Literature Research Collection, University of Minnesota.

8. Laidlaw to Brown, February 29, March 30, April 6, and May 14, 1924, in the W. W. Charters Papers, University of Minnesota. Because Laidlaw's Bunyan stories were collected in Ontario and have no clear Wisconsin ties, they have not been included in the appendix here.

9. Brown to Mellor Hartshorn, March 15, 1934, in the W. W. Charters Papers, University of Minnesota.

10. Terpening to Brown, January 7, 1929, in *Museum Curators' Correspondence*, Series 972, at the Wisconsin Historical Society (spelling slightly adjusted here to improve comprehension).

11. Most of Terpening's letters are in *Museum Curators' Correspondence* (Series 972) and box 5 of the Charles Brown Papers (Wis Mss HB) at the Wisconsin

Historical Society; a few are in the Charles Brown letters in the W. W. Charters Papers, Children's Literature Research Collection, University of Minnesota. Most of the tales are in Wis Mss HB, box 5.

12. These are all in the Charles Brown Papers, Wis Mss HB, box 5.

13. *Wisconsin: Stability, Progress, Beauty*, Volume 4 (Chicago: The Lewis Publishing Co., 1946), 259–261; *Capital Times* (Madison, WI), April 29, 1930, 8.

14. Brown to John F. Chetlain, January 5, 1928, in *Museum Curators' Correspondence*, Series 972, at Wisconsin Historical Society; Brown to Mellor Hartshorn, March 15, 1934, in the W. W. Charters Papers, Children's Literature Research Collections, University of Minnesota.

15. *Wisconsin State Journal*, November 4, 1937, 4; Brown to Marjorie O'Kelliher, October 10, 1935, in *Museum Curators' Correspondence*, Series 972, Wisconsin Historical Society; Harold Miner, *Essay and Letters, 1941–1942*, SC1243 in the Wisconsin Historical Society.

16. *Capital Times* (Madison, WI), January 19 and May 27, 1928, July 25, 1930; *Folklore Project Records, 1935–1937*, WI Mss IZ, Wisconsin Historical Society; *Wisconsin State Journal*, October 29, 1937, 4.

17. Lomax, July 17, 1936, in *Folklore Project Records, 1935–1937*, WI Mss IZ, Wisconsin Historical Society; *Appleton Post-Crescent*, November 30, 1937.

18. U.S. Works Progress Administration. *Federal Writers' Project. Records, 1936–1939: Folklore Wisconsin* (Washington, DC: Library of Congress Photoduplication Service, 1984). Microfilm 19045: reel 5, frames 306–311.

19. Ibid., reel 6, frames 670–675; *Capital Times* (Madison, WI), April 29, 1930, 8.

20. *Records, 1936–1939: Folklore Wisconsin*, reel 6, frame 674; Crosshaul interview, *Milwaukee Journal*, June 1943, in Children's Literature Research Collection, University of Minnesota, mss TM25, box 16.

21. Miner, *Essay and Letters*, 5–6; *Wisconsin State Journal*, October 29, 1937, 4 and November 29, 1937, 4; Brown to Robert Halpin, November 10, 1937, in *Museum Curators' Correspondence*, Series 972, Wisconsin Historical Society.

22. Miner, *Essay and Letters*, 7, 28–29; Jack Lyons to Miner, May 1, 1942, and "Marie" to Miner, June 3, 1942, both filed with Miner, *Essay and Letters*.

23. C. Brown to Charters, August 26, 1941, and D. Brown to Charters, September 11, 1947 and March 19, 1948, all in the W. W. Charters Papers, Children's Literature Research Collection, University of Minnesota.

24. Wayland D. Hand, "North American Folklore Societies," *The Journal of American Folklore* 56, no. 221 (July–September 1943), 190–191.

25. George Slecht, *Cal Crosshaul Interpreting the Oral Literature of the Lake States Lumberjack* (Hudson, WI: Northern Forest Baking Bureau, [1939?]); Crosshaul is identified as Slecht in Dorothy Brown's acknowledgments in *What Say You of Paul?*; Brown to Charters February 23, 1941, in the W. W.

Charters Papers, Children's Literature Research Collection, University of Minnesota; Dorson's "In the News, part I" contains several other Wisconsin examples.

26. *Wisconsin State Journal*, October 26, 1935; Brown, *Paul Bunyan and Tony Beaver Tales*, 1; *Paul Bunyan, American Hercules*, 1.

27. Compiled from acknowledgments in the Brown's publications and interview summaries, notes, and unpublished correspondence at the Wisconsin Historical Society and the Children's Literature Research Collection, University of Minnesota.

28. The full texts of all of them can be seen at www.wisconsinhistory.org.

29. Ethel Falk to D. Brown, February 3, 1947, D. Brown to Charters September 11, 1947; Charters to D. Brown, October 31, 1947, all in the W. W. Charters Papers, Children's Literature Research Collection, University of Minnesota; D. Brown to Charters, November 28, 1947; March 19, April 29, June 18, and July 14, 1948, all in the W. W. Charters Papers, Children's Literature Research Collection, University of Minnesota.

30. D. Brown to Charters, March 19 and July 14, 1948, in the W. W. Charters Papers, Children's Literature Research Collection, University of Minnesota.

31. Charters to D. Brown, September 8, 1947, in the W. W. Charters Papers, Children's Literature Research Collection, University of Minnesota.

32. *Wisconsin Magazine of History* 79, no. 4 (Summer 1996): 269, and 28, no. 2 (December 1944): 133.

CHAPTER 10

1. Fishwick, "Sons of Paul," 278.

2. Hutchinson, "The Birth of Paul Bunyan," *Forest History* 16, no. 3 (1972): 45–46. 3. W. H. Hutchinson, "The Caesarean Delivery of Paul Bunyan," *Western Folklore* 22, no. 1 (January 1963): 2–3.

4. Hutchinson, "Birth of Paul Bunyan," 46.

5. Hutchinson, "Caesarean Delivery," 8.

6. Hutchinson, "Birth of Paul Bunyan," 48.

7. Ibid., 47–48.

8. Quoted in Max Gartenberg, "Paul Bunyan and Little John," *Journal of American Folklore*, LXII (October–December, 1949): 447.

9. See Hoffman, "What Does the Symbol Symbolize?" in *Paul Bunyan* and Dorson, "Paul Bunyan in the News, 1939–1941."

10. Charles Albert Albright [P. S. Lovejoy], "Chronicle of Life and Works of Mr. Paul Bunyan," *American Lumberman*, June 17, July 8, August 12 and 26, September 30, November 11 1916, August 11, 1917, and June 29, 1918; Lee J. Smits, "The Epic Lumberjack. He Did Wonders. Let's Collect Yarns. Do You Know Any?" *Seattle Star*, November 17, 18, 19, 20, 22, 23, 24, 25, 26, 27, and 29, 1920; Rourke, "Paul Bunyon [*sic*]," 176–179.

11. Laughead, *Marvelous Exploits*, 4 and 23.
12. Fenska to Charters, June 13, 1941, in the Children's Literature Research Collection, University of Minnesota.
13. Biographical information from National Archives and Records Administration, *Old German Files, 1909–1921* (Publication M1085), "Investigative Case Files of the Bureau of Investigation, 1908–1922," Case No. 8000-41576: 24 (Fenska); *Syracuse Herald,* July 15, 1921, 13; Laughead, *Marvelous Exploits*, 4.
14. William Laughead to Dorothy Brown, February 6, 1942, in the W. W. Charters Papers, Children's Literature Research Collection, University of Minnesota; Hutchinson, "Caesarian Delivery," 9.
15. William Laughead to Dorothy Brown, February 6, 1942, in the W. W. Charters Papers, Children's Literature Research Collection, University of Minnesota; Laughead to E. Shephard May 5, 1923, Esther Shephard Papers, University of Washington, Box 3, folder 5.
16. Hubert Langerock, "Twenty-Five Years of Eight-Hour Propaganda," *International Socialist Review*, May 1914, at www.marxists.org/subject/mayday/articles/eighthour.html.
17. Laughead to E. Shephard, May 5, 1923, Esther Shephard Papers, University of Washington, Box 3, folder 5.
18. Hubert Langerock, "The Wonderful Life and Deeds of Paul Bunyon," *The Century Magazine* 106, no. 1 (May 1923): 33.
19. Maunder, "The Making of a Folklorist," 18.
20. Ibid., 1, 4, 6–9.
21. Ibid., 11, 16–18.
22. Ibid., 11–12, 17; the reference Stevens recalled was to Victor Shawe, "When Finn Meets Finnegan," *Saturday Evening Post* 194 (June 3, 1922): 8–9.
23. Maunder, "Making of a Folklorist," 18.
24. Ibid., 16–17.
25. Ibid., 10, 12.
26. Ibid., 11.
27. "Preliminary Guide to the Esther Shephard Papers, 1852–1972" at the University of Washington; her first husband, who died in 1915, was named Shepard (without an "h"), and her second was named Shephard, leading to a certain amount of bibliographic confusion; Shephard to Lovejoy, May 7, 1921, and January 4, 1922, in the Lovejoy Papers at the Archives of Michigan, box 31 folder 1 and box 30 folder 13, respectively.
28. "Ledger of Income and Expenditures, 1899–1930," Wisconsin Academy, *Records, 1869–1989*, Wis Mss 429 in the Wisconsin Historical Society Archives, box 5, folder 7; Esther Shephard, *Paul Bunyan* (New York: Harcourt Brace, 1924): xi–xii.
29. Lovejoy to W. W. Charters, July 5, 1941, in the W. W. Charters Papers at the children's Literature Research Collection, University of Minnesota; the

lengthy Lovejoy-Rourke correspondence in boxes 30 and 31 of his papers in Lansing, Michigan, details the 1920 *New Republic* article and their possible collaboration.

30. "Preliminary Guide to the Esther Shephard Papers, 1852–1972"; *New York Times*, April 19, 1925.

31. James Stevens, "Mythical Hero of Loggers. Logger Deserts Ax for Pen," *Los Angeles Times*, June 28, 1925, 26.

32. Maunder, "Making of a Folklorist," 12.

33. Hutchinson, "Birth of Paul Bunyan," 49; Matthew Joseph Bruccoli, *F. Scott Fitzgerald: A Descriptive Bibliography*, rev. ed. (Pittsburgh: University of Pittsburgh Press, 1987), 64–72.

34. "America's Only Folk-Lore Character: Paul Bunyan, Mythical Hero of the Logging Camps, and the Exploits of His Husky Axemen at Last Find a Permanent Place in Literature and College Classics," *The American Weekly*, October 30, 1927, 8. The copy I examined ran in the *Chicago Examiner*.

35. OCLC WorldCat; Maunder, "Making of a Folklorist," 14; James Cloyd Bowman, *The Adventures of Paul Bunyan* (New York: The Century Co., 1927), 7.

36. O'Malley to D. Brown, May 13, 1948, in the W. W. Charters Papers, Children's Literature Research Collection, University of Minnesota.

37. "An Interesting Letter. Lumberjacks and River Hogs," *Banner-Journal* (Black River Falls, WI), January 23, 1935.

38. *Evening Telegram* (Superior, WI), February 4, 1935; *Daily Tribune* (Wisconsin Rapids, WI), March 19, 1938; Brown to Charters, March 25, September 23, 1944, in the W. W. Charters Papers, Children's Literature Research Collection, University of Minnesota.

39. Walls, "The Making of the American Logger"; Harty, "Legendary Landscapes."

40. Biographical introductions to the registers of the papers of Stevens and Shephard at the University of Washington, Seattle, WA.

41. Lovejoy to Charters, July 5, 1941, in the W. W. Charters Papers, Children's Literature Research Collection, University of Minnesota.

42. Watt to W. W. Charters, August 21, 1942, in the W. W. Charters Papers, Children's Literature Research Collection, University of Minnesota; author's interview with Barbara Friend, Northampton, MA, October 6, 2007.

CHAPTER 11

1. Stevens, *Paul Bunyan* (1925), 2.

2. Quoted in Dorson, "Paul Bunyan in the News, 1939–1941," part III, 259 and in *Minnesota History* 21, no. 3 (June 1940): 176; and in Gladys Haney, "Paul Bunyan Twenty-Five Years After," *Journal of American Folklore* 55, no. 217 (July–September 1942): 156. Laughhead's incoming Bunyan cor-

respondence at the Forest History Society in Durham, NC, came to light only after this book went to press, and was not examined for this chapter.

3. Dorson, *Jonathan Draws the Long Bow.*

4. Stevens, *Paul Bunyan* (1948 edition), 10a.

5. Maunder, "Making of a Folklorist," 15.

6. "The Paul Bunyan Tales," *Minnesota History* 21, no. 3 (June 1940): 176–177; C. A. Roos, "The Trail of the Lonesome Pine: Reminiscences of the Days of the Lumberman on the St. Croix," *Balsam Lake (WI) Ledger*, November 23, 1916.

7. Theodore C. Blegen, "With Ax and Saw: A History of Lumbering in Minnesota," *Forest History* 7, no. 3 (1963): 13; William Lass, *Minnesota: A History* (New York: W. W. Norton & Co., 1998): 183.

8. Gifford Pinchot to P. S. Lovejoy, October 28, 1920, in Lovejoy Papers, Archives of Michigan, Lansing, MI, box 31, folder 1.

9. Stevens, *Paul Bunyan* (1925), 4–5.

10. Laidlaw to Brown, March 26, 1925, in the Charles Brown correspondence, W. W. Charters Papers, Children's Literature Research Collection, University of Minnesota.

11. Loehr, "Some More Light on Paul Bunyan," 407.

12. Hutchinson, "Caesarian Delivery of Paul Bunyan," 3.

13. Laughead, *Introducing Mr. Paul Bunyan of Westwood, Cal.; Daily Pioneer* (Bemidji, MN), May 1, 1940.

14. W. W. Charters, "Paul Bunyan in 1910," *Journal of American Folklore* 57, no. 225 (July 1944): 188–189; William MacGillivray, "Round River" [prose], *Oscoda Press*, August 10, 1906; James MacGillivray, "The Round River Drive" [prose], *Detroit News*, July 24, 1910; "The Round River Drive" [poem], *American Lumberman*, April 25, 1914: 33; Mary Jane Hennigar, et al., "The First Paul Bunyan Story in Print," *Journal of Forest History* 30, no. 4 (1986): 175–181; D. Laurence Rogers, *Paul Bunyan: How a Terrible Timber Feller Became a Legend* (Bay City, MI: Historical Press, 1993); "When Paul Bunyan Crashed the Headlines," *Milwaukee Journal*, February 10, 1948, 14.

15. Charles E. Brown, "Paul Bunyan a Wisconsin Product, Without Doubt," *Wisconsin State Journal*, October, 26, 1935; Kent to Brown, November 9, 1938, in W. W. Charters Papers, Children's Literature Research Collection, University of Minnesota; Charles E. Brown, *American Folk Lore. Paul Bunyan Tales...* (Madison, WI: 1922); Kortenhof, *Long Live the Hodag*, 43.

16. Brown to Edward J. Felz, May 27, 1936, in *Museum Curators' Correspondence*, series 972, Wisconsin Historical Society.

17. Henry Thoreau, *The Maine Woods* (Boston: Ticknor and Fields, 1864), 3, 129.

INDEX

Page numbers in *italics* indicate photographs and illustrations.

A

accidents, logging, 14, 42–44

adoption of Bunyan by diverse groups, 3–4

advertising: early use of Bunyan tales, 3, 70; mid-1920s publication of Bunyan tales, 52; and popularization of Bunyan, 147–148, 160; present-day use of Bunyan, 5–6; Red River Lumber Company and, 130–132

African Americans, 36–38, 89, 169, 193

Albright, Charles (pseud.) *see* Lovejoy, Parrish, 134, 140

Alft, William, 34, 37

allotment policy, 36

alteration of tales for publication, 66, 94, 110, 111, 116, 133

America and Bunyan as cultural icon, 1, 3–4, 110, 148–149, 160

American Folk Lore (Brown), 113–114

"American Hercules", 52

American Lumberman, 89–90, *90*, 101, 103, 134, 158

American Mercury, 137, 138

American uniqueness of Bunyan tales, 108–109

Ames, Carleton, 56

Anderson, Julius (fict.), 170

animals belonging to Paul Bunyan, 180–184

appeal of Bunyan, 3–6, 8, 149

Ashland, Wisconsin, 46

Au Sable River, 85, 158

audience: effect on printed tales, 96–97, *96*; gullibility, 56, 57, 60, 67; and humor in tales, 95; national audience for tales, 86–87, *88*, 89

B

Babe the Blue Ox: Brown's use of name, 116; in Bunyan tales, 170, 173–174, 177, 198; crooked road tale, 181; described, 180, *180*; fishing tale, 205; logjam tale, 181; made into soup, 189; naming of, 65, 132; shoeing of, 186, 214; stretchable yokes and harness tales, 179–180, 181–182

Bacon, Charley (fict.), 170

Balch, James, 124

Barbeau, Marius, 29, 30

Barrett, W. W., 124

Index

Dick, Pete, 132
Dictionary of English Literature (Watt), 99
dinner horn tales, 191, 192, 211, 217
Disney version of Bunyan, 4–5
distortion of Bunyan tales for publication, 66, 94, 110, 111, 116, 133
Dobre, Frank, 124
dogs in Bunyan tales, 183, 208–209, 215
Dorson, Richard: criticism of Bunyan craze, 4; on folklore and learning, 53; on lumberjack creed, 48–49; on origins of tales, 6, 29; on raw nature of tales, 63; tall tales survey, 152; on Upper Peninsula logging tales, 55
doughnuts in Bunyan tales, 189–190
"down-cutter" machine, 190
Down East loggers, 33
Drake, Horace, 14
drunkenness: in Bunyan tales, 184, 195; hog-proof fence tale, 182–183; loss of Bunyan tales regarding, 48; spring revels and, 45–47
Duluth Herald, 86
Duluth News Tribune, 83, *85*, 86, *90*, *91*
Dyer, Harry, 37, 124

E
early logging stories: overview, 9–10; dating of earliest Bunyan tales, 65–68; and European folktales, 102, 107–108; Wisconsin as source of Bunyan tales, 2, 6–7, 10, 31, 154, 157, 158
Eastman brothers, 156–157
eating in Bunyan tales, 191–192
Eau Claire Telegram, 69, 106
Edick, Dave, 170
Elmer, Paul Bunyan's dog (fict.), 183
employment in Wisconsin logging industry, 25
entertainment in logging camps, 40–41, *41*, 54, *59*
ethnic background of Wisconsin lumberjacks, 33–35
European folktales, 102, 107–108
exaggerated style of Bunyan tales, 30, 53–54, 108

F
fabrication of new Bunyan tales, 111
"fakelore", 4
farming in Bunyan tales, 209
fear and Bunyan tales, 5, 8, 71, 95
Federal Anti-Obscenity Act, 97
Federal Writers' Program funding, 120
Felton, Harold, 128, 146

Index